RECONSTRUCTION TO REFORM

Texas Politics, 1876–1906

Reconstruction to Reform

TEXAS POLITICS, 1876-1906

By ALWYN BARR

UNIVERSITY OF TEXAS PRESS, AUSTIN & LONDON

International Standard Book Number 0-292-70135-7
Library of Congress Catalog Card Number 73-165911

Printed by The University of Texas Printing Division, Austin
Bound by Universal Bookbindery, Inc., San Antonio

For Nancy, Juliana, and Alicia

CONTENTS

ILLUSTRATIONS

Maps

PREFACE

This study began as an attempt to fill the gap in Texas political history between the existing works on Reconstruction and the Constitution of 1876 and those about the twentieth century which generally began with the election of 1906 following major changes in the election law. Several biographies of political figures and monographs on specific parties or political topics are available for the late nineteenth century, but no full-scale account encompassing the entire period. In addition to historiographical bounds, however, adoption of the constitution and passage of the voting act thirty years later mark the chronological limits of an era in which the electorate and electoral rules differed from the periods before and after.

In the late nineteenth and early twentieth centuries Texas politics reflected the turmoil of a state and nation moving away from sectional politics to grapple with the closing of the frontier, the complete commercialization of agriculture, domination of the economy by industrialization, and the rapid urbanization of a once overwhelmingly rural country. Texans approached these changes as opportunities or problems depending on their economic and cultural interests, the range of political ideas and personalities available to them, and the historical traditions from which they came. The interaction between Texans and both the federal government and the national political parties and their leaders also affected the course of politics on each level. My goal has been to unravel and evaluate the influence of these factors.

A major function of the expanding historical profession in the United States during the twentieth century has been detailed testing on the regional, state, and local levels of broad historical generalizations about periods and movements in national life. This study provided an opportunity to develop such comparisons, contrasts, and connections between events in Texas and those throughout the South and the nation, especially as analyzed in recent studies of railroad regulation, the Populist and progressive movements, and ethnic and religious group politics. It also offered an opportunity to evaluate the standard interpretations of the period in general histories of Texas. These questions led me to doubt first the wide acceptance of Democratic views about Republican failures during Reconstruction and Democratic successes afterward, with special reference to carpetbagger involvement, the increased state debt, and support for public schools. The effort to regulate rail lines developed not only on an agrarian base, but also with the backing of many merchants and shippers in Texas urban areas, the state's emerging industrialists, and some railroad men.

The third-party movements of the period did not represent a simple progression of the same men from the Grange into the Greenback party and on within the Populist fold, because Texas Grange leaders never endorsed the third-party movements. Campaign cooperation between Republicans and Greenbackers or Populists makes far more sense than has generally been granted because the Negro tenant farmers and laborers who formed a majority of Texas Republicans faced problems quite similar to those of white third-party members. My research suggests also that Texas Populists hardly fit the mold of backward-looking reactionaries, with antiforeign and anti-Semitic views, howling over imaginary ills and offering no useful reforms as they have been pictured by some modern critics.

Many works on politics in this period of Texas history slight the role of Negroes, yet they dominated the Republican party for over a decade and formed a crucial swing vote in the hotly contested elections of the 1890's. The exclusion of black Texans from the electorate through the use of force by white men's associations, the white primary among Democrats, a Lily-white movement within the Republican party, and the poll tax previously had remained largely unexplained.

E. M. House, who dominated Texas politics at the turn of the century, seems miscast as a moderate progressive, since he supported the more conservative of the real Democratic contenders for political offices, personally favored the gold standard, maintained strong business ties, and helped write watered-down Democratic state platforms that frequently avoided substance. Texas Democratic progressivism, briefly under Hogg and again in the early twentieth century, seems to fit a southern and midwestern pattern of well-organized urban middle class pressure groups loosely coordinated at times with farmer, labor, business, or professional organizations on a variety of individual issues, with prohibition often the only unifying factor in the latter period. Despite their failings, which helped keep alive a Republican minority and produce third-party challenges, Texas Democrats retained the support of most voters through a well-developed but flexible party organization, an understanding of the varied economic and cultural interests of different regions and ethnic and religious groups, and increasing efforts to use federal power and patronage to meet the needs of their constituents.

Texans influenced national politics on several occasions. John H. Reagan led the congressional struggle for railroad regulation in the seventies and eighties, while Roger Q. Mills became a Democratic expert in Congress on the tariff during the eighties and nineties. Texas Democrats helped swing their national party in favor of silver coinage in the crucial election of 1896. A Greenbacker from Texas reunited his party in 1880 as its vice-presidential nominee. But Texas Populists, reluctant to leave the Democratic party in 1891, helped divide the People's party in 1896 because they feared a coalition with Democrats. Republicans in Texas reflected more than influenced national party politics, as in 1896 when McKinley supporters in the national convention ousted N. W. Cuney as state party leader. Perhaps most important, the state consistently formed part of the solid South upon which national Democratic leaders relied and therefore at times slighted in patronage and legislation.

I wish to express my appreciation to Professor Barnes F. Lathrop of The University of Texas at Austin, who originally suggested this study and provided thoughtful advice and constructive criticism. For their assistance I am also indebted to the late Professor Andrew Forest Muir of Rice University; Professor J. Reuben Sheeler of Texas

Southern University; Mrs. Rosalie Hutcheson Bosworth, Mr. Edward C. Hutcheson, and Mrs. Harry H. Tinch of Houston; Mr. Wilton Woods of Seguin; Mrs. Richard T. Betts and Mr. James P. Newcomb, Jr., of San Antonio; Professor Donald Everett of Trinity University; Mr. Chilton O'Brien of Beaumont; Dr. Llerena Friend, Dr. Chester Kielman, Professor H. Wayne Morgan, Professor Joe B. Frantz, and Mr. Henderson Shuffler of The University of Texas at Austin; Professor James A. Tinsley of the University of Houston; Professor William Campbell of the University of the South; Professor James Day of The University of Texas at El Paso, former director of the Texas State Archives; Professor Paul Casdorph of West Virginia State College; Mr. David Gracy and Professor James Reese of Texas Tech University; Colonel Jay A. Matthews, Jr., and Frances Parker of Austin; the staffs of the Texas Collection at Baylor University, the Dallas Historical Society, the Rosenberg Library of Galveston, the Library of Congress, the Southern Historical Collection of the University of North Carolina, the University of Oklahoma Library; and my wife, Nancy. A grant-in-aid from the American Association for State and Local History made it possible for me to complete my research.

ALWYN BARR

RECONSTRUCTION TO REFORM

Texas Politics, 1876–1906

1. THE PARTIES AND VOTERS IN 1876

EIGHT HUNDRED DELEGATES to the state Democratic convention poured into Galveston by train and by boat in January 1876. From their hotels and boardinghouses they strode the broad streets and flagstone walks or rode streetcars past the substantial commercial houses and showy homes to eat oysters at a dollar a dozen and to attend sessions of the convention during the day or performances at the opera house and theaters at night.[1]

Superficially the delegates seemed quite similar, since Confederate veterans, of Southern birth, with pre–Civil War Texas backgrounds, filled over 80 per cent of the positions of power in the convention—nominees for state offices, delegates to the Democratic National Convention, presidential electors, and members of the platform and state executive committees. About 80 per cent also listed themselves as attorneys. A clear majority had always been Democrats, but at least

[1] James P. Baughman, ed., "Letters from the Texas Coast, 1875," *Southwestern Historical Quarterly* 69 (April 1966): 501; clipping, Richard Coke, Scrapbook.

two prominent figures in the convention had been Whigs in the 1840's and 1850's, four had voiced Know-Nothing views in the mid-1850's, and two had opposed secession in 1860. Three of the state's six Democratic congressmen also had espoused Know-Nothing or Unionist beliefs before the Civil War.[2]

Democratic leadership in 1876 reflected quite accurately the history of Texas politics since annexation. Texans of the republic, primarily nonslaveholding small farmers from the South, tended to divide over administrative and legislative policies into Houston and anti-Houston or Lamar factions, around the two principal presidents during the years of independence. Sam Houston, a Jacksonian Democrat from Tennessee and hero of the Texas revolution, generally advocated economy and peace with Indian tribes and Mexico. Mirabeau B. Lamar, a Georgian, showed some Whiggish tendencies in his support of expansion, a national bank, and higher tariffs.[3]

At the time of annexation a Texan wrote with considerable accuracy: "We are all Democrats in Texas, since the glorious victory of that party, who fearlessly espoused our cause and nailed the 'Lone Star' to the topmast of their noble ship." Former Houston and Lamar supporters in nearly equal numbers proclaimed themselves Democrats in 1846, and that party won fifty-five of the eighty-six seats in the first state Legislature. The other members divided among several views or refused to label themselves. Actual organization of the Democratic party began in the presidential election of 1848 when Democratic electors defeated Whig opponents by a majority of two to one. The Democrats carried all but three counties along the South Texas coast, though the Whigs showed some strength in most urban commercial centers and several agricultural and ranching counties in East and South Central Texas. Texans exhibited a passionate interest in the congressional dispute during the late 1840's over slavery

[2] This analysis is based upon biographical sketches in Walter P. Webb and H. Bailey Carroll, eds., *The Handbook of Texas,* of about half the leaders listed in Ernest William Winkler, ed., *Platforms of Political Parties in Texas,* pp. 174–176. See also Roscoe C. Martin, "The Grange as a Political Factor in Texas," *Southwestern Social Science Quarterly* 6 (March 1926): 367.

[3] Stanley Siegel, *A Political History of the Texas Republic.*

in the territories because it involved questions concerning the boundary between Texas and New Mexico and payment of the debts of the Texas republic. The state sent a representative to the southern convention at Nashville in 1850 and spoke boldly of resistance to any redrawing of its disputed western boundary. Yet the Compromise of 1850, which paid the Texas debt and granted New Mexico territory east of the Rio Grande, won general support from Texas senators and congressmen. Democrats extended their margin to three to one in the presidential election of 1852. They carried every county and continued in easy control of the state government and congressional delegation as the Whig party collapsed in the mid-1850's.[4]

In 1854 the aggressive new American or Know-Nothing party forced Texas Democrats to organize fully for the first time. In a time of increasing sectional tension over the Kansas-Nebraska Bill, which at least in theory opened new territories to slavery, the Know-Nothing party provided a new political home for Union men from both the Whig and Democratic parties and received the support of Houston, a United States Senator. Many Texas Know-Nothings, however, shared their party's hostility toward immigrants and Catholics, though it seems to have been aimed as much at the waves of immigrants who strengthened northern abolitionist views as at such groups within the state. Nevertheless Texas Germans and Mexicans naturally strengthened their attachment to the Democratic party in response to the apparent threat. In 1855 the Know-Nothings elected mayors in Austin and Galveston, captured one of the two congressional seats, and won one-third of the places in the Legislature, but lost the gubernatorial race. Thoroughly aroused, the Democrats swept the 1856 state and national elections by a two-to-one margin,

[4] Winkler, *Platforms*, pp. 15–36, 43–44; Randolph Campbell, "The Whig Party of Texas in the Elections of 1848 and 1852," *Southwestern Historical Quarterly* 73 (July 1969): 17–34; Avery O. Craven, *The Growth of Southern Nationalism, 1848–1861*, pp. 95, 98, 106; Holman Hamilton, *Prologue to Conflict: The Crisis and Compromise of 1850*, pp. 192, 197, 198. A comparison of W. Dean Burnham, *Presidential Ballots, 1836–1892*, pp. 764–813, with Barnes F. Lathrop, *Migration into East Texas, 1835–1860*, pp. 25, 100, indicates no correlation between Whig strength and sources of migration or slaveholding.

the widest in the South. Know-Nothings carried only three counties in East Texas and four in South Central Texas, though they showed some strength in most of Central and East Texas.[5]

By 1857 Know-Nothing party organization had collapsed in Texas and its members had entered the Democratic party, which shifted state political contests from the realm of party to that of faction. Houston lost his senate seat in 1857, because he believed the Kansas-Nebraska Act was unlikely to open the territories to slavery and opposed its passage. The same year he failed in an attempt to defeat the regular Democratic nominee for governor who held strong states' rights views. In 1859 Houston reversed that decision in a successful gubernatorial campaign based on his personal popularity, Unionism, opposition to commercial and planter efforts at reopening the African slave trade, and promise of better frontier protection against Indian raids.[6]

In the days following John Brown's raid into Virginia late in 1859 secessionist sentiment grew rapidly in Texas as it did in the entire South. Texas delegates to the Democratic convention in Charleston, South Carolina, in the spring of 1860 endorsed demands for congressional defense of slavery and bolted rather than accept Stephen A. Douglas of Illinois as their presidential candidate. At Richmond later they joined in the separate nomination of Vice-President John C. Breckinridge of Kentucky for president. Failure by the government to provide adequate frontier protection, and summer fires, blamed on abolitionists, provided states' rights men with further arguments for separation if a Republican won the presidential election of 1860. John Bell of Kentucky defeated Houston for the Constitutional Union party nomination, but carried only three counties in the German and

[5] W. Darrell Overdyke, *The Know-Nothing Party in the South*, pp. 27–30, 62, 89, 117, 154, 163, 229. The conclusion that Know-Nothings came from both the Whig and Democratic parties is based on a comparison of the Know-Nothing leaders listed in Ralph A. Wooster, "An Analysis of the Texas Know-Nothings," *Southwestern Historical Quarterly* 70 (January 1967): 414–423, with the lists of previous Whig and Democratic leaders in Winkler, *Platforms*.

[6] Charles W. Ramsdell, "The Frontier and Secession," in *Studies in Southern History and Politics*, pp. 63–73; Earl Wesley Fornell, *The Galveston Era*, pp. 215–225.

Mexican sections of Southwest Texas as he lost the state by a margin of three to one, the smallest Unionist percentage in the South. When Houston refused to call a convention to consider secession, states' rights men formed their own meeting, endorsed by the Legislature, which submitted a separation ordinance to public vote in the spring of 1861. It received three-to-one support and carried all but eighteen counties, seventeen of them in North and Central Texas where settlers were primarily from the border South, Germany, and Mexico.[7]

Most Texans, including some prewar Unionists, fought for or supported the Confederacy under the leadership of antebellum Democrats who held a majority of state and Confederate political offices during the Civil War. Other Unionists, who refused to take sides or secretly favored the United States, found themselves liable to mob violence, trial and imprisonment or hanging, or forced departure from the state. The most decided Unionists joined the United States Army to fight for the return of Texas to the Union.[8]

When the war ended in 1865 A. J. Hamilton, a former United States congressman from the western district of Texas who had joined the Union army, received appointment as provisional governor to organize civil government and call a new constitutional convention. That body, representing the various existing opinions in Texas but predominantly the views of the recent Confederates, recognized the death of secession and slavery, granted limited rights to Negroes, and cancelled the state's war debt. James W. Throckmorton, a Unionist turned Confederate, won the governor's chair with 49,277 votes to 12,168 for E. M. Pease, an ex-Democratic governor turned Unionist, in a campaign fought along wartime Unionist-Confederate lines. After the inception of military rule in 1867 General Philip Sheridan removed Throckmorton—as an impediment to Reconstruction—and

[7] Ramsdell, "The Frontier and Secession," pp. 74–79; Craven, *Growth of Southern Nationalism*, pp. 322, 327, 331, 334, 375–377; Ollinger Crenshaw, *The Slave States in the Presidential Election of 1860*, pp. 92–99, 284–295, 298; Ralph A. Wooster, *The Secession Conventions of the South*, pp. 121–135.

[8] Claude Elliott, "Union Sentiment in Texas, 1861–1865," *Southwestern Historical Quarterly* 50 (April 1947): 449–477; Charles Robert Lee, Jr., *The Confederate Constitutions*, pp. 45–50, 158; Wilfred Buck Yearns, *The Confederate Congress*, pp. 236–244.

appointed Pease in his place. Pease served until 1869 when he resigned because of differences with the military commander of Texas.

In 1868, after the enfranchisement of Negroes and the temporary disfranchisement of some former Confederates, Republicans dominated the new constitutional convention with seventy-eight of the ninety members though they included only nine black men and six to eight postwar immigrants from the North, or "carpetbaggers." Out of the convention came not only a new constitution guaranteeing Negro voting rights but also two Republican factions, one led by Hamilton and the other by a second Union brigadier from Texas, E. J. Davis. In the ensuing gubernatorial contest Hamilton and the "conservative" wing appealed for Democratic support, while Davis and the "radical" wing had the backing of most Negroes. Davis won a narrow victory with 39,901 votes to 39,092 votes for Hamilton in a campaign filled with charges of fraud by both sides.[9]

The Davis administration, which lasted four years, continuously suffered from political bickering. Democrats charged extravagance and gross abuse of power, especially in appointments, control of the state police, and declarations of martial law. Davis found himself plagued with a variety of difficult problems such as frontier protection, lawlessness, widespread refusal to pay taxes, and bitter political opposition. The Democrats won back all four congressional seats in 1871 with a total vote of 74,841 to 50,562 for the Republicans. In 1872 the Democrats captured a majority of the Legislature, and Horace Greeley, running as a Liberal Republican with Democratic endorsement, carried the state over regular Republican U. S. Grant by almost 20,000 votes; but he lost the national election. Democrat Richard Coke defeated Davis for governor in 1873 by polling 85,549 votes to 42,663. Davis protested the election on a legal technicality, but President Grant refused to intervene and Coke took office in January 1874.[10]

Republican efforts to create a political majority based heavily on black votes conjured up fears of Negro social equality which drove into the Democratic party many former Whigs and Unionists who

[9] Charles W. Ramsdell, *Reconstruction in Texas*, pp. 121–132.
[10] W. C. Nunn, *Texas under the Carpetbaggers*, pp. 313–317.

did not object to a somewhat expanded and centralized state government. This emotional issue produced a lasting connection between white supremacy and the Democratic party which muted internal efforts at change and lengthened the psychological leap for those who might seek a new political home.

The Democratic majorities in the Legislatures of 1873 and 1874 clearly outlined the political philosophy of their party in several enactments. They replaced the partially Negro state police with an all-white ranger force which included a number of former state policemen. The Democrats abolished the Republican school system as too centralized in its administration and replaced it with a weak substitute which left many children of the state without adequate schools for years to come. The Legislature drastically cut state salaries and expenditures, met debt payments by issuing high-interest bonds, and converted monetary aid for railroads into grants of public land. In the effort to undo Republican measures the legislators also stripped the governor of his powers to declare martial law and to appoint certain state officers. Finally they called for a constitutional convention to meet in 1875.[11]

The new constitution, drawn up after lengthy debates in 1875, represented primarily the views of an agriculture- and law-oriented Democratic majority of southern background and extensive political experience. Almost half acknowledged membership in the state Grange—which since its founding in 1873 had reached a peak strength of about 45,000 out of the state's electorate of approximately 250,000—easily the largest organized interest group in Texas. Like the Democratic legislators before them, the delegates saw their task basically as the prevention of any repetition of what they believed to be administrative and financial excesses by the Republican administration of 1870–1874. The convention placed strict limitations on state debt, salaries, taxes, and educational expenses. In addition it made more public offices elective while shortening terms and restricting powers, abolished state banks, and placed potential restraints on corporations and railroads.[12]

[11] Marion H. Farrow, *The Texas Democrats*, pp. 53–81.

[12] S. D. Myres, Jr., "Mysticism, Realism, and the Texas Constitution of 1876,"

Several of the state's newspapers opposed specific articles, although most favored adoption. Such prominent citizens as Webster Flanagan, a Republican member of the convention, and Ashbel Smith, a Democratic politician and Houston physician, joined in the attack. Critics assailed the public school article as financially inadequate, the judicial article as cumbersome with niggardly salaries, the railroad regulatory article as unfriendly, and other sections for being anti-immigration and for containing low executive salaries. In response, at a proconstitution rally held in Austin, Democratic Governor Richard Coke offered generally favorable comments, which several other Democratic leaders echoed in print. Despite differences over some aspects of the constitution, Texas Democrats in 1876 basically stood for white supremacy, states' rights, and decentralized government, with a mixture of suspicion and attraction toward business and transportation developments.[13]

Though lifelong Democrats and fairly typical southern Democratic views dominated the party as it met in convention in 1876, division might arise from several sources. Size alone militated against complete accord. The delegates in Galveston represented two-thirds to three-fourths of Texas citizens, who had grown in number from 602,432 in 1860 to 818,579 in 1870 and to over one million by the mid-1870's, as immigrants, mainly white Southerners, poured into the frontier state. Most of them settled north of the Guadalupe River and east of San Antonio, Austin, and Fort Worth, in an area of generally good soil and of rainfall adequate to support small, self-sufficient farmers. In this heavily settled region only the counties in the piney woods of Southeast Texas along the lower Sabine, Neches, and Trinity rivers and a few in Central and Northeast Texas failed to produce thousands of bushels of corn. A few counties from Waco north to the Red River supplemented their corn production with

Southwestern Social Science Quarterly 9 (September 1928): 166–184; John S. Spratt, *The Road to Spindletop*, pp. 12–14; J. E. Ericson, "The Delegates to the Convention of 1875," *Southwestern Historical Quarterly* 67 (July 1963): 22–27; Seth Shepard McKay, *Seven Decades of the Texas Constitution of 1876*, pp. 47–142.

[13] McKay, *Seven Decades*, pp. 145–168.

wheat and oats. Market prices for all three grain crops declined by one-fifth to one-third in the depression of the 1870's. But grain growing, primarily for local consumption, dominated Texas agriculture in the early 1870's.

Commercial agriculture expanded rapidly and land prices increased steadily with the postwar growth of Texas railroads. The ring of sledgehammers driving spikes into ties sounded across much of the settled region in the 1870's as Texas track mileage increased from 341 miles in 1865 to 1,578 miles in 1873 and stretched from Houston to Austin, Waco, Dallas, Palestine, Longview, and Liberty, from Marshall to Dallas, and from Denison across the Indian Territory to Kansas. Most Texas farmers and merchants by the mid-1870's could ship to or from the population centers of the nation, either directly north and east or through Houston to Galveston by rail, and from Galveston north and east by ship.

Cotton production then developed with only minor variations in the same counties of Central, North, and Northeast Texas which produced most of the state's grain crops. By 1873 Texans grew more cotton than they had in 1860 and more than any other southern state in the mid-1870's. Cotton prices fell during the depression of the 1870's, however, from seventeen and nine-tenths cents per pound in 1871 to nine and nine-tenths cents per pound in 1876. Texans produced sugar, the state's only other commercial crop, in as significant quantities as before the war only in Brazoria and Fort Bend counties on the lower Brazos River south of Houston.

Overall farm production had revived by the mid-1870's, but the number of farms increased from 42,891 in 1860 to 174,184 by 1880, while the average size of farms decreased over 27 per cent. Tenant farming and sharecropping had developed rapidly after the war, by Negroes, in place of slave labor on plantations, and by white immigrants who could not immediately afford to purchase land. By 1880, 37.6 per cent of Texas farmers would rent the land they tilled. The vast majority of white farmers voted for the Democratic slate in 1876, but a potentially important political division existed between landowning and nonlandowning agrarians.

As the United States Cavalry and Texas Rangers brought an end to raids by Indians in West Texas and by border bandits along the Rio Grande in the 1870's, cattlemen and sheepherders expanded their already considerable holdings in land and animals. Ranching represented a significant element in the economy of two areas in Texas at that time. One area included the coastal counties from Liberty to Cameron and inland to Fayette and Wilson counties. The other included the counties along the Red River from Lamar to Wichita, stretching southwest to Scurry County, southeast to Freestone County, and south along the frontier to Kimble County. Sheep raising did not overlap ranching to any extent, since it constituted a major economic factor primarily in the South Texas counties along the Rio Grande from Starr to Kinney, east to Nueces County on the coast, and north to Bandera and Gonzales counties with scattered pockets as far north as Coleman County on the frontier and Bosque County west of Waco. Cattle drives north to Missouri and Kansas railheads had begun in 1866 and continued into the 1880's, even after the expansion of Texas railroads, because trailing cattle north proved more economical. The panic of 1873 cut into cattle prices and reduced the drives for a few years but never completely stopped the flow. Wool prices remained generally low, however, because no railroads penetrated South Texas to ease the transportation problem facing sheep raisers. Cattlemen and sheep raisers clashed in areas where they contested for control of public grazing land, but both opposed the advance of the farmers who divided up and plowed under the grasses so crucial to their herds. Political divisions could easily result from either conflict. Cattlemen generally backed the Democratic party, but sheep raisers offered less uniform support because their interests in tariff protection ran counter to party doctrine.

Texas business grew, in step with the dominant agricultural facets of the state's economy, in the 1870's. Manufacturing establishments —generally local cotton or woolen mills or craftsmen producing brooms, leather goods, wagons, farm implements, furniture, and food products—had increased from 938 in 1860 to 2,399 in 1870 and had almost doubled the value of their products. Exports of cotton, lumber, wool, and hides by Texas commercial houses primarily in Texas ports and railroad centers expanded steadily through the

1870's. Galveston alone almost doubled its exports from over $14.8 million in 1870 to more than $26.6 million in 1881. To facilitate and share in the economic growth of the state, Texans increased the number of private banks from fifteen in 1868 to eighty-nine in 1876 (a depression decline from 104 in 1874), and founded ten national banks by 1874. Most Texas manufacturers, lumbermen, bankers, shippers, and railroad men considered themselves Democrats. Yet they might find themselves aligned against each other on such political issues as tariffs or railroad regulation, or together in opposition to the agricultural interests on such other questions as business taxes. While attorneys representing rural constituencies would hold an overwhelming majority of the positions of leadership in the Democratic convention of 1876, three land speculators, five bankers, and ten railroad attorneys or stockholders would also occupy positions of prominence. Among them were the nominee for lieutenant governor, seven of twenty-eight delegates to the national convention, and three of eight presidential electors. Clearly their influence far exceeded their numerical strength within the electorate.[14]

In 1876 the Texas economy approached the threshold of major change, with the development of commercial agriculture, expanded cattle and sheep production, better national transportation links, and an increased number of local industries. Nevertheless it remained a predominantly rural, preindustrial economy which produced essentially raw materials. At such a transitional stage in their economic development Texas agrarians and other shippers did not face the problems which led to demands for state regulation of business and transportation corporations by their counterparts in the more settled midwestern farm region. Yet the state's economic changes moved toward such a clash.

[14] Spratt, *Road to Spindletop*, pp. 3–12; Nunn, *Texas under the Carpetbaggers*, pp. 135–165; Avery L. Carlson, *A Monetary and Banking History of Texas*, pp. 39, 43; Fred A. Shannon, *The Farmer's Last Frontier*, p. 415; U.S., Tenth Census, 1880, III, *Agriculture*, 204–206, 239–242, 276–278, and V, *Cotton Production*, 665–668. For sketches of business-oriented delegates to the state Democratic convention in 1876 see Webb and Carroll, *Handbook of Texas*, I, 128–129, 354–355, 568–569, 686–687, 802, and II, 105, 673–674, 832, 891–892; and Robert C. Cotner, *James Stephen Hogg*, pp. 178, 187, 310.

Industrial, commercial, and transportation advances in turn produced urban growth of 75 per cent to 100 per cent in the 1870's for the major Texas towns—Austin, Dallas, Fort Worth, Galveston, Houston, Marshall, San Antonio, Sherman, and Waco—though Galveston maintained its claim to being the largest, with 22,248 citizens. Varied sources of growth and rivalries between towns in some areas of the state suggested potential political differences. Galveston remained the chief port and the most urbane and ostentatious city in Texas. But Houston, the major railroad town, proved a constant commercial rival with more cooperative and progressive citizens who sought to deepen Buffalo Bayou to accommodate seagoing ships. San Antonio remained the most diverse and cosmopolitan city, the largest military depot in the state, the commercial center for South Texas cattle and sheep raisers, and the staging point for most trade with Mexico. Austin had developed primarily as the focus of state government. Railroad expansion had made the other large towns regional commercial centers and stimulated their growth. Dallas and Fort Worth in North Texas clearly viewed each other as rival transportation centers from the beginning.

The growing number of urban Texans found available to them an increasingly varied life. Skilled jobs and professional positions expanded in number and diversity. With labor specialization and economic problems in the 1870's came the organization of a few unions—there were fourteen in Galveston and six in Houston by 1876. A wider range of professionally created products—clothes, medicines, tools, furniture, books, utensils, and luxury items—appeared in more specialized shops. Daily newspapers replaced weekly or semiweekly papers as their subscription lists grew. Schools increased in number and size as well as in the levels of instruction they offered. Social life included baseball, fairs, chicken or fish fries, barbecues, fireworks on holidays, billiards, bowling, cock fights and dog fights, and wrestling. Traveling circuses, professional actors and singers, and public lecturers added varying degrees of sophistication to city life. The frontier had not entirely passed from the urban scene, however, for newspaper editors still carried their wars of words into the street at times, and Oscar Wilde found his speaking engagements interrupted on various occasions by electrical failure, noisy spectators, and the ringing of a saloon bell nearby.

By contrast most Texans who lived in rural areas made their own clothes, furniture, tools, and utensils. They supplemented a basic diet of cornbread and pork with vegetables from a garden and dove, quail, buffalo, bear, deer, turkey, or pigeons from hunting. Patent medicine and a few other items they could not create came from general stores in small towns. Their children attended one-room schools a few months a year between harvesting and planting seasons. Rural Texans in their limited spare time read weekly papers from the county seat and entertained themselves with picnics, logrollings, quilting parties, and dances. If local law enforcement seemed too weak, the citizens might form a vigilance organization to deal with horse or cattle thieves. Clearly, political differences could develop with the cities, whose rapid growth and greater ties to the interdependent national economy increasingly separated them from the still largely self-contained rural areas.[15]

The Democratic state administration and the proposed state constitution allowed virtual autonomy for county and city governments, whose officials in turn won their positions in unrestricted local elections. Most organized urban areas functioned through an aldermanic system with aldermen representing geographical wards. Local candidates could know their constituents better than those seeking higher offices; therefore, personalities played a greater role and individuals became independent candidates and voters more frequently in city and county elections. Texas towns, especially near the frontier, often waged heated campaigns over the continuation of open gambling and prostitution. Some "reformers" represented only a self-interested change in administration rather than a change in fundamental practices. County politics became most bitter over contests for the county seat or for railroad connections. To carry the day opponents resorted

[15] *Texas Almanac*, 1966–1967, pp. 134–137; Kenneth W. Wheeler, *To Wear a City's Crown*; Wayne Gard, *Rawhide Texas*, pp. 39–55, 96–120, 142–150; Nuun, *Texas under the Carpetbaggers*, pp. 237–244; James V. Reese, "The Early History of Labor Organizations in Texas, 1838–1876," *Southwestern Historical Quarterly* 72 (July 1968): 13–14; Lloyd Lewis and Henry Justin Smith, *Oscar Wilde Discovers America*, pp. 364–365.

to fraud, to cowboys imported from outside the county to vote, or, along the Rio Grande, to Mexican "voters" from across the river. City and county issues frequently outweighed state or national ones within a specific area. Local factions gained broader importance as they sought the aid of candidates for state and congressional offices and in turn lent them support in their campaigns.[16]

Ethnic and religious differences provided further potential divisions among the Democratic majority in Texas. Anglo Americans of southern background would form about two-thirds of the state's 1,591,749 citizens by 1880 and a majority in most counties north of the Nueces River and east of the Pecos River. Among the Anglo majorities Southern Methodists slightly outnumbered Southern Baptists, but together they formed a majority of all Protestant Texans and over 40 per cent of all church members in the state. The two major Protestant groups shared, with some variations, evangelical views in opposition to government involvement in broad social problems or religious issues, though they had less qualms about legal enforcement of individual morality on questions of gambling and drinking. Together their members dominated political offices in Texas. Among Anglo Texans, Presbyterians and Episcopalians represented only 11 per cent and 2 per cent respectively.

The Anglo majority shared a sense of cultural superiority based on victory in the Texas revolution, ten years of independence as a republic, and almost exclusive control of the institution of slavery in the state. No Civil War devastation or defeats on Texas soil dimmed that assumption. Frontier expectations unavailable to other Southerners provided Texans with a source of relief from the burden of Reconstruction resentment. Anglo Texans exhibited basically American and southern traits in somewhat exaggerated form. They appeared "strongly individualistic and egalitarian, optimistic and utilitarian, volatile and chauvinistic, ethnocentric and provincial," and "much under the influence of older rural and moral traditions."

German immigrants numbered 35,347 by 1880, while their sons

[16] R. D. Holt, "Texas Had Hot County Elections," *West Texas Historical Association Year Book* 24 (1948): 3–26; Oliver Knight, *Fort Worth*, pp. 112–117; C. L. Sonnichsen, *Pass of the North*, pp. 345–379.

and daughters probably equaled that figure. Together they formed significant minorities in several counties from Gillespie County north of San Antonio to Austin County west of Houston in South Central Texas. Most Germans counted themselves among the Lutherans, who comprised 3 per cent of the state's Protestants, or the Catholics, who comprised 17 per cent of all church members in Texas. Regardless of their religion, Germans exhibited almost complete opposition to government interest in social and religious questions, since their views on the morality of drinking ran counter to those of many native-born Protestants. From native Anglos they could expect some suspicion and social discrimination, but general acceptance as part of the white majority. In the 1870's white Protestants overwhelmingly favored the Democratic party. But the German voters aligned themselves almost evenly with each party.

Mexican immigrants to Texas counted 43,161, but Texans of Mexican descent probably outnumbered them. Together they formed a significant majority of the state's Catholic population and majorities or large minorities in the counties south of the Nueces River and west of the Pecos River. Mexican vaqueros and laborers along the Rio Grande seemed susceptible because of economic dependence and the language barrier to manipulation by large landowners and their own local leaders. Yet religion clearly influenced their actions, for most prominent Anglo politicians of the region either came from Catholic backgrounds or adopted the faith after their arrival. Most poor Mexicans faced considerable suspicion if not hostility from native Anglos, based on cultural differences heightened by the Texas revolution and later clashes. Immigrants—predominantly Germans and Mexicans, but also some Irish, English, French, Dutch, Swiss, Poles, Italians, Spanish, Czechs, and Swedes—collectively constituted from 10 per cent in Austin to 33 per cent in Galveston of the population in Texas cities, where they served primarily as skilled and unskilled laborers.

By 1880 Negroes formed the largest ethnic minority in Texas with 393,384 citizens. Black majorities existed in eleven counties along the lower Brazos and Colorado rivers and in three counties in Northeast Texas along Cypress Bayou where the plantation system had been most highly developed before the Civil War. Large Negro minorities lived in several other counties along the rivers in Central and East Texas. Black Regular Baptists outnumbered the three black Methodist sects with 19 per cent and 10 per cent respectively of church members in Texas. Though both groups held theological views similar to their white counterparts, neither gave the same degree of support to puritanical reforms such as prohibition. Most Negroes supported the Republican party, but Democrats sought their backing in city, county, and district elections, where they sometimes formed majorities or represented large swing blocs between contesting white factions. From native Anglos black Texans could expect an attitude of superiority coupled with broad social discrimination as a result of racial views reinforced by relationships regulated for years by slavery.[17]

Ambition to hold office, a drive basic to all politicians, found expression on every level of Texas politics and added another source of possible division within the Democratic party. A visitor to Galveston in 1875 observed that "aspirants for the positions of public servants are abundant, and need no solicitations to take upon themselves the onerous duties of mayor at four thousand a year, or those of alderman at seven dollars per sitting." Potential candidates for state office also seemed likely to grow in number as the threat of Republican opposition faded. Once Democrats had won back most local and state offices they found themselves besieged by applicants for state appointive positions as their opponents had been before them. If the national party could recapture the presidency, Democratic senators and congressmen from Texas would have a voice too in the selection of federal judges, attorneys, marshals, customs collectors, postmasters, and internal revenue collectors. Clearly control of patronage at every level played a key role in the development and maintenance of the loose

[17] U.S., Tenth Census, 1880, I, *Population*, 408, 494–495; U.S., Eleventh Census, 1890, IX, *Religious Bodies*, 165–166, 176–177, 245–246, 451–452, 461, 468, 482, 517–518, 549–550, 562, 589–590, 662–663, 687, 717–718; Rufus B. Spain, *At Ease in Zion*, pp. 131–139, 232–233; D. W. Meinig, *Imperial Texas*, pp. 89, 55–57, 62–63.

factions which supported and promoted personal and regional ambitions within the party.[18]

After routine organizational activities and some speeches exhorting party unity in the early moments of the Democratic convention, the politicians turned to the selection of candidates for state offices. For a second term as governor they unanimously renominated Coke, a Virginia-born lawyer and former Confederate captain who had strong Grange support. The tall, ungainly governor, with his broad-brimmed, floppy felt hat, long-tailed coat, huge walking stick, and penetrating voice presented an appealing figure to his largely rural constituents. Behind the colorful exterior existed a politically astute man of some ambition who carefully blended anti-Republican retrenchment views with a touch of rural progressivism and an understanding of the need for improved transportation and business facilities in the state. Most segments of the party found him acceptable to one degree or another; those who did not refused to oppose him for lack of an equally popular candidate, or for fear of being charged with an attack on party unity. When three challengers withdrew to ensure harmony, rotund Richard B. Hubbard, another ex-Confederate officer, originally from Georgia, received renomination for lieutenant governor, despite criticism for his activities as an attorney for the International Railway Company. Contests followed for the lesser state offices, with the convention exhibiting its deepest feelings in the nomination over all preconvention candidates for state treasurer of H. H. Boone, a maimed Confederate veteran.[19]

The short, rather vague platform consisted only of general issues of broad appeal to Texas Democrats: protection against border bandits, defense of states' rights and home rule, and united opposition to the Republican national administration. The platform committee tried to

[18] Baughman, "Letters from the Texas Coast, 1875," p. 504.

[19] McKay, *Seven Decades*, pp. 168–171; Richard Coke to O. M. Roberts, November 8, 26, 1875, Oran M. Roberts Papers; *Dallas Herald*, January 8, 1876; *Galveston Weekly News*, January 3, 10, 1876; O. Douglas Weeks, "The Texas-Mexican and the Politics of South Texas," *American Political Science Review* 24 (August 1930): 610–611; Norman G. Kittrell, *Governors Who Have Been*, pp. 61–67.

meet opposition to the weak education article of the proposed constitution by declaring maintenance of public schools a duty of the Legislature. In keeping with the retrenchment spirit of the new constitution, the 1876 platform omitted 1873 planks favoring immigration and support for railroads. The convention sidestepped an outright endorsement of the new constitution, however, tabling such a motion in the interest of party harmony. For similar reasons it avoided the controversial question of whether the federal government should resume specie payments for greenbacks in 1879, as voted by Congress in 1875.[20]

Texas Republicans convened in Houston on January 12, amidst bickering between federal officeholders, generally from the old "conservative" faction of the party, and supporters of former Governor E. J. Davis, including most Texas Negro voters. Over three hundred delegates arrived from sixty-eight counties, mainly areas of Negro strength along the lower Brazos and Colorado rivers and in Northeast Texas, or of prewar Unionism north of Dallas along the Red River and in Central Texas between Austin and San Antonio, along the Rio Grande, and in the Hill Country, where many sheep raisers also favored protective tariffs. Negroes formed about 90 per cent of the party in Texas. The other 10 per cent consisted of Anglos, Germans, and Mexicans, about equally divided.[21]

The platform, adopted after limited discussion, opposed the new constitution, emphasizing the weak public school article, the awkward and burdensome judicial system, and the unfriendliness to immigration and internal improvements. The party policy statement went on to endorse the Grant administration and its policies, attack the state Democratic administration as uneconomical, call for en-

[20] *Galveston Weekly News,* January 10, 1876; Winkler, *Platforms,* pp. 174–176.

[21] Republican Party, Texas, *Proceedings of the Republican Convention of the State of Texas, 1876,* pp. 4–11; *Galveston Weekly News,* January 3, 1876; C. B. Sabin to E. M. Pease, October 10, 1875, E. M. Pease Papers; Homer Lee Kerr, "Migration Into Texas, 1865–1880" (Ph.D. diss.), pp. 5–22; Allen W. Trelease, "Who Were the Scalawags?" *Journal of Southern History* 29 (November 1963): 445–468.

forcement of the laws against Ku Klux Klan activity, and suggest ad valorem taxes rather than occupational taxes on the state level.[22]

When the convention turned to the selection of candidates for state offices, Davis, now chairman of the central committee, declined the gubernatorial nomination; the choice then went to William M. Chambers. A native of Virginia, Chambers had come to Texas during the 1840's, served in the Confederate army, and been impeached but acquitted for his actions as a Republican district judge in the 1870's. The nomination for lieutenant governor—refused by Webster Flanagan—went to F. W. Minor of North Texas. The delegates selected to the national convention belonged with one exception to the Davis faction.[23]

Southern-born or pre–Civil War immigrants to Texas, about equally divided between former Unionists and Confederate veterans, formed two-thirds of the Republican leadership—nominees, delegates to the national convention, presidential electors, convention officers, and platform committee members. Negroes, despite their overwhelming majority within the party, provided only a small percentage of its leaders. Lawyers constituted half of the delegates with the other half a scattering of editors, teachers, farmers, and merchants.[24]

Texas political parties in 1876, like those in other southern states, continued divided over Reconstruction issues of race, state finances, and state administration. When the Democrats had regained control in 1874 they had reduced the number of Negro officeholders, the level of state expenditures, and the exercise of state authority. The relatively low percentage of Negro population, except in a few counties, stimulated little effort in comparison to most southern states to centralize government controls or restrict the suffrage as means of re-

[22] Winkler, *Platforms*, pp. 177–179.

[23] Republican Party, Texas, *Proceedings, 1876*, pp. 21–25; *Galveston Weekly News*, January 17, 24, 1876.

[24] This analysis is also based on a check of the leaders listed in Winkler, *Platforms*, pp. 177–179, against biographical sketches in Webb and Carroll, *Handbook of Texas*, and in a variety of biographical volumes listed in Texas Historical Survey, "Index to Biographical Studies of Texans" (ms.).

ducing black political power. Intimidation and fraud did exist on the local level in some areas between races and between factions. Despite possible conflicts of interest and cases of incompetence, Texas Democrats provided no immediate examples of the corruption common to many southern Bourbon regimes.

Lone Star Democratic leaders did include some men with clear railroad, business, and banking interests, which received generally favorable consideration from the party in the 1870's. Former Whigs occupied fewer positions of prominence in the party than in most other southern states, however, because of the historical Democratic dominance in Texas politics. Representatives of agrarian interests shared political power to a greater extent than in most southern states because of the higher percentage of rural population and the level of farmer organization. The state Grange ranked second in size only to that in Kentucky and clearly influenced the constitutional convention in 1875.[25] Conflict between business and agricultural interests had not developed to any degree prior to 1876 because of the calls for Democratic unity during Reconstruction and the quite recent nature of most business expansion, especially of the railroads, which stimulated a change from subsistence production of food crops to commercial cotton raising.

The unwieldy bulk and diversity of the party suggested other possible future divisions between East and Central Texas farmers, West Central Texas cattlemen, and Southwest Texas sheep raisers; between urban and rural dwellers; and between the Anglo Methodist and Baptist majority and the major minorities: Negro Baptists and Methodists, Mexican and German Catholics, and German Lutherans. Factions interested in group or personal advantage in politics also had begun to form around such popular individuals as Governor Richard Coke. In 1876 Democrats still emphasized unity and Reconstruction issues, though the relatively young, postwar leadership represented a new generation which already had begun to show greater interest in economic questions.[26]

[25] Theodore Saloutos, *Farmer Movements in the South, 1865–1933*, p. 33.

[26] C. Vann Woodward, *Origins of the New South, 1877–1913*, pp. 1–22, 51–74.

Most Negroes and lesser numbers of Mexicans, Germans, and Anglos formed the Republican party, which took more favorable stands on civil rights, business development, and public schools. Based on the election of 1873, all hope of victory on the state level had been swept away, since the party represented only about one-third of the Texas voters, less than anywhere else in the South except Georgia. Under those conditions the factions which had developed out of different views on Reconstruction continued to wrangle over federal patronage. Leaders of both the conservative and radical wings remained predominantly white pre–Civil War Texans despite the fact that blacks formed the vast majority of party membership in Texas.[27]

For the men who made up the political parties of Texas, 1876 offered a complete array of campaigns from the local to the national level. Those campaigns in turn would test whether Reconstruction issues of race and philosophy of government would continue to divide Texans along existing party lines or whether political realignment would develop from the numerous economic, regional, and cultural differences which lay beneath the surface of past coalitions.

[27] Vincent P. De Santis, *Republicans Face the Southern Question*, p. 262.

2. THE CAMPAIGNS OF 1876

For Texans the year 1876 held the prospect of enough electoral campaigns to satisfy the most energetic and ambitious politicians. In February a state election would accept or reject the new constitution in addition to selecting a governor, lesser administrative officers, and a new Legislature. The new Legislature would then choose a United States senator in May. Finally, at the usual time in November, the voters would cast their ballots for congressmen and president. For Democratic party leaders these elections presented the challenge of maintaining or expanding their majority over the Republican opposition. To some Democrats the campaigns offered an opportunity for personal advancement. The wide margin of recent Democratic victories opened the way for new divisions within the party over economic and social issues previously muted by Reconstruction politics. If the Democrats divided over ambitions or issues, the Republicans might renew their hopes of victory or at least gain some influence by supporting a Democratic faction. The elections represented a potential period of transition for parties, politicians, and voters.

In the state campaign of 1876 Democratic candidates Richard Coke and Richard Hubbard spoke widely, contrasting their administration with that of E. J. Davis, which they characterized as wasteful, turbulent, and undemocratic. Republican gubernatorial candidate William Chambers made little effort to campaign. His running mate, F. W. Minor, did speak in Dallas opposing the constitution and attacking the Democrats as the party that had forced Sam Houston from office in 1861. Only 9 of the 186 newspapers in Texas identified themselves with the Republican party.

Several Republican leaders spoke against the constitution along the lines suggested by their platform. In reply, Coke, other Democratic candidates, and most newspapers favored the constitution as a general improvement, with weaknesses, especially the judicial article, susceptible to amendment. The *Houston Telegraph* and the *Austin Statesman* continued to attack its Granger-inspired retrenchment reforms as excessive. At least some of the opposition also stemmed from railroad and business interests that feared its potentially regulatory features.[1]

On the constitution Texans cast 136,606 votes for and 56,653 against, with twenty counties—mostly Republican—giving majorities against. In the immediate future there would be continued criticism of the judiciary article but no amendment of it. The school article, which allowed only community schools and no local school taxes, would prove uneven in application and require amendment in 1883 to allow district schools outside towns and local taxes to provide adequate support.

In the race for state offices Coke defeated Chambers 150,681 to 47,719, and other Democrats won by similar margins. The Demo-

[1] William Neal Ramey to O. M. Roberts, January 20, 1876, Oran M. Roberts Papers; James A. Ware to Ashbel Smith, December 31, 1875, Ashbel Smith Papers; *Galveston Weekly News*, February 7, 14, 1876; George P. Rowell, *American Newspaper Directory, 1876*, pp. 218–221; Oran M. Roberts, "The Political, Legislative, and Judicial History of Texas for Its Fifty Years of Statehood, 1845–1895," in Dudley G. Wooten, ed., *Comprehensive History of Texas, 1685–1897*, II, 218.

cratic vote had increased 65,000 over 1873, the Republican only about 5,000. The Democratic ratio thus had risen from two to one in 1873 to three to one in 1876. The Republicans carried only sixteen counties—two in Northeast Texas and eleven in Southeast Texas, all but one with Negro majorities, and three in the Hill Country west of San Antonio with its sheep raisers and old German Unionist element.[2]

Though Democratic strength appeared overwhelming at the state level, local campaigns displayed considerable variety in activities and results. In Dallas and elsewhere Democrats felt so confident of their majority that they did not concentrate their strength by making formal nominations for local offices. A proliferation of candidates resulted, allowing Republicans to unite behind one man with a chance of success. In Bexar County and certain other areas where Democrats made official nominations, independent Democrats took the field in opposition to views or actions of the official nominees. The *Galveston News* praised Negro Republicans for joining independent Democrats to elect city and county officers. The fusion failed, however, to elect a Negro, N. W. Cuney, state representative. The *Hempstead Messenger* reported that Negroes "voted as they were advised [to] by their present employers." In several rural counties Grangers either controlled the Democratic nominations or nominated their own candidates. Republicans in some Rio Grande Valley counties contested Democrats for Mexican votes. Democrats and Republicans in Houston imported voters from outside the county. A mixed set of officers, composed of Democrats, Republicans, and independents, resulted, as in several other counties and towns.[3] Clearly the

[2] Seth Shepard McKay, *Seven Decades of the Texas Constitution of 1876*, pp. 172–180; D. W. Ogletree, "Establishing the Texas Court of Appeals, 1875–1876," *Southwestern Historical Quarterly* 47 (July 1943): 5–18; Frederick Eby, *The Development of Education in Texas*, pp. 171–174, 194–197.

[3] *Dallas Herald*, February 5, 12, 19, 1876; *Galveston Weekly News*, January 17, February 7, 14, 21, 28, 1876; W. D. Oney to Ashbel Smith, February 7, 1876, Smith Papers; Diary, January 28, 29, February 15, 16, 1876, William Pitt Ballinger Papers; R. F. Mann and Jesse A. Sumpter to Richard Coke, April 17, 1876, Executive Correspondence.

diverse interests within the preponderant Democratic majority in the state had already produced internal unrest.

The new Legislature, like its predecessor, included three Republicans and one independent among its thirty-one senators. The house counted six Republicans and six independents among the ninety-three members, compared to ten Republicans in the previous Legislature. Of the overwhelming Democratic majority ten admitted to former Whig views and nine to being Grangers. Business and professional men, primarily attorneys, formed a majority of the body, with sixty-four members, while agriculturalists numbered forty-four. Southerners by birth, including eleven natives of Texas, constituted over 90 per cent of the membership; Confederate veterans held at least half of the seats, Negroes only five.[4]

Among its first duties the new Legislature faced the election of a United States senator to replace the incumbent Republican, Morgan C. Hamilton. A variety of political factions, economic interests, and geographical areas hoped to influence or control the decision. Several congressmen and state Democratic leaders had been mentioned in newspaper rumors during 1875 and early 1876, but the contest narrowed to Governor Coke, Congressman John Hancock, and former Supreme Court Justice John Ireland.

The balding, forty-six-year-old Coke had developed a position of considerable power because of his Grange support and control of state patronage.[5] Hancock, a big man with black hair, eyes, and mustache, from Alabama, had opposed the secession of Texas in 1861. After the Civil War he had become a successful lawyer with business views and served three terms in Congress as a Democrat from the Central and West Texas district around his home in Austin.

[4] John Cardwell, *Fifteenth Legislature. Sketches of Legislators and State Officers, 1876–1878; Daily Democratic Statesman* (Austin), May 2, July 16, 1876; Nat Q. Henderson, comp., *Directory of the Members and Officers of the Fourteenth Legislature of the State of Texas.*

[5] Richard Coke, Scrapbook; O. M. Roberts, "Historic Texas," April 1876, Roberts Papers; Norman G. Kittrell, *Governors Who Have Been*, pp. 61–67; Allen Johnson and Dumas Malone, eds., *Dictionary of American Biography*, IV, 278–279.

His pre–Civil War views gave him strength in some old Unionist areas and made him less repugnant than other Democrats to Texas Republicans.[6] Ireland, a slender, stern man born in Kentucky in 1827, had been a Know-Nothing and a Confederate major. Friends called him "Old Tige," "Honest John," and the "Sage of Seguin"; opponents preferred "Ox-cart John," a reminder of his opposition to a railroad bill while in the state senate. In the fall of 1875 he had resigned as chairman of the state Democratic executive committee to avoid a conflict of interests in his senate race. His strength lay primarily in South Texas around his home in Seguin, and in East Texas where he was considered "*a staunch southern man, a Bourbon.*"[7]

Coke, although quite popular, met considerable opposition from those who suspected that he might give up the governorship soon after reelection. Some newspaper editors accused him of hoping to use it as a stepping-stone to the Senate; others suggested a combination of Granger-railroad interests to elect Coke a senator, which would make Hubbard governor. That prospect alone stimulated a few newspapers that had backed Coke for governor to oppose his election as senator. Actually Coke had desired reelection as governor to vindicate his often-criticized administration, while privately indicating an interest in the position of senator if it were offered without his seeking it. To secure the votes of those who feared Hubbard's influence if governor, Coke promised, if elected senator, not to resign as governor before March 1877, when Hamilton's term officially ended. In addition Coke worried that Congressman James W. Throckmorton might be gathering support for Hancock in North Texas.[8]

Critics of Coke's administration called attention to the increased

[6] Walter P. Webb and H. Bailey Carroll, eds., *Handbook of Texas*, I, 763–764; Diary, 1909–1918, Horace Chilton Diaries, p. 434; Richard Coke to A. C. Gray, March 2, 1876, Earl Vandale Collection.

[7] Amory R. Starr to W. S. Coleman, May 3, 1876, Henry Raguet Papers; Kittrell, *Governors Who Have Been*, pp. 81, 90–92; Johnson and Malone, *Dictionary of American Biography*, IX, 493–494.

[8] Richard Coke to A. C. Gray, June 15, 1875, March 2, 1876, Vandale Collection; *Galveston Weekly News*, February 7, March 27, April 10, 24, May 8, 1876.

state debt; the continuing lawlessness in many sections of the state; grant of the state printing, in alleged disregard of lower bids, to the *Houston Telegraph*, a Coke organ; and the rumors that he and D. C. Giddings had divided the fee of a commission sent to recover the value of state indemnity bonds in Europe. The *Galveston News* also suggested that Coke had bartered gubernatorial acceptance of certain bills for senatorial votes in the Legislature. Coke defended himself in a message of April 19 and through friendly newspapers. The debt increase resulted from the issuance of bonds to pay pensions to veterans of the Texas revolution; he had tried to reorganize the Texas Rangers for frontier defense and law enforcement; and the charges concerning public printing and the commission funds were groundless.[9]

Perhaps the most persistent criticism of Coke stemmed from the status of his candidacy, especially in relation to that of John Ireland. In December 1875 Ireland wrote Coke that he planned to run and received in reply a letter wishing him well. But Ireland's friends failed to get a pledge from Coke that he would not enter the race. At the state Democratic convention rumors hinted at an Ireland-backed resolution requiring that the nominee for governor pledge himself to serve out his term in office. But Coke opposed such an idea and it was not adopted. From the state election to the legislative session, Ireland used Coke's original letter to prove that the governor had broken a promise of support. Finally, to allay doubts concerning the correspondence, Coke placed it before a caucus of his supporters in the Legislature, offering to withdraw if they thought the letter compromised his candidacy.[10]

John Hancock's Civil War Unionism, a source of some strength, also created considerable opposition, for many ex-Confederates felt,

[9] *Galveston Weekly News*, March 13, April 10, May 1, 1876; *Waco Daily Examiner*, April 16, 1876; Roberts, "Political History of Texas," in Wooten, *Comprehensive History*, II, 218–219; Richard Coke, Scrapbook.

[10] Richard Coke to A. C. Gray, March 2, 10, 18, 1876, August 27, 1877, Gustave Cook to Gray, April 21, 1876, Vandale Collection; Diary, March 18, 1876, Ballinger Papers; *Galveston Weekly News*, April 24, May 1, 1876; "What Senator Coke Said of John Ireland in 1877," broadside, A. W. Terrell Papers, Archives, Texas State Library.

with Coke, that Hancock was "*not* a representative man of this people." In February he denied that he had asked for command of Union Negro troops to invade the Rio Grande Valley during the Civil War. Trying to turn his position again into an asset, Hancock noted in a Washington interview that Northerners resented the increasing southern sentiment against former Unionists—a situation that might hamper the Democratic party on the national level by keeping alive bloody-shirt issues. Hancock also denied charges aimed at casting doubt on his postwar allegiance to Democratic views. His business and banking connections, a source of strength in Texas towns, also cost him support in rural areas.[11]

John Ireland, besides his argument with Coke over the best-wishes letter, faced newspaper accusations that he had opposed adoption of the new constitution. The *Dallas Herald* taxed him also with having advocated a legislative grant of twenty sections of land per mile of track in exchange for the bonds of the International Railway Company, to promote its extension through Austin to San Antonio and South Texas, his home area. And Ireland feared that the other United States senator from Texas, Sam Bell Maxey, was supporting Coke to avoid the possibility of facing him in a future senatorial race. The *Houston Age* argued in Ireland's behalf that he, unlike his two opponents, had resigned the office he held before seeking the senate seat. But Ireland's greatest strength and the greatest source of opposition to him proved to be his public image, which was, as the *Sherman Register* put it, that of an "impracticable Bourbon" who "draws all his inspiration from the war and the period antedating it."[12]

On May 1 the Legislature had the candidates speak in their own behalf. Coke and Ireland offered short, noncontroversial statements. Hancock spent over two hours defending himself against various charges, many of which, he said, emanated from the Ireland camp.[13]

[11] Richard Coke to A. C. Gray, March 2, 1876, Vandale Collection; John Hancock to Guy M. Bryan, April 17, 1876, Guy M. Bryan Papers; *Galveston Weekly News,* March 20, April 3, 17, 24, 1876.

[12] *Galveston Weekly News,* May 1, March 13, 27, 1876; John Ireland to O. M. Roberts, October 23, 1879, Roberts Papers.

[13] *Houston Daily Telegraph,* May 2, 1876.

Balloting began on May 3, the first vote being Coke, forty-nine; Ireland, thirty-nine; Hancock, twenty-nine; and former Governor Fletcher Stockdale, a possible compromise candidate, five. Coke's support came from North and Central Texas with scattered backing in East and West Texas. Ireland's votes came from South, East, and Northwest Texas with a few counties in Central and North Texas. Hancock's came from Central and West Texas, the Republican districts on the coast and in Northeast Texas, and from the cities. The second ballot on May 4 showed only minor shifts: Coke, fifty-two; Ireland, thirty-six; Hancock, twenty-eight; and Stockdale, four. In a caucus that day the trailing candidates apparently decided to concentrate their vote on Ireland. But in the balloting on May 5, after Stockdale and Hancock withdrew, enough of their West and Central Texas votes, and even a few original Ireland votes, shifted to Coke, giving him the election, sixty-eight to forty-nine. Coke's personal popularity, resulting from his victory over the Republicans in 1873, the agriculture-oriented retrenchment efforts of his administration, and his moderate political image compared to those of his two major opponents contributed to the governor's success. When Hancock withdrew, several of his supporters chose to go to Coke rather than to Ireland.[14]

After Coke's election attention turned to the Republican and Democratic national conventions. The Republicans met at Cincinnati in mid-June 1876. On national issues the Texas delegates expressed more interest in the protection of personal freedom in the South than in the financial question, although E. J. Davis did speak in favor of specie resumption. In the early balloting for a presidential nominee a majority of the Texans supported Oliver P. Morton of Indiana, a Radical. But on the sixth ballot A. B. Norton led the beginnings of a Texas shift to Rutherford B. Hayes of Ohio, a moderate reformer who had been a classmate of Norton's at Kenyon College. Before the convention another of his college friends, the staunch

[14] Texas, Legislature, Senate, *Journal*, 15th Legislature, Reg. sess., pp. 122–123, 127–128, 131–132; Richard Coke to A. C. Gray, March 2, 1876, Vandale Collection; *Waco Daily Examiner*, April 29, 1876; *Galveston Weekly News*, May 8, 15, 1876.

Texas Democrat Guy M. Bryan, had suggested to Norton that he support Hayes. On the seventh ballot Hayes received the nomination with 384 votes, including 15 of the 16 cast by Texans. The selection of Davis as national committeeman seemingly settled the question of Republican party leadership in Texas for the ensuing four years.[15]

The Democratic National Convention began in St. Louis on June 27 with the question of specie resumption a major issue. By Act of Congress in 1875 all "greenbacks," paper money issued during and after the Civil War with no gold or silver backing, were to be made payable in coin in 1879. The result would be deflationary, forcing debtors to pay back dollars of greater value than those they had borrowed. Naturally it had aroused much opposition in the growing West and rebuilding South. The Texas delegation supported a compromise platform demand for repeal of the specie resumption date, which allowed different interpretations in hard- and soft-money areas, but opposed a proposed demand for complete repeal of the act. A Texan seconded the nomination for president of Samuel J. Tilden, governor of New York, and the Texans gave him ten and a half of their sixteen votes on the first ballot and their whole vote on the second ballot, when he won the nomination. The Texans had opposed a strong stand for or against specie resumption in the platform and had acquiesced in the selection of an Easterner to promote a party victory in the national election. Former Governor Fletcher Stockdale, a South Texas land and railroad promoter, won reelection as the Texas member of the Democratic National Committee.[16]

In the fall campaign the six Democratic congressmen from Texas came home to defend their records and seek reelection. They shared similar views in favor of federal appropriations to improve Texas

[15] Republican Party, National Convention, 1876, *Proceedings*, pp. 64–65, 84–109; Paul Casdorph, *A History of the Republican Party in Texas, 1865–1965*, pp. 36–37; Richard C. Bain, *Convention Decisions and Voting Records*, pp. 102–104, Appendix D.

[16] Bain, *Convention Decisions*, pp. 106–107; *Galveston Weekly News*, July 3, 17, 1876; Democratic Party, National Convention, 1876, *Official Proceedings*, pp. 115–117, 137, 144–146; Irwin Unger, *The Greenback Era*, pp. 308–310; Deolece Parmelee, "Forgotten Prologue—Fletcher Summerfield Stockdale," *Texana* 2 (Fall 1964): 169–170.

rivers and harbors, the transfer of federal troops from the South to the Texas frontier, and lower tariffs to benefit Texas consumers rather than high tariffs for the protection of eastern industries. Each position had practical economic and political bases, though support of river and harbor bills represented a shift from at least partial opposition to internal improvments in the antebellum period. The Texans ignored any states' rights implications, however, to press for improved water transportation both as an end in itself and because they hoped it might also lower railroad rates. Only on the question of specie resumption did they differ strongly, with David B. Culberson, Roger Q. Mills, John H. Reagan, and James W. Throckmorton favoring repeal of the act, while John Hancock and Gustavus Schleicher supported its provisions. Yet local issues and personalities offered the Republicans their only hope of challenging the tremendous statewide Democratic majority on the congressional level.

In the First Congressional District of East Texas incumbent John H. Reagan, former postmaster general of the Confederacy, but still only forty-eight years old, again received the Democratic nomination over ex-congressman and railroad executive W. S. Herndon. Reagan, a Granger-style reformer, defeated Republican L. W. Cooper, a Georgia-born attorney and former Texas legislator and district judge, in the November election by 13,697 votes to 6,416. Cooper carried only one of the district's twenty-two counties.[17]

Democrats of the Second Congressional District in Northeast Texas renominated incumbent David B. Culberson, a Georgia-born lawyer and ex-Confederate colonel, to face Republican Stillwell H. Russell. A native of Texas, a Confederate veteran, and a former district attorney, Russell carried only Harrison and Marion counties. Culberson won, 17,326 to 9,130.[18]

[17] U.S., Congress, *Congressional Record*, 44th Cong., 1st sess., pp. 5231–5232; Ben H. Procter, *Not Without Honor*, pp. 207–214; H. L. Bentley and Thomas Pilgrim, *The Texas Legal Directory for 1876–77*, p. 45; James W. Truit to W. W. Spivey, July 15, 1876, James W. Truit Papers; *Galveston Weekly News*, August 21, December 25, 1876.

[18] *Galveston Weekly News*, September 25, December 25, 1876; Johnson and Malone, *Dictionary of American Biography*, IV, 586–587; *Biographical Encyclopedia of Texas*, pp. 98–99.

Incumbent Democrat James W. Throckmorton—a pre–Civil War Unionist but a Confederate veteran and a conservative governor after the war—met opposition in the Democratic Third Congressional District convention at Dallas because he was connected with the Texas and Pacific Railway Company and because he had opposed Tilden's nomination for president. Three counties apparently felt slighted in the railroad's limited construction program, but could not prevent Throckmorton's renomination. In the general election, by a vote of 24,138 to 1,283, he overwhelmed the Republican challenger J. C. Bigger, a thirty-two–year–old Ohio-born Union veteran, who had practiced law in Dallas for only a year.[19]

The Fourth Congressional District in Central Texas seemed a possible scene of Democratic internal strife. Charles Stewart, a Houston attorney and Confederate veteran who had withdrawn in favor of Roger Q. Mills in 1874, appeared ready to contest his renomination. But Mills, an ex-Confederate colonel and Corsicana attorney who had been born in Kentucky, announced his candidacy on July 1 and built up enough strength to receive the nomination by acclamation on August 30. Mills then faced Republican J. P. Osterhout, a Pennsylvania-born attorney and editor who had migrated to Texas in the 1850's and served in the Confederate army and as a district judge in the 1870's. The victory went to Mills, 20,731 votes to 8,639, with Osterhout carrying only four counties.[20]

In the Sixth Congressional District of Southwest Texas incumbent Democrat Gustavus Schleicher, a three-hundred-pound surveyor-engineer who had served in the Confederate army, won unanimous renomination. With strong support from cattlemen and from his fellow Germans, he defeated former Unionist and Republican Secretary of State of Texas James P. Newcomb, editor of the *San An-*

[19] Claude Elliott, *Leathercoat*, pp. 237–242; *Memorial and Biographical History of Dallas County*, pp. 383–384; *Galveston Weekly News*, December 25, 1876.

[20] *Galveston Weekly News*, June 26, August 7, December 25, 1876; *Waco Daily Examiner*, July 1, August 31, 1876; Myrtle Roberts, "Roger Quarles Mills" (M.A. thesis); *Memorial and Biographical History of McLennan, Falls, Bell, and Coryell Counties, Texas*, pp. 880–881.

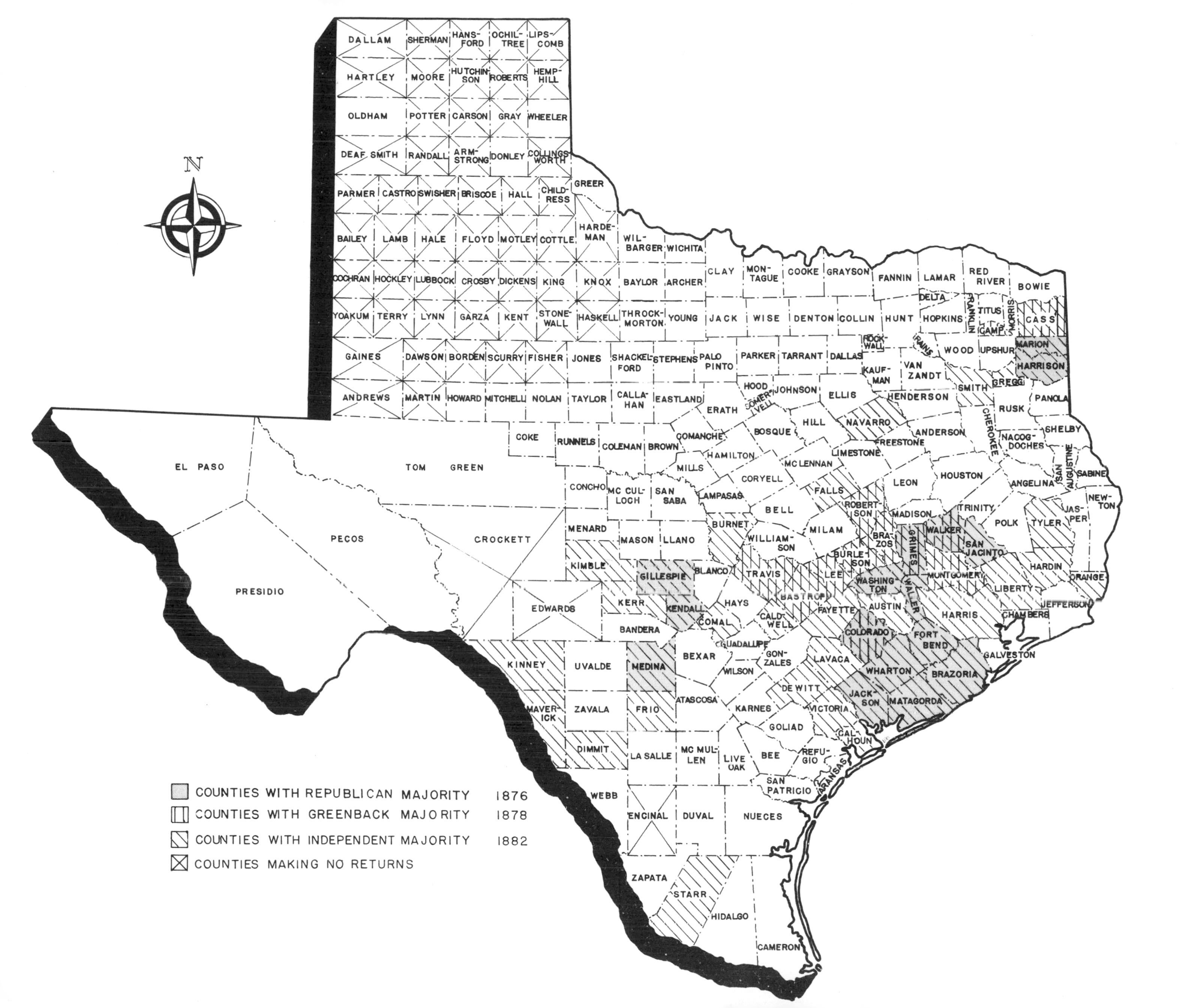
N
DALLAM
SHERMAN
HANS-FORD
OCHIL-TREE
LIPS-COMB
HARTLEY
MOORE
HUTCHIN-SON
ROBERTS
HEMP-HILL
OLDHAM
POTTER
CARSON
GRAY
WHEELER
DEAF SMITH
RANDALL
ARM-STRONG
DONLEY
COLLINGS-WORTH
PARMER
CASTRO
SWISHER
BRISCOE
HALL
CHIL-DRESS
GREER
BAILEY
LAMB
HALE
FLOYD
MOTLEY
COTTLE
HARDE-MAN
WIL-BARGER
WICHITA
COCHRAN
HOCKLEY
LUBBOCK
CROSBY
DICKENS
KING
KNOX
BAYLOR
ARCHER
CLAY
MON-TAGUE
COOKE
GRAYSON
FANNIN
LAMAR
RED RIVER
BOWIE
YOAKUM
TERRY
LYNN
GARZA
KENT
STONE-WALL
HASKELL
THROCK-MORTON
YOUNG
JACK
WISE
DENTON
COLLIN
HUNT
DELTA
HOPKINS
FRANKLIN
TITUS
CAMP
MORRIS
CASS
GAINES
DAWSON
BORDEN
SCURRY
FISHER
JONES
SHACKEL-FORD
STEPHENS
PALO PINTO
PARKER
TARRANT
DALLAS
ROCK-WALL
RAINS
WOOD
UPSHUR
MARION
HARRISON
KAUF-MAN
VAN ZANDT
GREGG
ANDREWS
MARTIN
HOWARD
MITCHELL
NOLAN
TAYLOR
CALLA-HAN
EASTLAND
ERATH
HOOD
SOMER-VELL
JOHNSON
ELLIS
HENDERSON
SMITH
PANOLA
RUSK
EL PASO
COKE
RUNNELS
COLEMAN
BROWN
COMANCHE
BOSQUE
HILL
NAVARRO
ANDERSON
CHEROKEE
SHELBY
TOM GREEN
HAMILTON
MILLS
FREESTONE
LIMESTONE
NACOG-DOCHES
MC LENNAN
CORYELL
LEON
HOUSTON
SAN AUGUSTINE
SABINE
CONCHO
MC CUL-LOCH
SAN SABA
LAMPASAS
FALLS
ANGELINA
NEW-TON
PECOS
CROCKETT
MENARD
BURNET
BELL
ROBERT-SON
MADISON
TRINITY
POLK
TYLER
JAS-PER
MASON
LLANO
WILLIAM-SON
MILAM
BRA-ZOS
GRIMES
WALKER
SAN JACINTO
KIMBLE
GILLESPIE
BLANCO
TRAVIS
BURLE-SON
LEE
WASHING-TON
MONTGOMERY
HARDIN
PRESIDIO
EDWARDS
KERR
KENDALL
HAYS
BASTROP
FAYETTE
AUSTIN
WALLER
LIBERTY
ORANGE
JEFFERSON
HARRIS
CHAMBERS
BANDERA
COMAL
CALD-WELL
COLORADO
FORT BEND
GALVESTON
KINNEY
UVALDE
MEDINA
BEXAR
GUADALUPE
GON-ZALES
WILSON
LAVACA
WHARTON
BRAZORIA
MAVER-ICK
ZAVALA
FRIO
ATASCOSA
KARNES
DE WITT
VICTORIA
JACK-SON
MATAGORDA
GOLIAD
CAL-HOUN
DIMMIT
LA SALLE
MC MUL-LEN
LIVE OAK
BEE
REFU-GIO
ARANSAS
SAN PATRICIO
WEBB
ENCINAL
DUVAL
NUECES
ZAPATA
STARR
HIDALGO
CAMERON
COUNTIES WITH REPUBLICAN MAJORITY 1876
COUNTIES WITH GREENBACK MAJORITY 1878
COUNTIES WITH INDEPENDENT MAJORITY 1882
COUNTIES MAKING NO RETURNS

tonio Republican, 11,254 votes to 2,711, without losing a single county.[21]

In those five districts straight Democratic-Republican contests, waged primarily on the basis of old Reconstruction issues and rhetoric, ended with predictable results.[22] But elsewhere there appeared signs of the changing times.

In the Fifth Congressional District of South Central Texas, Seth Shepard, a young Brenham attorney and former state senator, opened the race for the Democratic nomination. George P. Finlay, a Galveston attorney, Confederate veteran, and ex-state senator, joined him as a candidate. Incumbent John Hancock then returned from a political speaking engagement in New York City to campaign for renomination. At the district convention in August, Hancock's opponents—stimulated in part by his intemperate speech before the Legislature during the senatorial election—centered their support upon Shepard, next on Finlay, then on Shepard again as the voting remained deadlocked for three days. Finally, after the ninety-first ballot, both sides agreed on D. C. Giddings, an ex-Confederate colonel and Brenham banker.[23]

In September the *Bastrop Advertiser* shook the Democratic party by announcing with regret that its "honored and beloved townsman," G. W. "Wash" Jones, would oppose Giddings as an independent candidate. A former Unionist who had become a Confederate colonel, Jones had served as Democratic lieutenant governor in 1866–1867. Jones toured the district attacking Giddings for the high fee he had received for the recovery of state bonds in Europe and for his partisan comments against Republicans while claiming to speak

[21] E. J. Davis to J. P. Newcomb, July 19, 1876, J. L. Haynes to Newcomb, September 4, 1876, James P. Newcomb Papers; Christine Schott, "Gustavus Schleicher," *West Texas Historical Association Year Book* 28 (1952): 50–70; Webb and Carroll, *Handbook of Texas*, II, 275; *Galveston Weekly News*, September 4, December 25, 1876.

[22] *Galveston Weekly News*, September 4, 25, 1876.

[23] *Ibid.*, June 26, August 7, 14, 21, 28, 1876; Diary, August 14–19, 1876, Ballinger Papers; Johnson and Malone, *Dictionary of American Biography*, XVII, 74–75; Webb and Carroll, *Handbook of Texas*, I, 599, 686–687.

for harmony. Jones also criticized the convention system for producing the nomination of men the people did not favor, and the Legislature and Lieutenant Governor Hubbard for questionable acts connected with railroad land grants and for alleged bribery.[24]

Giddings responded with charges that Jones had Republican support and campaigned as an ex-Unionist in some areas and as an ex-Confederate in others. Throughout the race rumors spread that E. J. Davis would announce, hoping that the Democratic split would permit a Republican victory. Late in October, however, the Republican congressional executive committee endorsed Jones. Democratic tensions eased only when it became apparent several days after the election that Giddings had won, 15,286 to 13,277. Jones had received majorities in seven rural counties between Galveston and Austin because of his exceptional ability as an orator, plus a combination vote of small farmers, both Negro Republican tenants and white "Old Jackson Union Democrats." The defeat of Hancock in the convention upset some, while others opposed the nomination of Giddings or his equally business-oriented predecessor. Afterward accusations of false dealing and nonsupport racked the Democratic party within the district.[25]

Tilden carried Texas with 106,382 votes to 45,013 for Hayes, who won only three counties in deep East Texas, ten along the coast and lower Brazos River, two in the Hill Country, north of San Antonio, and two in the Rio Grande Valley—all generally Republican in the 1870's except for the politically unpredictable counties of South Texas. But Hayes went on to win the national election on the basis of contested returns from Louisiana, Florida, and South Carolina. In the ensuing dispute several Texas congressmen denounced the decision by the national electoral commission in favor of Hayes. All except Mills voted to accept it, however, motivated by desire for a peaceful solution and by a Republican compromise offer of aid to the

[24] Webb and Carroll, *Handbook of Texas*, I, 924; *Galveston Weekly News*, September 4, 25, October 9, 16, 1876.

[25] *Galveston Weekly News*, September 4, October 16, 30, December 25, 1876; James Shaw to E. M. Pease, October 16, 1876, E. M. Pease Papers; John Hancock, *Reply to the Attacks Made on Him by Col. Giddings on 4th November, and Col. Flournoy on 6th November, 1876, at Galveston, Texas.*

Texas and Pacific railroad, removal of the last federal troops from the South, and consideration of southern interests in the distribution of federal patronage.[26]

Through their senators and congressmen and through Hayes's friend Guy M. Bryan, Texas Democrats made some inroads into Republican control of federal offices in the state at the local level. They failed to gain any major appointments, however, despite efforts to place Hancock in the cabinet, Galveston attorney William Pitt Ballinger on the Supreme Court, and Bryan himself in the United States ministry at Mexico City.[27]

The campaigns of 1876 in Texas politics exhibited many lingering aspects of Reconstruction on every level. But the year actually represented a period of transition. The size and diversity of the Democratic majority led to internal divisions, based on personal ambitions, and the appearance of independent candidates in local elections, as in other southern states where Democrats clearly dominated. Internal divisions produced factions which would contest for position and power again in the future. The independents met with some success as Republicans resorted to fusion with Democratic factions. Thus attention began to turn away from issues based on Civil War views or race toward those involving economics, personalities, and local differences.

[26] Roger Mills to A. C. Gray, January 31, 1877, Vandale Collection; Procter, *Reagan*, pp. 215–216; C. Vann Woodward, *Reunion and Reaction: The Compromise of 1877 and the End of Reconstruction*, passim, especially p. 215; W. Dean Burnham, *Presidential Ballots, 1836–1892*, pp. 765–813.

[27] Ernest William Winkler, ed., "The Bryan-Hayes Correspondence," *Southwestern Historical Quarterly* 27 (July and October 1923): 63, 72–73, 165; Charles C. Tansill, *The Congressional Career of Thomas Francis Bayard, 1869–1885*, p. 193.

3. THE GREENBACK CHALLENGE

AN EAST TEXAN summarized widely held views when he wrote in 1878: "Money is hardly to be had, at all, outside of the Banks. And there the interest is ruinous. I know of nobody making money in our Country." In the 1870's the Texas cotton crop, raised primarily in the area north of the Nueces River and east of Fort Worth and Austin, provided the greatest source of wealth and employment, either directly or indirectly, for most Texans of that decade.[1] But cotton prices had begun to fall in 1874 because of the pervasive effects of the Panic of 1873. Initiated by the failures of eastern banking houses and stimulated by international wars and excessive railroad construction, business expansion, and speculation, the panic resulted in the United States in a nationwide depression which

[1] Henry W. Lightfoot to Sam Bell Maxey, June 1, 1878, Sam Bell Maxey Papers; Vera Lea Dugas, "A Social and Economic History of Texas in the Civil War and Reconstruction Periods" (Ph.D. diss.), p. 674; John S. Spratt, *The Road to Spindletop*, pp. 60–75, 83.

lasted until 1879. In addition Texas farmers felt apprehensive about the outcome of ever-nearing specie resumption with its deflationary effect. Such fears appeared most frequently among the numerous tenants and sharecroppers, including many of the recent and usually indebted immigrants, mainly from the South, who constituted over 37 per cent of all Texas agriculturists. The drought which struck much of Texas in 1878 compounded both problems.[2]

Increased economic problems did not necessarily mean major changes in Texas politics, however, for a variety of reasons. With a Republican state administration only four years in the past, Democratic party solidarity still appeared impressive despite the success of a few independent and fusion candidates in 1876. Many Texas farmers believed that through the Grange and its leaders and the politicians associated with it they had a real voice in the legislation and administration of the state by the Democrats. And on the national level the senators and five of the six congressmen from Texas had joined other Westerners and Southerners against resumption and for controlled inflation through free coinage of silver.[3]

But if economic conditions alone did not create explosive problems for Texas, they combined with local issues and personal ambitions to provide the basis for heated political differences. During 1877 and 1878 attention focused on the race for the Democratic gubernatorial nomination. By January 1878 the field had narrowed to Congressman James W. Throckmorton and Governor Richard B. Hubbard, who had taken office when Coke resigned to assume his senate seat in 1877. Support for the tall, angular Throckmorton came primarily from his home district in North Texas, where his efforts to encourage the Texas and Pacific Railroad and his combination of prewar Unionism, Confederate service, and a gubernatorial term which had

[2] Spratt, *Road to Spindletop*, pp. 41–42, 56, 111–113; Irwin Unger, *The Greenback Era*, pp. 342, 385; Samuel Lee Evans, "Texas Agriculture, 1880–1930" (Ph.D. diss.), pp. 310–311, 319; Ralph A. Smith, "The Grange Movement in Texas, 1873–1900," *Southwestern Historical Quarterly* 42 (April 1939): 300–301.

[3] Unger, *Greenback Era*, pp. 342, 355, 362; Roscoe C. Martin, "The Grange as a Political Factor in Texas," *Southwestern Social Science Quarterly* 6 (March 1926): 368–374.

been abbreviated by military order in 1867 made him a sentimental favorite. Hubbard, a stocky three-hundred pounder with a deep sonorous voice, known to his friends as "Jumbo," developed his greatest strength in East Texas, around his Tyler home, and in West Texas, where his connections with the advancing International Railway were acceptable. Throckmorton stood to lose some support because Senator Maxey, again looking ahead to potential opponents in 1881, would help swing a bloc of Northeast Texas counties away from him. But Throckmorton might gain in Central Texas, where the chairman of the Democratic state executive committee, Joseph D. Sayers, appeared to be pooling strength with Throckmorton and perhaps with Ireland, seeking the nomination for lieutenant governor.

Both gubernatorial candidates faced a variety of charges in the press. Throckmorton, the *Galveston News* suggested, wished to use the office of governor merely as a stepping-stone to the United States Senate. The newspapers reviewed his connections with the Texas and Pacific and lodged a new charge of involvement in fraud against him. Hubbard's critics attacked him for having represented several railroads in their legal affairs, and for having failed as governor to put down lawlessness. In addition they accused him of cowardice during the Civil War, of appropriating private funds to his own use, of making appointments to promote his political future, and of accepting bribes for a penitentiary lease. Most of the charges against each man resulted from public distrust of technically legal dealings, which bordered on conflicts of interest between the individual and the state. The highly partisan campaign allowed neither candidate to approach the state Democratic convention with an untarnished reputation.

Few substantive issues separated the two men. Both favored frontier protection, railroad construction, reduction of the state debt by refunding at lower interest rates, and general retrenchment in state government, with more efficient taxes. Throckmorton did make the more direct appeal to farmers, announcing that he supported remonetization of silver on the national level and greater taxation of such relatively untaxed property as railroads, instead of relying primarily upon land.[4]

Newspapers mentioned several other candidates, but only William W. Lang, sturdy, plainspoken grand master of the state Grange and member of the Legislature, actually entered the contest. His candidacy immediately came under the newspapers' fire as an apparent effort by the Grange to control the state government completely, and opponents charged Lang with using his Grange position to promote his personal ambitions. On the eve of the state Democratic convention Hubbard held a slim lead of forty-nine counties with 366 votes instructed for him, to Throckmorton's twenty-two counties with 304 votes, and Lang's five counties with 103 votes.[5]

On the second day of the convention at Austin in July, voting began on the gubernatorial nominees, after the candidates had spoken and the convention had defeated, 883⅔ to 579⅓, a pro-Throckmorton minority report from the credentials committee to seat one delegate from each unorganized county. The first ballot gave Hubbard 670 votes, Throckmorton 560, and Lang 240, with a two-thirds majority required for nomination. When Lang withdrew on the third day, two-thirds of his support swung to Throckmorton. On the fourth day Throckmorton lost ground slowly but steadily through the thirteenth ballot, then withdrew. Opponents of Hubbard renominated Lang, however, and the voting continued, despite suggestions from Hubbard supporters that he be nominated after leading through fourteen ballots. During the fifth day the opposition withdrew Lang and searched widely for another candidate. Finally they settled on Thomas J. Devine, a slight, graying San Antonio attorney who looked like a clergyman but proved unacceptable to some delegates because

[4] Claude Elliott, *Leathercoat*, pp. 253–267; George Raymond Nielsen, "Richard Bennett Hubbard, 'The Demosthenes of Texas'" (M.A. thesis), pp. 25–81; Norman G. Kittrell, *Governors Who Have Been*, pp. 76, 78; Biographical Notes, Horace Chilton Diaries, p. 317; *Galveston Weekly News*, February 11, April 1, June 24, 1878.

[5] *Galveston Weekly News*, January 21, 28, April 1, June 17, 1878; E. H. Cushing to Ashbel Smith, May 31, 1878, Ashbel Smith Papers; Elliott, *Leathercoat*, p. 266.

of his connections with the International Railway. Hubbard continued to increase his lead through the eighteenth ballot, when he received 906 of the 1,002 votes needed. Fearing his nomination, the opposition offered to take any compromise candidate acceptable to his supporters, but the Hubbard men refused. Devine then regained the lost ground and led on ballots twenty-two through twenty-seven. At last the Hubbard and Devine caucuses selected a conference committee to choose a compromise candidate. This joint committee also adopted a two-thirds rule and then balloted. John H. Reagan received fifteen votes; John Ireland, five; Roger Mills, three; William P. Ballinger, a Galveston attorney, two; Charles Stewart, one; and Oran M. Roberts, chief justice of the state supreme court, one. The Hubbard caucus learned that Reagan probably would not accept, because of his bill in Congress for railroad regulation, while the Devine group, thinking that the Hubbard faction favored Reagan, decided to support Roberts. Roberts then led for three ballots in the joint committee, which finally adopted a majority rule and presented him to the convention as the compromise candidate. It nominated him by acclamation. Texas Democrats had reached the brink of a major division amid the clash of personal factions tinged with mild agrarian-business overtones. Suddenly aware of the developing crisis they hastily stepped back for the sake of party unity.[6]

One young Democrat described the "tall, gray bearded, gray headed," rather awkward Roberts as "a notable and to some extent a ludicrous figure . . . a man that everybody laughed at and everybody loved and venerated." He had been born in South Carolina, educated at the University of Alabama, and elected to the state supreme court in Texas. Roberts had been president of the Texas secession convention and a Confederate colonel before his return to the state bench as chief justice in 1874 earned him the affectionate

[6] Elliott, *Leathercoat*, pp. 267–275; John H. Reagan, *Memoirs*, p. 246; Oran M. Roberts, "Political, Legislative, and Judicial History of Texas," in Dudley G. Wooten, ed., *Comprehensive History of Texas, 1685–1897*, II, 225–228; Biographical Notes, Chilton Diaries, p. 56; Diary, July 20, 1878, William Pitt Ballinger Papers; *Galveston Weekly News*, July 22, 1878, Seth Shepard McKay, "The Texas State Democratic Convention of 1878," *West Texas Historical Association Year Book*, 12 (1936): 3–10.

title of "Old Alcalde." Considered a "long and tedious" speaker even by some supporters, Roberts held legalistic small government views which made him popular with most Texas farmers, attorneys, and businessmen. His background and apparent lack of political ambition made him an ideal compromise candidate. Texas Democrats had resorted to a figure and a philosophy from the past in their failure to evolve a new consensus on state administrative policies for the future.[7]

The convention did adopt a platform which to some degree reflected the changing times. The "commercial and industrial stagnation" of the nation resulted from "the pernicious financial legislation of the Republican party . . . demonetizing silver and decreeing the destruction of legal tender paper." The Texas Democrats suggested repeal of the Resumption Act, free coinage of silver, use of United States currency in place of national bank notes, reduction and taxation of the government's bonded debt, and a revenue tariff rather than a protective one. W. H. Hamman and R. S. Pridgen of the platform committee urged the convention to go still further by calling for the issuance of greenbacks equal to existing United States treasury notes and bonds and acceptable for payment of the nation's bonded debt, much of which could be paid only in coin. The convention refused.[8] On purely state issues new planks favored regulating railroad rates, exempting farm products in the hands of the farmer from taxation, prohibiting convict labor outside the penitentiaries, and avoiding state government expenses in excess of revenues.

While Democrats held back from complete endorsement of greenbacks, however, ardent paper-money advocates in Texas had begun to form Greenback clubs—local chapters of the National Greenback party. Farmer and labor groups in the Midwest had created the organization in 1874 to oppose resumption. It polled only 80,000 votes in the presidential election of 1876, but continuing depression,

[7] Chilton Diary, 1909–1918, pp. 410, 412; Lelia Bailey, "The Life and Public Career of O. M. Roberts, 1815–1883" (Ph.D. diss.); Diary, October 25, 1878, Ballinger Papers.

[8] Ernest William Winkler, ed., *Platforms of Political Parties in Texas*, pp. 183–186; McKay, "Texas State Democratic Convention of 1878," pp. 8–9.

labor unrest, dissatisfaction over the election, and fears of the deflationary effect of specie resumption caused it to grow rapidly in 1877.[9]

Independent clubs in North Texas had advocated paper money during the state campaign of 1876. In the spring of 1877 the new party began to organize in Texas. Supporters established a Greenback club and a paper, the *Texas Capital*, in Austin in September. The paper immediately advocated fusion between the Greenback club and the local Workingmen's club. In October, when membership in the Greenback club reached one hundred, both clubs endorsed various independent candidates for local offices. About half of the candidates won. At least fifty-nine clubs existed in the state by November.[10]

Enthusiasm ran high among Texas Greenbackers in 1878. A succession of organizational meetings, like the one attended by one hundred persons at Waelder in Gonzales County on February 16, enabled the secretary of the state executive committee to report, in early March, 127 clubs and an average of 200 new supporters each week. J. W. Jennings of Denison represented Texas at the February 1878 convention in Toledo, Ohio, where several hundred delegates attended from twenty-eight states. He said that many Texans held Greenback views but that most of them still remained in the Democratic party—a statement Greenbackers at home strongly disputed. An Independent Greenback convention in Austin on March 12 drew about forty delegates from fourteen counties, mostly in Central Texas. Predominantly farmers and mechanics, about equally divided between ex-Democrats and ex-Republicans, the delegates included ten Negroes. The convention adopted a platform emphasizing their financial views, appealed to the Grange for support, and took steps to increase cooperation among the clubs represented there.[11]

[9] Solon J. Buck, *The Agrarian Crusade*, pp. 81–89; Fred E. Haynes, *Third Party Movements since the Civil War*, pp. 106–124.

[10] *Texas Capital* (Austin), September 16, 23, October 28, November 4, 13, 18, 25, 1877, April 28, 1878; Roscoe C. Martin, "The Greenback Party in Texas," *Southwestern Historical Quarterly* 30 (January 1927): 161–177; *Dallas Herald*, January 8, 1876.

[11] *Texas Capital*, March 10, 17, 1878; *Galveston Weekly News*, March 11, 18,

In April state executive committee chairman W. A. H. Miller reported 250 clubs in Texas, including 7 white clubs and 5 Negro clubs in Milam County, 17 in Travis County by June, and 9 in Guadalupe County by July. Picnics and speakers served to attract new members. In June the new party showed its strength in Grimes County by dividing the local ticket with the Democrats in a gentlemen's agreement. During the summer the movement spread over southern, central, western, and northern Texas. After the bitter Democratic convention struggle many felt that if the Greenbackers selected a prominent candidate for governor, they could develop enough support among Republicans and dissatisfied Democrats, especially Grangers, to threaten strongly the Democratic control of Texas.[12]

Two hundred and seventeen delegates representing 482 Greenback clubs—70 of them for Negroes—opened a state convention at Waco on August 7. They came almost exclusively from the farming areas and major towns of the state. The meeting ousted a white delegate for refusing to sit with the several Negroes present, though it later readmitted him. Farmers or men in farm-related occupations filled at least half of the positions of leadership, attorneys about one-third, and a scattering of other professional men or skilled laborers the rest. A few of the Greenback leaders had business connections which marked them as speculators or promoters seeking to ease their debt payments in the midst of the depression or to facilitate easier credit for business expansion. Over four-fifths had been born in the South, most of them in Kentucky, Tennessee, Missouri, or Maryland, and at least two-thirds had come to Texas before the Civil War. Their average age was about forty-five. Perhaps half had served in the Confederate army, but only a limited number had been Republicans or Grangers.[13] Texas Democratic leaders contrasted significantly only

1878; Frederick Kemp Dixon, "A History of Gonzales County in the Nineteenth Century" (M.A. thesis), pp. 75–76.

[12] *Texas Capital*, April 21, 28, June 30, July 7, 14, 21, August 4, 1878; *Galveston Weekly News*, June 10, July 8, 29, August 5, 1878.

[13] *Galveston Weekly News*, August 12, 1878; Winkler, *Platforms*, pp. 187–190: the analysis of Greenback leadership rests upon information about 46 of the

because attorneys formed a clear majority, and because they held a limited advantage in political experience.

The platform adopted by the convention called for abandoning the old parties and uniting "in the National Greenback Labor party to save business men from bankruptcy, the working classes from starvation, the whole country from revolution, and the Nation from repudiation." On the national level it attacked resumption, demonetization of silver, repeal of the income tax, national banks, and importation of "servile" Asiatics "as crimes against the people." In Texas the Greenbackers opposed the use of convicts to compete with mechanics and laborers, land grants to railroads and corporations, "odious and unjust" state taxes on occupations and smokehouses, and excessive state offices and salaries. Turning to the positive side, the platform advocated an income tax and a revenue tariff in national politics. For Texas it favored the reestablishment of public schools, railroad regulation, the funding of state bonds at 4 per cent, frontier protection, low maximum rates for state and county taxes, and a larger homestead exemption. Above all else the party demanded the issuance of greenbacks that should be legal tender for all debts, including United States bonds, and equal in value to the United States treasury notes in circulation. The call for more currency in circulation stemmed in part from the existence of only twelve national banks and eighty-five private banks to serve the financial needs of one and a half million Texans—figures well below the national average. Delegates hoped the platform would warm the hearts of Texas farmers and laborers who faced a combination of debts and falling prices. It construed the legality of greenbacks even more broadly than the Democrats did and suggested more measures in behalf of farmers and laborers on the state level. It also appealed to Negro voters, especially by the strong public school plank.[14]

---

129 men listed. The information is from *A Legislative Manual for the State of Texas,* 1879; Will Lambert, comp., *Pocket Directory of the Seventeenth Legislature of Texas*; and biographical sketches in Walter P. Webb and H. Bailey Carroll, eds., *Handbook of Texas,* and various biographical volumes listed in Texas Historical Survey, "Index to Biographical Studies of Texans" (ms).

[14] Avery L. Carlson, *A Monetary and Banking History of Texas,* pp. 39, 43;

By unanimous vote the Greenbackers nominated for governor William H. Hamman—signer of the minority platform report in the state Democratic convention and a prominent railroad and land developer of Robertson County. A tall, forty-eight–year–old attorney, born in Virginia, he had come to Texas in the 1850's, had favored secession, and had become a Confederate officer. His Democratic opponents considered him "a man of some ability and a most untiring . . . worker," but of course thought him "impracticable and visionary." For lieutenant governor the convention selected James S. Rains, a sixty-one–year–old native of Tennessee, former member of the Missouri legislature, and southern officer in the Civil War. He had come to Texas in the 1860's and settled as a farmer-attorney in Kaufman County, where he had tried to promote a railroad. For commissioner of the general land office the delegates nominated Jacob Kuechler—a pre–Civil War German immigrant, a Unionist, and Republican land commissioner in the Davis administration—the only other nominee of more than local prominence. The Greenbackers selected two other former Republicans among the men to serve as congressional district chairmen.[15]

Hamman began his campaign with a speech at Austin on August 24. He emphasized the need for greenbacks to provide credit for paying debts, and suggested fifty dollars per person as a proper amount to be issued without fear of depreciation. His speaking tour scheduled debates with Roberts and other Democrats at Seguin on September 10, with D. B. Culberson at Jefferson, with Roberts again at Longview and Jacksonville, and with Lang at Tyler. Rains and other state candidates also stumped for the party as did the four Greenback congressional candidates.[16]

Campaign oratory by Texas Greenbackers extolled the advan-

Allyn A. Young, *An Analysis of Banking for the United States*, p. 3; Winkler, *Platforms*, pp. 187–190.

[15] Winkler, *Platforms*, p. 187; Richard Coke to O. M. Roberts, August 15, 1878, Oran M. Roberts Papers; Ada Margaret Smith, "The Life and Times of William Harrison Hamman" (M.A. thesis); *Galveston Weekly News*, August 12, 19, 1878; *Texas Capital*, August 11, 1878; *Dallas Daily Herald*, September 11, 1867; Webb and Carroll, *Handbook of Texas*, I, 975.

[16] Smith, "Hamman," pp. 146–163; *Texas Capital*, October 6, 1878.

tages of greenbacks to increase the amount of currency in circulation. They charged the two older parties with domination by eastern and foreign financiers, including "German Jews, the Rothschilds, and English capitalists." Yet similar attacks by Democratic candidates against Republicans establish such statements as common southern and western political stereotypes of bankers and bondholders rather than evidence of anti-Semitism.[17]

Greenbacker calls for Republican support did not go unanswered. In July E. J. Davis announced to a Greenback meeting in Austin that he had become an opponent of resumption. Then on August 13 after the Greenback state convention, Davis proclaimed his support of the Greenback party, saying "The best thing to be done for the future of Texas is to break down the Democratic party . . ." A majority of the Republican state executive committee agreed and chose to make no nominations for state offices. But a dissident faction, including several national bankers and federal officeholders who feared the Davis element and the Greenbackers, held a small convention in Dallas. They nominated a straight Republican ticket with A. B. Norton for governor and Richard Allen of Houston, a Negro contractor and former legislator, for lieutenant governor.[18]

Through their campaigns the Greenback candidates developed a variety of supporters across much of the state. The Greenback press provided the new party with a means of spreading its views. Besides some Travis County newspapers, others in Montague, Milam, Comanche, Leon, Dallas, Galveston, Cass, Tarrant, Lee, Falls, and Grayson counties supported the movement. Yet despite the sudden birth of such Greenback sheets, the overwhelming majority of the Texas press remained openly or tacitly Democratic.[19]

Negro and white Greenback clubs organized in Harris County; mechanics, contractors, laborers, and small merchants joined the new

[17] *Texas Capital*, August 25, 1878.

[18] *Ibid.*, July 28, September 1, 1878; *Galveston Weekly News*, August 19, 1878; Winkler, *Platforms*, pp. 190–193.

[19] George P. Rowell, *American Newspaper Directory*, 1879, pp. 326–331; *Texas Capital*, March 31, September 1, October 6, 1878; *Galveston Weekly News*, September 2, October 14, 1878; *Waco Daily Examiner*, October 8, 29, 1878.

party in Houston. A rump Workingmen's party, led by former Republican editor and railroad developer J. G. Tracy, threatened to split the Houston Greenbackers, however, until the selection of a compromise ticket restored harmony. Republicans in neighboring Montgomery County endorsed the local Greenback nominees. In Burleson County white subsistence farmers constituted the strength of the new party. Farmers, ranchers, and skilled workmen made up the Greenback ticket in Travis County. In Waco the new party held a large barbecue attended primarily by Negroes; black Greenbackers were active in Walker and Waller counties; and Negroes made up one-third of those present at the Greenback convention of the Second Congressional District in Northeast Texas. Small farmers or ranchers and laborers of various types in the towns, including a high percentage of Negroes in both groups, apparently dominated the membership of the party.[20]

Democrats began to express worries over the growing Greenback challenge in the spring of 1878. The *Galveston News* declared the new party basically weak because Texas Democrats overwhelmingly shared the same general views. The *Houston Age*, openly antagonistic, compared Greenback clubs to the Loyal League of Reconstruction.[21] After the Democratic state convention the gubernatorial nominee, Roberts, accepted the advice of political friends to tour Central and North Texas to make himself better known and to counter increasing Greenback strength. In his speeches he charged the Republicans with legislation, especially resumption, favoring monopolies at the expense of the people; he attacked the Greenback party as a northern, not a southern, product, including Republicans, Negroes, and disaffected Democrats; and he said that to pay off national bonds with unredeemable paper currency would be un-

[20] *Galveston Weekly News*, August 5, 19, 26, September 2, 9, 16, 23, 30, October 7, 21, 28, 1878; *Texas Capital*, September 1, 29, 1878; Frank MacD. Spindler, "Concerning Hempstead and Waller County," *Southwestern Historical Quarterly* 59 (April 1956): 457; H. F. Gillette to Ashbel Smith, August 1, 1878, James Burke to Smith, September 13, 1878, Smith Papers.

[21] E. H. Cushing to Ashbel Smith, April 29, 1878, Smith Papers; *Galveston Weekly News*, March 25, April 15, 1878.

constitutional. On state issues Roberts reiterated the Democratic platform promises of reduced expenses and greater efficiency.[22]

Other leading Democrats, including Senators Coke and Maxey, joined Roberts on the stump. Their speeches ranged from attempts to out-greenback the Greenbackers to violent attacks on them as predominantly ex-Republicans or Democrats with crackpot financial views. Maxey drew a partially inaccurate but politically useful comparison of greenbacks with the "continentals" of the American Revolution, Confederate paper money, and the "redbacks" of the republic of Texas. Congressmen Culberson, Reagan, and Mills, who were unopposed for renomination, concentrated on the contest with the Greenbackers.

In the fall the Greenbackers offered no candidate against Reagan, who fought them politically but shared their views on most issues. Culberson and Mills faced Greenback opponents in their East and Central Texas districts, however, as did Olin Wellborn, the Democratic nominee in Throckmorton's old North Texas district. Henry F. O'Neal and E. M. Daggett, former legislators who were third-party candidates, conducted active local campaigns.[23]

In South Central Texas, Democrats of the Fifth Congressional District revived their conflict of 1876 over personalities and Unionism when John Hancock entered the race for the nomination in April 1878. Seth Shepard, who had withdrawn in favor of Giddings two years before, again opposed Hancock. Delegates to the convention at Brenham in August waged another heated contest, but Shepard withdrew on the ninth ballot. Hancock's strength came primarily from Galveston and Austin. Several leading Democrats soon attacked him

[22] *Galveston Weekly News,* September 2, 1878; A. W. Terrell to O. M. Roberts, July 31, 1878, Roberts Papers; Roberts to J. W. Truit, December 2, 1878, James W. Truit Papers; Bailey, "Life and Career of O. M. Roberts," pp. 280–285; Smith, "Hamman," p. 147; Roberts, "Political History of Texas," in Wooten, *Comprehensive History of Texas,* II, 231.

[23] Richard Coke to O. M. Roberts, August 15, 1878, Richard Hubbard to Roberts, August 27, 1878, Roberts Papers; Ashbel Smith to S. B. Maxey, September 13, 1879, Maxey Papers; Webb and Carroll, *Handbook of Texas,* I, 453; Eugene C. Barker and Ernest William Winkler, eds., *A History of Texas and Texans, by Frank W. Johnson,* III, 1257; *Galveston Weekly News,* June 24, August 12, September 9, 16, October 7, 1878.

as a former Know-Nothing and Unionist who had opposed the Confederacy and refused to back Giddings in 1876. His straddling views in favor of both increased currency and sound money also came under severe criticism. He campaigned actively, calling the Greenbackers alarmists and arguing that issuance of greenbacks would virtually repudiate the national debt and destroy public and private credit. Like most Texas congressmen he favored federal aid to improve Texas harbors—especially Galveston, in his district.[24] Hancock also faced the most serious challenger of the Democratic rule in "Wash" Jones, who had been narrowly defeated as an independent candidate in 1876. Jones opened a campaign on greenback principles in April 1878 and continued to speak throughout the summer and fall, engaging in debates with his opponent and appealing openly to Negro as well as to white voters.[25]

In the Sixth Congressional District Democrats found themselves caught up in a bitter internal struggle. Congressman Schleicher had been the only Texan in 1876 voting against bills to repeal specie resumption and to resume limited silver coinage, both aimed at increasing the amount of money in circulation. To him it seemed that "here in Texas our party from fear of the Greenbackers has taken a greenback mongrel platform and stands on no ground whatever." Considerable unrest developed in the farming area east of San Antonio because of Schleicher's votes in Congress. By April 1878 many persons were urging John Ireland to oppose him. The district convention met at San Antonio in July and, after five days of deadlock, with Schleicher leading but unable to obtain a two-thirds majority, adjourned without a nomination. Campaigning then began in earnest and continued into October, even though Schleicher became ill at various times. Schleicher claimed to have procured harbor surveys and better mail service for his district and to have worked for rail-

[24] *Galveston Weekly News*, April 15, June 24, July 15, August 12, 19, 1878; Diary, July 1, 2, August 4–9, 11, 1878, Ballinger Papers; Guy M. Bryan to A. Bryan, September 1, 1878, Guy M. Bryan Papers; Democratic Party, Texas, Galveston, *To the People of the Fifth Congressional District, State of Texas*; *Waco Daily Examiner*, August 27, 1878.

[25] *Galveston Weekly News*, April 29, May 6, 27, June 3, 10, September 30, 1878; *Texas Capital*, March 17, 1878.

roads, for a tariff on wool, and for frontier protection. He believed that resumption would increase gold circulation, that the Bland silver bill would simply depreciate currency, and that greenbacks would destroy credit. Ireland he attacked as a former Know-Nothing who had once opposed the San Antonio–bound International Railway and would do nothing for frontier protection. In reply Ireland denied any anti-German sentiment, said Schleicher actually had done little for frontier defense, and continued to berate his opponent's views on resumption and silver coinage.[26]

Because of its own internal dissensions and the strong farmer appeal of the opposition, Democratic party success rested to a considerable extent on continued support from the Grange. Grange interest in social events and a return to diversified farming set it apart from the Greenback party emphasis on political solutions to the problems of commercial agriculture. In the spring, while Grand Master Lang sought the Democratic gubernatorial nomination, Greenback efforts proved generally unavailing among Grangers. After his defeat in the state convention, Lang still refused a request to run for governor as an independent and campaigned for Roberts. The *Waco Examiner*, considered the voice of the Texas Grange, announced that it favored reform within the Democratic party, although "we are just as good a Greenbacker as the Georgetown *Era*." Thus the Democrats retained strong farm support, while offering at the same time some more conservative views, especially on national bonds, to avoid alienating the railroad interests and the businessmen.[27]

The final days of the campaign witnessed several acts of intimidation. In Montgomery County seventy-five armed Democrats drove away two Greenback speakers. The incident came after local

[26] G. Schleicher to Thomas F. Bayard, August 19, 1878, Thomas F. Bayard Papers; U.S., Congress, *Congressional Record*, 45th Cong., 1st sess., pp. 241, 632; *Waco Daily Examiner*, August 27, 1878; *Galveston Weekly News*, February 4, March 25, April 8, June 24, July 1, 22, 29, August 5, 26, September 2, 9, 23, October 7, 1878.

[27] *Texas Capital*, May 12, June 2, 1878; *Waco Daily Examiner*, August 23, 1878; William W. Lang to O. M. Roberts, August 1, December 20, 1878, F. S. Stockdale to Roberts, August 27, 1878, James Burke to Roberts, September 1, 1878, Roberts Papers.

charges and countercharges of misappropriating funds, illegally influencing elections, and threatening opponents. The thwarted Greenbackers upon their return to Houston swore out federal warrants against nineteen Democrats, who were arrested but later released. At Hearne several Negro Greenbackers kept Republican Richard Allen from speaking, and a Democratic candidate for the Legislature later struck his opponent on the head with a pistol. Near Marshall masked men broke up a Republican meeting. In Austin and Houston Greenbackers feared that bogus ballots were substituted for real ones, while Galveston Democrats claimed that Negro votes were purchased by the opposition.[28]

Roberts and the Democratic ticket swept the statewide elections with 158,933 votes to Hamman's 55,002 and Norton's 23,402. Hamman carried twelve counties in Central and Northeast Texas; Norton, seven counties of Northeast and Southeast Texas and one in the Hill Country. Hamman carried three of fourteen counties with Negro majorities and five of thirteen with black minorities of 40 per cent or more. Norton won seven counties with Negro majorities; Roberts carried two others by pluralities. Greenbackers and Republicans together reduced the Democratic margin to two to one from three to one in 1876. Greenback votes had come primarily from farming areas with Baptist and Methodist, Anglo and Negro majorities, especially where Republican or Unionist views had made dissent more acceptable, and from predominantly working-class urban wards of similar ethnic and religious composition. Lack of widespread labor organization as well as the cultural and religious views of immigrant workers kept other labor wards from joining the shift to the new party.[29]

[28] Diary, November 6, 1878, Ballinger Papers; William Alexander to G. W. Jones, November 14 [1878], E. M. Pease Papers; *Galveston Weekly News*, October 28, November 4, 11, 1878; *Texas Capital*, December 15, 1878; T. J. Renfro, *Thirteen Years of Radical Misrule.*

[29] Information on labor voting came from a comparison of ward votes as they appeared in the *Galveston News*, November 19, 1878, *Austin Weekly Democratic Statesman*, November 14, 1878, and *Waco Daily Examiner*, November 7, 1878; with occupations of voting age males living in each ward, as listed in U.S., Tenth Census, 1880, Population, for Galveston and Travis counties, Texas, microfilm,

In three of the congressional races Democrats won by margins of two, three, and four to one. In the fifth district, however, Hancock lost to Jones, 19,721 to 21,101. Jones's success came because of his oratorical ability, his mixed Unionist-Confederate background, his Greenback views, and Republican support. In the contest between Democrats in the sixth district Schleicher won over Ireland, 19,199 votes to 15,671. Schleicher had the backing of German Lutherans and Catholics, San Antonio businessmen, Hill Country sheepmen, and powerful ranchers and landowners below the Nueces River who controlled the votes of their Mexican Catholic laborers and vaqueros. Ireland, enjoying Greenback and some Republican support, did carry eighteen predominantly evangelical Anglo and Negro farming counties north of the Nueces and east of San Antonio.[30] Greenbackers in Central and East Texas elected two state senators, ten representatives, and several local officials, especially in Travis and Harris counties. Greenback inroads on the Democratic vote allowed the election of four Republican state senators, nine representatives, and a number of county officers.[31]

Schleicher died shortly after his victory over Ireland. In the spring election that followed, Henry Maney, a Tennessee-born Republican county judge, ran as a Greenbacker against Columbus C. Upson, a New York–born Confederate veteran and San Antonio attorney. Despite Maney's quiet efforts to develop Republican and German support, Upson, a Democrat who accepted the position of the state platform on greenbacks, won with the votes of most former backers of Schleicher and Ireland.[32]

The University of Texas Library; and John Sleeper and J. C. Hutchins, *Waco and McLennan County, Texas, Containing a City Directory of Waco.*

[30] Texas, Legislature, Senate, *Journal*, 16th Legislature, Reg, sess., pp. 70–77; Texas, Secretary of State, *Report*, 1878, pp. 68–69; *Galveston Weekly News,* July 22, September 23, October 14, 1878; Charles L. Lege to O. M. Roberts, July 31, 1878, A. W. Terrell to Roberts, November 11, 1878, Roberts Papers; Henry Maney to J. P. Newcomb, October 2, November 8, 1878, James P. Newcomb Papers.

[31] *A Legislative Manual for the State of Texas*, 1879; Spindler, "Concerning Hempstead and Waller County," p. 457; *Texas Capital*, November 10, December 15, 1878.

[32] *Texas Capital*, March 30, 1878; Henry Maney to J. P. Newcomb, March 25,

Their victories notwithstanding, Democrats faced major problems of patronage as requests for appointive positions continue to increase. One Roberts supporter found the outlook so dismal he predicted "the Dem[ocratic] party in this state is on the wane. Unless we had a thousand or two offices to partially supply the demand the party will go to pieces, or rather melt away and the meltings go to Republicans and Greenbackers, more to the latter."[33]

In March 1879 a large Texas delegation attended the national convention of the Union Greenback Labor party, a factional organization representing all Greenback clubs. Hamman served as temporary president; B. J. Chambers of Johnson County won election to the national executive committee; and the delegates reported 658 clubs in Texas, a number exceeded only in Missouri and Illinois.[34]

Greenback members in the Sixteenth Legislature offered bills generally reflecting their farmer-labor views. They opposed the use of convicts outside prisons, the dog tax, which fell heavily on tenant farmers, railroad land grants, sale of large blocks of cheap public land, and a poll tax as a voting requirement. They favored funding the bonded debt, liens to protect artisans and mechanics, maximum school appropriations, lower ad valorem taxes, and an income tax. One of them claimed during the regular session: "The greenbackers have made a good record for the party in this Legislature, the democrats themselves admit it, we have their respect . . ." In Congress Jones opposed a silver-coinage bill because he favored greenbacks, but he joined other Texans against the recharter of national banks and for river and harbor appropriations that included Texas ports.[35] Greenbackers found themselves too weak in the Texas Legislature

1879, John L. Haynes to Newcomb, April 5, 1879, Newcomb Papers; *Galveston Weekly News*, March 31, April 14, 21, 1879.

[33] John C. Robertson to O. M. Roberts, November 8, 1878, Roberts Papers.

[34] *Texas Capital*, March 16, 1878.

[35] W. N. Linton to James R. Davis, March 4, 1879. N. H. Davis Papers; Texas, Senate, *Journal*, 16th Legislature, Reg. sess., pp. 12, 13, 93–94, 115, 593; Texas, Legislature, House of Representatives, *Journal*, 16th Legislature, Reg. sess., pp. 124, 227, 232, 283, 493, 509, 626, 660–661, 738; Edward McPherson, *A Handbook of Politics for 1882*, pp. 28, 141–142, 176–177; *Bastrop Advertiser*, August 9, 1879; *Texas Capital*, June 29, October 27, 1879.

and in Congress, however, to accomplish anything except in coalition with sympathetic Democrats.

During 1879 Greenback clubs continued to organize despite poor communication between state and local leaders and confusion over factional fights in the national party. Greenback congressional district conventions met to promote enthusiasm in preparation for the campaigns of 1880. Hamman debated Culberson and Wellborn several times in North Texas. At Weatherford, after a heated exchange, Wellborn struck the Greenback leader with his fist. Jones toured Central Texas after his return from Congress in July. Newspapers supported the Greenback party by the early fall in Wills Point, McKinney, Sulphur Springs, Longview, Brenham, Burnet, and in Hill County. In November several Greenbackers won city offices in Austin, including former Republican J. C. DeGress as mayor. Yet Democrats felt that as 1879 ended the new party had reached its peak or might even be dying out.[36]

Early in 1880 Greenback support seemed stable but limited. The state Grange defeated a Greenback motion by a vote of twenty-six to twenty-four, although some East Texas Granges merged with Greenback clubs. Republican E. J. Davis renewed his advocacy of fusion with the Greenbackers, but the Republican state convention in March left the decision for later action. In April Dallas elected a Greenback mayor, despite a Democratic majority among the aldermen.[37]

A large delegation went from Texas to the national convention of Greenback clubs at St. Louis, where B. J. Chambers received the nomination for vice-president. The Greenback party reaffirmed his selection in national convention at Chicago in June to help restore harmony with the club faction and to increase the party's appeal in

[36] F. P. Rogers to W. H. Hamman, May 30, 1879, John Friery to Hamman, December 28, 1879, William H. Hamman Papers; Horace Chilton to John H. Reagan, August 11, 1879, D. B. Culberson to Reagan, September 25, 1879, John H. Reagan Papers; S. B. Maxey to Ashbel Smith, November 14, 1879, Smith Papers; *Texas New Era* (Longview), July 19, 26, October 4, 11, 1879; *Bastrop Advertiser*, July 26, 1879; *Texas Capital*, August 17, September 21, October 5, November 5, 1879.

[37] Winkler, *Platforms*, pp. 195–197; *Galveston Weekly News*, January 22, April 8, 1880.

the South. Chambers thus became the first Texan ever to receive a party nomination for a national office. A tall, gray-haired native of Kentucky, Chambers had been a surveyor, land dealer, banker, and farmer since migrating to Texas in 1837. He had been defeated for the state Legislature in 1878 but continued as an active speaker, writer, and organizer for the new party, which led to his election as national committeeman and then to the vice-presidential nomination.[38]

Later in June about 140 Greenbackers met in a state convention at Austin, renominating Hamman for governor and Kuechler for land commissioner. New men, again of only local prominence, received the other nominations for state offices. The delegates adopted a platform similar to that of 1878, except for planks opposing road, poll, and ad valorem taxes; the Sunday law and the Bell Punch Tax on liquor by the drink, unpopular acts of the last Legislature; and any interference with voting.[39]

The Greenbackers began their campaign with an overnight meeting in Dallas on July 15–16. It featured picnics, torchlight parades, and speeches by party leaders, including Hamman, Jones, and two Greenback candidates for Congress, Jerome C. Kearby, a Confederate veteran and former Dallas district attorney who was a native of Arkansas, and John T. Brady, a Maryland-born Houston attorney, businessman, and former legislator.[40] But word that an accident would keep vice-presidential candidate Chambers away lessened their enthusiasm. Jones spoke widely in North Texas during the summer before returning to his district in Central Texas to campaign for reelection to Congress. Greenbackers established several newspapers, and prospects appeared at least hopeful until late summer. Then the Republican state executive committee met at Hearne on August 25 and nominated a state ticket headed by E. J. Davis. It apparently based the decision against fusion with the Greenbackers

[38] *Galveston Weekly News*, June 17, 24, 1880; *Texas Capital*, March 22, 30, 1880; Alwyn Barr, "B. J. Chambers and the Greenback Party Split," *Mid-America* 49 (October 1967), 276–284.

[39] Winkler, *Platforms*, pp. 198–201.

[40] Webb and Carroll, *Handbook of Texas*, I, 204–205, 940.

upon the known opposition of some Republicans to Greenback views and upon hopes that an active campaign in a national election year might return federal patronage to the Davis faction of the state party. Thereafter Greenbackers continued to campaign through the fall, but with little chance of success except on the congressional or local level.[41]

Democratic spirits had been at low ebb in the spring of 1880. Several Democratic newspapers and legislators criticized Governor Roberts's support of large land sales at low prices, his veto forcing the public school appropriation to be cut from one-fourth to one-sixth of the state's general revenues, and other economy measures to reduce the state debt. Possible opponents of Roberts for the gubernatorial nomination included State Senator Charles Stewart of Houston, who argued that the Legislature had provided for increased revenue to cover both the school appropriation and debt reduction. The opposition to Roberts soon shifted, however, behind Lieutenant Governor Joseph D. Sayers. In an interview in March, Sayers advocated a larger school appropriation, land sales to settlers rather than to corporations, better frontier protection, and aid to immigration—measures he felt would produce growth and increased wealth.[42]

To minimize conflict the Democrats decided to hold one convention to select delegates to the national convention at Cincinnati and another to choose state candidates. An April convention sent an uninstructed delegation to the national convention. Most Texas delegates leaned toward Winfield Scott Hancock of Pennsylvania, because of his favorable actions while military commander of Texas during Reconstruction. Nine of the sixteen Texas votes went to Hancock on the first ballot at Cincinnati, eleven on the second ballot, and sixteen when the switch that produced his nomination began after the second ballot. In addition most of the Texans opposed Hancock's strongest rival, Senator Thomas F. Bayard of Delaware, a hard-

[41] *Galveston Weekly News*, July 22, 29, August 5, 12, 19, September 23, 1880; E. J. Davis to "Sir," July 28, 1880, broadside, Pease Papers; E. J. Davis to J. P. Newcomb, November 13, 1880, Newcomb Papers; Winkler, *Platforms*, p. 197; Smith, "Hamman," pp. 171–176.

[42] *Galveston Weekly News*, January 1, 29, February 5, 12, April 1, 1880.

money eastern Democrat who had helped kill the Warner silver bill of 1879.[43]

Sayers and Roberts continued in July to speak on state issues. Roberts emphasized that the state debt should be paid while maintaining the other functions of state government and not raising taxes. Sayers replied that the increase in state revenues came from acts passed prior to Roberts's administration, that overall expenditures had not decreased, and that, instead of decreasing the debt by paying off older bonds with cash from the state treasury, the administration had issued new bonds. When the Democratic nominating convention opened on August 10, the Roberts faction was in control. A compromise platform vaguely endorsed public schools and the promotion of immigration. The convention soundly defeated efforts to include more specific statements on those and other views held by Sayers, however, and renominated Roberts on the first ballot.[44] The real key to Roberts's success lay in his efforts to lighten the taxes that landowning farmers paid by reducing state expenditures and by finding revenue elsewhere, especially through the sale of public land. Although in some ways shortsighted, his measures had an irresistible and immediate financial appeal exceeding even that of greenbacks.

Their internal problems settled or at least patched up, the Democrats turned full attention to the Greenbackers and Republicans. Candidates on all levels took the stump, confident in most areas of success over divided opposition. Leading Democrats continued to speak until the November election, but only Seth Shepard, who opposed "Wash" Jones, faced a real chance of defeat.[45] In the gubernatorial race Roberts won by 166,101 votes to 64,382 for Davis and

[43] *Ibid.*, January 15, July 1, 1880; George Clark to O. M. Roberts, February 10, 1880, Roberts Papers; John Hancock to Thomas F. Bayard, November 29, 1879, April 23, 1880, Bayard Papers; Richard C. Bain, *Convention Decisions and Voting Records*, p. 119; Charles C. Tansill, *The Congressional Career of Thomas Francis Bayard, 1869–1885*, pp. 231–234; Winkler, *Platforms*, pp. 197–198.

[44] Winkler, *Platforms*, pp. 201–206; *Galveston Weekly News*, July 8, 15, August 12, 19, 1880.

[45] *Galveston Weekly News*, August 5, 19, 26, September 2, 9, 30, October 21, 28, 1880; Seth Shepard to J. H. Reagan, August 8, 31, 1880, Reagan Papers.

33,721 for Hamman. Davis had carried twenty-three usually Republican counties, mostly in South Central Texas, a few in South and Northeast Texas. Hamman led only in Walker County. Together they increased the non-Democratic vote from 33 per cent in 1878 to 37 per cent in 1880. Because Davis reunited the Republican vote, Hamman supporters in 1880 more clearly represented the hard-core Greenback vote. Hamman received in excess of his statewide 13 per cent of the vote in fifty counties located almost entirely in the North and Central Texas farming area, including only two with Negro majorities and five with black minorities of 40 per cent or more. Anglo evangelical farmers formed the backbone of the Greenback party. To the Legislature Greenbackers elected only one senator and three representatives when fusion failed, while the Republicans elected one senator and eight representatives. In the congressional races Jones narrowly defeated Shepard by about 200 votes; the Democrats swept the other races by margins generally similar to those of 1878.[46]

Democratic presidential candidate W. S. Hancock carried Texas with 155,963 votes to 57,225 for James A. Garfield and 27,471 for the Greenbacker, James B. Weaver, but the Republican won the White House. The defeat stirred Guy M. Bryan to muse about the possibility that "the old Whig party might be revived; under that name men from the North and South might rally and act together without wounding sensibilities of any one, *and thereby form a National party.*" Democratic victories in the state and congressional campaigns ensured that such a course would not develop in Texas.[47]

Among its tasks the new Legislature would elect a United States senator since Maxey's term ended in 1881. With the Greenback defeat the race became one of personalities between the incumbent and other Democrats. By January 1881 Hancock, Reagan, and

[46] Texas, Senate, *Journal*, 17th Legislature, Reg. sess., p. 18; Texas, Secretary of State, *Report*, 1881, pp. 60–64; Lambert, *Pocket Directory, Seventeenth Legislature.*

[47] Robert C. Cotner and Watt P. Marchman, eds., "Correspondence of Guy M. Bryan and Rutherford B. Hayes," *Ohio State Archaeological and Historical Quarterly* 63 (October 1954), 367; Burnham, *Presidential Ballots*, pp. 765–813.

Roberts had eliminated themselves as potential candidates leaving Throckmorton to pursue a lifelong ambition against his fellow North Texan. Throckmorton tried to develop support among Roberts's followers by speaking for the governor in 1880 and did win some joint newspaper backing. He also denied Maxey's claims of credit for river and harbor appropriations. Both candidates faced conflict of interest charges because of their railroad connections. With little choice between the political views of the two contestants, the Legislature reelected Maxey 73 to 42.[48]

The Greenback party continued to hold conventions through 1884, but its effectiveness as an organization in Texas politics ended with the campaign of 1880. When the depression of the 1870's ended and specie resumption began, both in 1879, its goals seemed at the same time less necessary and less attainable. Moreover, opposition from the established Democratic party, to which many Texans felt emotional ties forged in the fires of Reconstruction politics, stunted Greenback growth in the state. Yet Greenbackers showed some insight into the economic problems of Texas and the nation, and, by concentrating on possible solutions, forced the Democrats to focus more attention on those issues. Democratic candidates, however, espoused views which ranged from virtual Greenbackism to more conservative positions. That flexibility and diversity produced a clear Democratic majority. The Democratic party, because it offered both reform and traditional stability, retained the support of the state Grange and of most landowning farmers of Anglo Baptist or Methodist background who still constituted a majority of the population and taxpayers in Texas. Democrats also continued to receive the votes of most businessmen, who seldom faced debts comparable to those of farmers, as well as of ranchers, who preferred the Democratic state land policy, which opened up vast new acreage to them. Those groups in turn controlled some votes of unorganized urban labor and Mexican Catholic laborers and cowboys in South Texas. Ties to the older parties, through local Mexican and Anglo Catholic politicians who spoke Spanish, easily resisted Greenback appeals which often seemed

[48] S. B. Maxey to Mrs. Maxey, September 6, December 19, 1880, January 19, 1881, Maxey Papers; Elliott, *Leathercoat*, pp. 279–283.

irrelevant to local problems. Democratic success stemmed, too, from that party's ability to retain the support of the landowning German Lutheran and Catholic farmers who opposed inflation and detected a prohibitionist strain among third-party advocates. Desire for cultural stability ranked with economic diversity as the crucial factors in Democratic victory.[49]

Greenbackers had made dissent again acceptable for an increased number of evangelical Anglo Texans and had appealed successfully at times through fusion agreements to nominally Republican voters. Tenants, heavily indebted farmers, and lesser numbers of organized laborers and businessmen interested in speculation or expansion formed the mass of Greenback voters. The Greenback challenge in Texas followed the general pattern for most southern states west of the Appalachians. There the Greenback clubs, based in the Midwest, exercised greater influence than in the Atlantic coastal states of the south. Texas Greenbackers showed greater strength than any of their counterparts except in Alabama and Arkansas, where the third party also failed to achieve statewide success.[50] Although local issues loomed large in some areas, Texas Greenbackers differed from other southern third-party men to a degree by the greater attention party leaders like Hamman and Chambers gave to national economic issues concerning finance. Even in defeat the Greenbackers had given wider circulation to some general views which would grow in popularity throughout the late nineteenth century and gain approval in the early twentieth century.

[49] Terry G. Jordan, *German Seed in Texas Soil*, pp. 116, 190–191.
[50] C. Vann Woodward, *Origins of the New South*, pp. 75–106.

4. THE INDEPENDENT MOVEMENT

UNSUCCESSFUL as they had been in the elections of 1880, Texas Greenbackers and Republicans represented over 37 per cent of the state's electorate. Many "progressives" within the Democratic party, who had opposed Roberts in 1880, continued restive even though the governor's renewed interest in public education —especially in the establishment of normal schools and the University of Texas—had quieted them to some extent.[1] A ray of hope for the minority parties and dissenting elements in Texas politics appeared when "Wash" Jones let it be known late in 1881 that he was considering a campaign for governor as an Independent, "anti-Bourbon candidate." The *Galveston News* supposed that Jones might be bluffing to keep the Democratic Legislature from reapportioning him out of his congressional seat. Rumors quickly spread that the national Republican administration would support Jones's candidacy. A

[1] *Texas New Era* (Longview), February 5, April 23, August 13, 1881; *Galveston Weekly News*, February 23, March 16, April 6, 1882; *Bastrop Advertiser*, October 29, 1881.

Greenback state senator said that his party and the Republicans would indeed unite behind an Independent ticket to defeat the Democrats, but he denied that their plan represented a Republican plot.[2]

Actual fusion of dissident groups began to be apparent as early as March 1882 when a Dallas mass meeting of men from all three parties nominated a local Independent ticket. Late in April, while the Legislature debated congressional redistricting, Jones announced for governor. In May, Jerome B. Robertson, a former Confederate general and ex-superintendent of the state bureau of immigration, also announced as an Independent. He shared the views of the "progressive" Democrats.[3]

Greenbackers brought in their national leaders to inspire the party faithful and to bolster their state campaign. Former Iowa Congressman E. H. Gillette arrived in January. James B. Weaver, presidential candidate in 1880, spoke on June 29 at the state Greenback convention in Fort Worth to about 140 delegates from thirty North and Central Texas counties. The convention then adopted a platform that included new planks charging the Democratic state administration with failure to support the public schools, sale of public land to corporations instead of to settlers, and repurchase of state bonds at a wasteful premium. It also added attacks on the Democrats for refusing to submit a prohibition amendment, taxing laborers' tools while exempting the cotton and sugar crops of the wealthy, and gerrymandering the state under the guise of redistricting. The Greenbackers deferred nominations until later.[4]

Four hundred Texas Republicans, about half of them Negroes, met in convention at Austin to hear E. J. Davis recommend support of Independent candidates for state offices. The delegates then adopted a platform incorporating his views and agreeing with the

[2] *Bastrop Advertiser*, December 24, 1881, January 7, 1882; *Galveston Weekly News*, January 12, 1882.

[3] *Galveston Weekly News*, March 9, May 4, 11, 1882; Harold B. Simpson, ed., *Touched with Valor*, pp. 19–21; *Bastrop Advertiser*, April 22, May 6, 1882.

[4] *Bastrop Advertiser*, June 17, 1882; *Galveston Weekly News*, January 5, 1882; Ernest William Winkler, ed., *Platforms of Political Parties in Texas*, pp. 206–208.

Greenback positions on public schools and public land sales. President Chester Arthur had foreshadowed Republican action in June when he announced his support of Independent movements in the South, including Jones's gubernatorial campaign in Texas. He had already removed two Texas Republicans as United States marshals because of their past opposition to fusion. That action directly followed Davis's spring visit to Washington and shifted federal patronage to his faction of the state party. Meeting in Corsicana on August 31, Greenback leaders also endorsed their earlier platform and the Independent candidates who favored its principles.[5]

In June, John Ireland remained the lone avowed Democratic candidate for governor. Antiadministration newspapers charged that Governor Roberts hoped to use the office as a stepping-stone to the United States Senate. West Texas legislators and friends, however, urged the "Old Alcalde" to run for a third term. John L. Henry, a Dallas attorney, received mention as a "railroad" candidate but declined consideration in May as did Congressman Mills.[6]

Since his earlier defeats, Ireland had developed a political position somewhere between Roberts and his Democratic opponents. He backed the governor's university bill and low taxes, but appealed to the "progressives" by favoring support for public schools, land sales to settlers only, public information to immigrants, and an end to repurchases of state bonds at premium prices. With farmers in mind, he also favored state regulation of railroads, national currency expansion, a revenue tariff, and abolition of national banks.[7]

As the time for the state Democratic convention approached, Ireland led in convention delegates, but several counties had instructed for Roberts. Supporters pressed Roberts to allow his renomination to

[5] Winkler, *Platforms*, pp. 212–215; *Galveston Weekly News*, March 23, May 18, June 22, 1882; E. J. Davis to J. P. Newcomb, April 10, 1882, James P. Newcomb Papers; Vincent P. De Santis, *Republicans Face the Southern Question*, p. 162; Stanley P. Hirshson, *Farewell to the Bloody Shirt*, p. 105.

[6] Lelia Bailey, "The Life and Public Career of O. M. Roberts, 1815–1883" (Ph.D. diss.), pp. 343–345; Myrtle Roberts, "Roger Quarles Mills" (M.A. thesis), pp. 39–40; *Galveston Weekly News*, March 23, April 6, May 11, June 1, 1882.

[7] *Galveston Weekly News*, June 22, 1882.

ensure Jones's defeat and to ward off possible dangers to Roberts's cherished projects—especially the recently created University of Texas. Roberts admitted differences with Ireland and mentioned Reagan as an alternate choice, but denied any desire for reelection. When the convention met in Galveston on July 18 the Roberts men caucused twice but learned on the afternoon of July 19 that Roberts definitely would not let his name be presented. Ireland then received the nomination by acclamation on a platform in general agreement with his views.[8]

Jones returned from Congress to open his campaign at Galveston on August 19. He attacked both old parties for avoiding issues and campaigning on prejudices, and especially the Democrats in Congress for vacillating on the question of greenbacks and for failure to defeat the protective tariff or national banks. Ireland and Hancock he accused of being former Know-Nothings. He favored improving public schools, promoting immigration, regulating railroads, and selling public lands only to settlers.[9]

Ireland began his campaign in Seguin on August 31 by defending the Democratic party, denouncing Republicans and Independents, and elaborating on the Democratic state platform. During the fall Ireland denied he had been a Greenbacker in 1878 and attacked Jones's Greenback views. Ireland also found it necessary to defend his own position on public schools, since previously he had favored a five-month term instead of ten and the use of public funds in support of denominational schools that did not require students to receive religious instruction.[10]

On September 2 the two candidates debated at Houston. Ireland admitted he had been a Know-Nothing but said he had left that party

[8] *Ibid.*, June 22, 29, July 13, 20, 27, 1882; John W. Harris to O. M. Roberts, June 11, 1882, Ashbel Smith to Roberts, June 15, 1882, S. W. Blount and others to Roberts, July 18, 1882, Oran M. Roberts Papers; Winkler, *Platforms*, pp. 208–211.

[9] *Galveston Weekly News*, August 24, 1882; *Bastrop Advertiser*, August 19, 1882.

[10] *Bastrop Advertiser*, August 26, September 9, 1882; *Galveston Daily News*, August 12, 13, September 5, 1882.

when he learned of its antiforeign views. The *Houston Post* described Ireland as an intelligent, well-prepared, and intense speaker, but rapid and monotonous in tone; Jones, like Lincoln, appeared awkward, earnest, shrewd, kind, and humorous. Instead of face-to-face confrontation with Jones, Ireland wisely spoke separately on an extended tour through East Texas and across North Texas in September, October, and early November. Jones followed him a day later with considerable success, debating several Democratic congressmen along the way. In mid-October, still hopeful, he advised a Republican supporter in South Central Texas that the Independents "must rely upon friends there while I contest with the Bourbon in his stronghold" of North and North Central Texas. Numerous Democratic leaders took the stump to counter the Independent thrust. As usual, many of their speeches predicted that opposition success would be in effect a Republican victory leading to "the horrors of ten years ago."[11]

On the congressional and local levels reapportionment complicated the situation. The state's population had grown from 818,579 in 1870 to 1,591,749 in 1880. Much of the growth consisted of new immigrants, three-fourths of them from the South. Five newly drawn congressional districts immediately became the scenes of close races within the Democratic party.[12] Only Reagan among the incumbent congressmen faced no convention contest.

In North Central Texas Wellborn met strong opposition for renomination from W. L. Crawford, resulting in part from the charge that Wellborn, as a former railroad attorney, did not represent the people. But Wellborn's supporters controlled the convention, seated a favorable delegation from Dallas, and nominated their man.[13] Wellborn then joined other Democratic congressmen of North, Central, and West Texas in campaigns against Greenbackers running as Independents. In the new Eleventh Congressional District of West

[11] Everett Young Seale, "John Ireland and His Times" (M.A. thesis), pp. 53–55; G. W. Jones to J. P. Newcomb, October 16, 1882, Newcomb Papers; Richard Coke, Scrapbook; *Galveston Weekly News*, September 7, 14, 28, 1882.

[12] Homer Lee Kerr, "Migration into Texas, 1865–1880" (Ph.D. diss.), pp. 26, 137; *Galveston Weekly News*, May 11, 1882.

[13] *Galveston Weekly News*, June 15, August 10, September 28, 1882.

Texas an open race included three Democrats and one Independent, a Granger.[14]

In East, South, and South Central Texas Democrats waged several hot convention contests. Around Houston, in the new First Congressional District, State Senator Charles Stewart faced State Representative J. C. Hutcheson. Stewart carried Harris County as the more favorable toward railroads and received the nomination to Congress when Hutcheson withdrew after thirty-three ballots.[15] A similar situation developed in the Third Congressional District. Richard B. Hubbard's supporters, including several railroad promoters, bolted the Smith County convention when it instructed for farmer-backed attorney Horace Chilton. Then the district convention deadlocked for fifty ballots among six candidates, four for railroad regulation. Finally the regulators pooled their strength to nominate James H. Jones.[16] Former Congressman John Hancock received the Tenth Congressional District nomination over incumbent Columbus C. Upson, running in a much altered district. Upson had been the only Texan to vote for the Republican-proposed tariff commission, because his sheep raising constituents in the Hill Country favored continued protective duties on wool. Upson's supporters withdrew from the convention claiming bad faith by Hancock, whom they had backed for chairman of the state convention. In the Seventh Congressional District, along the coast, Galveston attorney George P. Finlay won the nomination over a Rio Grande Valley candidate. Former Republicans provided the Independent opposition for Democrats in those East and South Texas areas where Republicans outnumbered Greenbackers. To promote their efforts, Independents had the support of about thirty Republican, Greenback, and Independent newspapers. One of them, the *Montague Age of Progress*, urged

[14] S. W. T. Lanham to "My Dear Brother," November 21, 1882, ms. in possession of Samuel Lanham, Galveston, Texas; *Weatherford Times*, June 3, 1882; *Galveston Weekly News*, October 26, 1882.

[15] *Houston Daily Post*, July 7, 8, 19, 23, August 9, 10, 12, 1882; *Galveston Weekly News*, May 25, August 17, 1882.

[16] *Galveston Weekly News*, July 13, August 24, 31, 1882; Robert C. Cotner, *James Stephen Hogg*, pp. 87–94; Diary, 1888–1894, Horace Chilton Diaries; J. M. Hairgrove to J. W. Truit, September 5, 1882, James W. Truit Papers.

Grangers, Farmers' Alliance members, Knights of Labor, and other laborers to unite on candidates against the Democrats.[17]

In the state election Ireland polled 150,809 votes to 102,501 for Jones. Jones carried forty-eight counties, mostly in his old congressional district of South Central and Southeast Texas but some in areas along the Rio Grande, in the Hill Country, and in Northeast Texas where Republican congressional nominees were strong. He ran well ahead of the Independent ticket. The Independent congressional candidates carried only thirty-eight counties, and the combined vote of the two candidates for lieutenant governor, Republican E. W. Morton and Greenbacker Andrew Young, fell almost 25,000 behind Jones despite the fact that their parties provided Jones's basic support. Internal tensions among Democrats over railroad legislation and over Roberts's renomination, German opposition to Ireland as a former Know-Nothing and rumored prohibitionist, Jones's personal and political popularity, and vote swapping in some areas—all of these contributed to Jones's showing, the best made against the Democrats between 1870 and 1894. Yet his defeat resulted from a failure to expand on the primary appeal of Greenback views among tenants and deeply indebted Anglo Baptist or Methodist farmers and organized laborers, combined with the attraction of fusion for nominally Republican, evangelical, Negro tenant farmers and laborers. Most Anglo Protestant ranchers, businessmen, and landowning farmers, Mexican Catholics, and German Lutherans and Catholics continued to provide Democrats with a substantial though somewhat reduced majority. If they had any doubts, the charge that Independents represented a return to Republican Reconstruction policies held them firmly in line.[18]

Greenback-Independents lost all the North and Central Texas congressional races, though some ran well because of Republican sup-

[17] Walter P. Webb and H. Bailey Carroll, eds., *Handbook of Texas*, I, 599; U.S., Congress, *Congressional Record*, 47th Cong., 1st sess., p. 3686; *Galveston Weekly News*, August 24, 31, September 14, October 5, 1882; N. W. Ayer, *American Newspaper Annual*, 1882, pp. 142–148, 379.

[18] *Galveston Daily News*, November 12, 15, 18, 22, 1882; Texas, Legislature, Senate, *Journal*, 18th Legislature, Reg. sess., pp. 22–23.

port. Republican-Independents generally met with similar results in East and South Texas. In the Tenth Congressional District old Reconstruction animosities helped Hancock defeat E. J. Davis although his protective tariff platform appealed to sheep raisers. In other counties Greenbackers traded their congressional votes to Hancock for Democratic gubernatorial votes for Jones.[19]

Thomas P. Ochiltree, a Confederate veteran, former United States marshal, and a personal friend of Presidents Grant and Arthur, achieved the only Republican-Independent success in the coastal district. From Washington, where he had been living for three years, Ochiltree announced for Congress in August, despite the opinions of Rio Grande Valley Republicans that a Spanish-speaking rancher would be a better choice. Ochiltree ran on a platform of support for river and harbor appropriations for all ports in the district and protection for wool growers, intimating influence through his personal and political connections with the Republican administration. His Democratic opponent took a position similar to Ochiltree's thus placing the issue on the level of potential success and personality, which gave the eccentric, charming, red-headed Republican a clear advantage. Ochiltree's boyhood tutor, who had become the Catholic bishop in San Antonio, helped swing Mexican support for his former student through his priests. Ochiltree won with 12,357 votes to 9,851 for Finlay. Ochiltree carried Galveston and seven other coastal counties—five were usually Republican—and five counties along the Rio Grande.[20]

Independents won one seat in the state senate and five in the house; and four Republicans also won seats in the house. Other

[19] E. J. Davis to J. P. Newcomb, August 19, 21, September 23, November 8, 11, 20, 1882, J. C. DeGress to Newcomb, October 19, 1882, Newcomb Papers; Texas, Secretary of State, *Report*, 1883, pp. 33–35.

[20] Texas, Secretary of State, *Report*, 1883, p. 34; J. L. Haynes to J. P. Newcomb, May 26, June 23, 1882, Newcomb Papers; *Galveston Weekly News*, June 8, August 3, November 16, 1882; *Dallas Weekly Herald*, July 31, 1884; George P. Finlay to O. M. Roberts, November 26, 1882, Roberts Papers; Webb and Carroll, *Handbook of Texas*, II, 299–300; Norman G. Kittrell, *Governors Who Have Been*, pp. 157–158; Claude H. Hall, "The Fabulous Tom Ochiltree," *Southwestern Historical Quarterly* 71 (January 1968): 347–376.

Independents and Republicans won local offices, although election irregularities again affected the results in some closely contested counties.[21]

Inspired by Jones's campaign in 1882, Greenback and Republican leaders discussed the possibility of solidifying their loose coalition into a new party; but apparently they could not reconcile all their differences, for nothing tangible resulted. Jones returned for his last session of Congress in the spring of 1883. Not until April 1884 did he speak out against Ireland's hesitation on the complicated question of fence cutting, a phenomenon Jones blamed on former Governor Roberts's policy of selling public lands in large blocks at low prices rather than small ones to actual settlers. He also denied that Greenbackism was dead, noting that many Democrats, such as Coke, were Greenbackers in principle. Charging that he had not received a fair count in 1882, Jones said he might again run if Ireland or Hancock were the Democratic candidate. Andrew Young became the first Greenbacker to announce for governor, however, before he left to attend his party's national convention at Indianapolis in May 1884.[22]

Interest in Independent candidates at all levels continued to develop during the summer in areas where Greenbackers and Republicans enjoyed appreciable strength. On August 26 at Waco, the Greenback state executive committee met with representatives of Central Texas counties to restate their platform. It included new planks condemning large leases of public lands, the stock law which seemed to them discriminatory against nonlandowners, and Democratic failure to regulate railroad rates. The group then selected presidential electors and endorsed Jones for governor. On September 2, at Houston, Texas Republicans, under the leadership of Negro labor organizer Norris Wright Cuney of Galveston, voted to support Independents for state offices. A few delegates, mostly white federal

[21] Will Lambert, comp., *Pocket Directory of the Eighteenth Legislature of Texas*; Willis H. Steed vs. M. C. Leslie, James K. Davis to Mayor of Austin, December 1, 1882, N. H. Davis Papers.

[22] E. W. Morten to W. H. Hamman, December 12, 1882, William H. Hamman Papers; *Bastrop Advertiser*, April 19, 1884; *Dallas Weekly Herald*, May 8, 29, 1884.

officeholders, bolted the convention when their minority report favoring a state ticket lost, 308 to 80. They then held a separate convention in Dallas that nominated a "straight-out" Republican ticket headed by A. B. Norton for governor. Responding to the endorsements of the Waco Greenback and Houston Republican conventions, however, "Wash" Jones announced for governor on September 7.[23]

The issues of land and national finance had caused considerable grumbling within the Democratic party. A special session of the Legislature met at Ireland's call in January 1884 to deal with the problems of free grazing on public land and fence cutting. It passed an act to meet both situations, but they remained key issues in several Democratic county conventions through the summer.

National leaders of the Independent Labor, Greenback, and Anti-Monopoly parties pressed John H. Reagan, an ardent advocate of farmers' views, to run for vice-president with their nominee, former Union general Benjamin F. Butler. But, although sympathetic, the Texas congressman refused, expressing continued hope that the stronger Democratic party would achieve the same goals.

At the Democratic state convention in June to select delegates to the party's national convention, leaders of both the agrarian and the "progressive" factions, among them Coke and Shepard, opposed sending another pro-Tilden delegation. The national convention, however, presented no real alternative to continued eastern domination. Thus the Texans split their votes equally between Thomas F. Bayard and Grover Cleveland on two ballots before acquiescing in Cleveland's nomination for the sake of party unity and a possible national victory.[24]

[23] *Dallas Weekly Herald*, August 28, September 4, 1884; E. S. Hicks to J. W. Truit, August 1, 1884, Truit Papers; *Bastrop Advertiser*, September 13, 1884; Winkler, *Platforms*, pp. 223–234.

[24] Winkler, *Platforms*, pp. 217–220; *Dallas Weekly Herald*, January 31, May 22, July 24, 31, 1884; Gerald Nash, ed., "Selections from the Reagan Papers: The Butler-Reagan Ticket of 1884," *Journal of Southern History* 21 (August 1955): 379–386; Richard C. Bain, *Convention Decisions and Voting Records*, p. 130; clipping, October 27, 1883, Richard Coke, Scrapbook; Seth Shepard to J. H. Reagan, June 3, 1884, John H. Reagan Papers.

Despite lack of unity on the state level and open opposition in some places, Ireland maintained his control of the party organization. As the time for the nominating convention approached in August he even chided potential opponents for holding back from the contest. Unable to produce a candidate, or even cohesion among themselves, the opposition made no effort to stop Ireland's selection. Backers of State Senator L. S. Ross refused to oppose Ireland, hoping for his support in 1886. The dominant farmer bloc then nominated State Senator Barnett Gibbs for lieutenant governor. One new platform plank opposed a herd law requiring constant watch over cattle to keep them from straying off the owner's land. Others favored a more comprehensive mechanics' and laborers' lien law, limitations on corporate landholdings, and regulation of railroad freight transportation.[25]

Ireland opened his campaign early in September; Jones, later that month. In an extensive speaking tour, the governor defended his administration, especially the lease law passed to help end free grazing and fencing of public domain, which had resulted in fence cutting. Jones attacked the Democrats for resorting to a lease law instead of allowing only settlers to purchase public lands, and for failure to abolish national banks. But Jones limited his campaign to Central Texas, apparently realizing that Democratic unity after their nominating convention, division among his own supporters, and Ireland's espousal of similar profarm sentiments reduced his own chances. On election day Ireland won with 210,534 votes to 88,230 for Jones and 24,485 for Norton. Jones carried twenty-two counties, mostly in Central and Southeast Texas, and Republican Norton carried six counties, mostly in the same area. Jones's lead of almost 30,000 over John L. Haynes, the Republican candidate for lieutenant governor, indicated Greenback strength within the Independent movement.[26]

Independent strength faded also in the Legislature, where only

[25] P. N. Bentley to J. W. Truit, May 20, 1884, Truit Papers; Joseph W. Baines to P. B. Muse, April 10, May 14, 1884, P. B. Muse Papers; Winkler, *Platforms*, pp. 220–223; *Galveston Daily News*, August 21, 1884.

[26] *Galveston Daily News*, September 3, 1884; *Bastrop Advertiser*, September 13, 27, October 4, 1884; *Galveston Weekly News*, October 2, 9, 1884; Texas, Legislature, Senate, *Journal*, 19th Legislature, Reg. sess., pp. 21–22.

two Independents and four Republicans won seats. On the congressional level five Democratic incumbents had virtually no opposition. In the other districts Republican candidates lost by margins of at least two to one. In the Seventh Congressional District, Ochiltree refused to run for reelection after Congress failed to pass the extensive river and harbor appropriations he had promised in his 1882 campaign. Republican Robert B. Rentfro, customs collector at Brownsville and a member of the Constitutional Convention of 1875, then entered the race against Democrat William H. Crain, a Cuero attorney and former state senator. One of the several Democrats who spoke for Crain, Senator Coke, used the Republican-proposed Blair Bill for federal aid to education to raise the emotional issues of states' rights and racial integration against Rentfro. Texas congressmen had uniformly opposed the Blair Bill, although several Southerners whose states had no public lands to use for the support of public education voted for it. Crain also had the support of James B. Wells, prominent land attorney and political leader of the Rio Grande Valley. Wells controlled the Mexican voters in the Valley as a fellow Catholic with paternalistic concern for their needs and through large landowners. He then supplemented the Democratic count with illegal voters imported across the river from Mexico. The district returned to the Democratic column, 15,471 votes to 9,486, with Galveston, Corpus Christi, and the Valley providing the margin of victory.[27]

When it became clear that they had captured the White House for the first time since the Civil War, a Texan wrote: "Democrats are still jubilant over Cleveland's election . . . There will be a great scramble for places, lots of petitions in circulation now for Post Offices, District Attornies [*sic*] and Marshalships. . . . I think

[27] E. H. Loughery, *Personnel of the Texas State Government for 1885*; Texas, Secretary of State, *Report*, 1885, pp. 28–35; Richard Coke, Scrapbook; M. Kennedy to J. B. Wells, July 13, 1884, W. H. Crain to Wells, August 29, 1884, M. L. Browne to Wells, November 3, 1884, James B. Wells Papers; James H. Thompson, "A Nineteenth Century History of Cameron County, Texas" (M.A. thesis), p. 121; Allen J. Going, "The South and the Blair Education Bill," *Mississippi Valley Historical Review* 44 (September 1957): 267–290.

Hubbard wants a cabinet position . . ." He did, and the Texas congressional delegation that had voted almost unanimously against civil service reform in anticipation of the victory besieged Cleveland with appeals for the appointment of Hubbard and hundreds of lesser office seekers. Requests for positions proved so great that bickering broke out among the Texas senators and congressmen trying to fulfill as many as possible to maintain and expand their political influence and support. Eventually major appointments went to Hubbard as minister to Japan and to W. W. Lang as consul at Hamburg, Germany. Former Confederate brigadier Henry McCulloch and others who failed to receive the positions they sought developed resentments which weakened their devotion to the Democratic party and provided an entering wedge for future division.[28]

Following its second and more complete defeat, the loose Independent coalition in Texas began to collapse as former Greenbackers started to return to the Democratic party in a period of greater prosperity and Democratic national success. Former Republicans had already begun to reestablish themselves as the opposition party on the congressional level in 1884. Yet the Independent movement had produced an even stronger challenge to Democratic domination in Texas than any opposition since Reconstruction. In the South only the momentary Independent victories in Virginia and Arkansas and a strong but unsuccessful contest in Mississippi ranked with Jones's campaigns in strength and determination. Like the Green-

[28] P. W. Walton to P. B. Muse, November 18, 1884, P. B. Muse Papers; U.S., Congress, *Congressional Record*, 47th Cong., 2nd sess., pp. 661, 867; Ira Hoogenboom, *Outlawing the Spoils*, pp. 248–249; John Ireland to Grover Cleveland, November 29, 1884, S. B. Maxey to Cleveland, December 5, 1884, Richard Coke and D. B. Culberson to Cleveland, December 8, 1884, Grover Cleveland Papers, series 2; W. P. Ballinger to Guy M. Bryan, March 31, 1885, Guy M. Bryan Papers; Henry E. McCulloch to J. W. Truit, January 20, 1884 [1885], Truit Papers; Webb and Carroll, *Handbook*, I, 857; II, 26. Letters of recommendation for the Democrats who received appointments as district judges, attorneys, and marshals in Texas indicate no clear pattern of exceptional influence by any politician or group of politicians. The appointees usually received the support of both senators, their own congressmen, and often several others, as well as several prominent state officeholders. U.S., Department of Justice, Appointment Papers.

back party from which they sprang in part, Independents had kept alive dissenting views and an opposition organization which would serve as partial bases for larger groups in the future.[29]

After their final success over the Independents, Texas Democrats could turn their attention to the first national Democratic administration in twenty-four years and to less partisan state issues. Their enthusiasm over Cleveland's victory did not extend to all of his ideas and attitudes. They appreciated his limited government views and his sympathy toward the South, but many agrarians exhibited little zeal for his business orientation, and most Texas Democrats disagreed with his support of civil service reform. They looked upon his administration with considerable hope, however, for it represented an opportunity to advance the party and at least some policies, such as tariff reduction, popular in Texas and the South. In state politics Democrats faced with some reluctance the pressing but potentially divisive issues of public land policy and prohibition.

[29] W. O. Campbell to T. S. Henderson, November 6, 1885, Thomas S. Henderson Papers; C. Vann Woodward, *Origins of the New South*, pp. 92–106.

5. PUBLIC LAND POLICY

TEXAS, UPON JOINING the Union in 1845, had retained its public land, a resource the state used to promote settlement, railroads, and education. Beginning in 1873, Democrats substituted grants of public land totaling 32,153,878 acres for state bonds Republicans had issued to railroad companies to stimulate construction in the state. Wisely, however, the Constitution of 1876 reserved half the state lands for the benefit of public schools.

Land policy became an issue again in the Roberts administration. Roberts, an honest, materially selfless man whose basic views had been formed in the antebellum South, believed strongly in limited government and rigid economy. He expressed primary concern over the state debt of $5,500,000, stemming mainly from an expansion of government functions during the Republican administration of E. J. Davis, a partial taxpayers' strike at that time, and extensive pensions to veterans of the Texas Revolution voted by the Democrats in 1874. Major weaknesses in the Texas tax system which retarded debt payment resulted from the failure by some persons to render their land for taxes, and undervaluation of other land by local taxing authorities. In 1880 census takers estimated property in the state at $725,000,000, while the assessed valuation stood at only $311,-470,000. In 1879 Roberts vetoed the appropriations bill, which devoted the constitutional maximum of one-fourth of state ad valorem tax revenues to maintain the public schools. He felt that the large school appropriation would leave the state with a deficit beyond its potential tax revenues because the lingering depression held them down. Any surplus funds he preferred to use for purposes of debt reduction.[1]

In the special session that followed, the Legislature cut the school appropriation to one-sixth of ad valorem revenues despite stiff opposition from most Republicans and Greenbackers from South Central and Southeast Texas, and from several Democrats, especially those from the major towns. They argued that the comptroller's estimate of revenues and disbursements for the next year left room for greater school appropriations, in view of the recent passage of new business and occupation taxes and the funding of state bonds at lower interest rates.[2]

To pay the state debt and provide additional funds for the public schools, the Legislature passed bills to sell unappropriated public lands at a minimum of fifty cents an acre, in unlimited amounts, and to sell school lands classed as farming lands, in blocks up to 640 acres, and that classed as grazing land, in blocks up to 1,920 acres, at one dollar an acre. Again Republicans and urban Democrats attacked the acts, though few Greenbackers and South Texas Democrats joined the opposition. Support for Roberts's veto and for the subsequent legislative action came from landowning farmers, who paid most of the state's taxes, as well as from potential land speculators,

[1] E. T. Miller, *A Financial History of Texas*, pp. 199–200, 207–214, 229–231; Oran M. Roberts, "Political, Legislative, and Judicial History of Texas," in Dudley G. Wooten, ed., *Comprehensive History of Texas, 1685–1897*, II, 234–237.

[2] E. T. Miller, "The Historical Development of the Texas State Tax System," *Southwestern Historical Quarterly* 55 (July 1951): 5–6; Texas, Legislature, House of Representatives, *Journal*, 16th Legislature, Called sess., pp. 226–227, 300, 305–306.

from opponents of public schools or Negro education, and from partisans of private or church schools.[3]

As a result of the smaller appropriation, public school enrollment decreased during the next two years and reached its 1879 level again only in 1884, despite steady population growth. Supporters of a larger public school appropriation and the sale of public land only to settlers then turned to Lieutenant Governor Sayers, who became a candidate for the Democratic gubernatorial nomination in 1880. But Roberts's strength, especially in most rural areas, ensured his renomination and the defeat of the platform planks stressing Sayers's views. At the same time, however, Roberts and his legislative supporters began to moderate their position on public education to placate opposition within the Democratic party. State Senator John Young Gooch, a Roberts man, advocated in the campaign of 1880 a return to maximum appropriations for public schools. And Roberts, in his 1881 inaugural address, emphasized the importance of public school and university education. The Legislature then increased the school appropriation again to one-fourth of the ad valorem tax revenues, broadened local control of schools to include the power to tax for improvements, and established the University of Texas during his second administration. The only change in public land-sale laws during Roberts's governorship, however, increased the price of watered school lands to $2.00 an acre and the amount of grazing land purchasable by one person from three to seven sections.[4]

[3] Texas, House, *Journal*, 16th Legislature, Called sess., pp. 234, 335; Texas, Legislature, Senate, *Journal*, 16th Legislature, Called sess., pp. 307–309; Lelia Bailey, "The Life and Public Career of O. M. Roberts" (Ph.D. diss.), pp. 287–303; *Austin Daily Democratic Statesman*, March 7, 1879; W. W. Lang to O. M. Roberts, March 16, 1879, J. M. Thompson to Roberts, May 5, 1879, J. M. Williams to Roberts, May 3, 1879, R. M. Jackson to Roberts, May 8, 1879, Rufus C. Burleson to Roberts, March 26, 1879, A. J. Hood to Roberts, May 17, 1879, Oran M. Roberts Papers; Frank Edgar Norton, "The Major Administrative Policies of Oran Milo Roberts" (M.A. thesis), pp. 114, 127; Roberts, "Political History of Texas," in Wooten, *Comprehensive History of Texas*, II, 238, 248.

[4] Frederick Eby, *The Development of Education in Texas*, pp. 175–176, 188–189; Bailey, "Life and Career of O. M. Roberts," pp. 314–339; Norton, "Administrative Policies of Roberts," p. 135; J. J. Hill to O. M. Roberts, March 14, 1880, R. H. West to Roberts, June 14, 1880, O. M. Roberts Papers; *Speech of Jno. Young Gooch*. See also Chapter 2.

By 1900 more than 3 million acres of unappropriated land had been sold for over $1.5 million. But since the state divided the resulting revenue between the public schools and payment of the public debt, it retired less than one-fifth of the debt existing in 1879 through land sales, even over a twenty-year period. The low price on state land opened the way for major investors, including out-of-state and foreign interests, to buy large sections of West Texas before settlers arrived. They circumvented acreage restrictions on the purchase of school lands by the use of borrowed names, and local county seat land "rings" often filed on the best lands for profitable resale rather than for settlement. Railroads found themselves forced to sell their lands at equally low prices or to set up dummy holding corporations to avoid forfeiting their acreage back to the state at the end of eight-year limitations written into the original grants. Finally, disabled Confederate veterans and widows, who received from the state 1,280 acres each in 1881 or a total of almost 2 million acres, also had to sell their land for extremely meager prices, averaging about fifteen cents an acre.[5]

Roberts undoubtedly believed it wise to sell the public lands because most of them could not be used for purposes other than ranching. But agricultural settlement, supported by barbed wire, the windmill, and dry farming, reached the plains in the 1880's and 1890's, causing land prices to rise despite setbacks from droughts. Thus Roberts's efforts, which reduced the state debt and increased the permanent school fund, also halted public school growth temporarily, cost the state revenue from land sales in the long run, and

[5] Reuben McKitrick, *The Public Land System of Texas, 1823–1910*, pp. 86–87; A. S. Lang, *Financial History of the Public Lands in Texas*, p. 58; Miller, *Financial History*, pp. 327, 331–332; Seymour V. Connor, "Early Land Speculation in West Texas," *Southwestern Social Science Quarterly* 42 (March 1962): 354–362; Roberts, "Political History of Texas," in Wooten, *Comprehensive History of Texas*, II, 248, 252–253; J. Fred Rippy, "British Investments in Texas Lands and Livestock," *Southwestern Historical Quarterly* 58 (January 1955): 331–341; Thomas L. Miller, "Texas Land Grants to Confederate Veterans and Widows," *Southwestern Historical Quarterly* 69 (July 1965): 59–65; Charles W. Ramsdell, Jr., "Memories of a Texas Land Commissioner, W. C. Walsh," *Southwestern Historical Quarterly* 44 (April 1941): 487–488.

retarded the settlement and development of West Texas by anyone except large ranchers and corporations.

In a partial reaction against Roberts's policies, the succeeding Ireland administration separated school revenues and general revenues in order to avoid future reductions of the school appropriation for the sake of debt payment. It also ended sales of large blocks of land, increased the selling price of public school lands, and established a Land Board to manage sales and leasing of public lands.[6]

A new problem, fencing and fence cutting, then arose to bedevil the governor and Legislature. In the early 1880's landholders, especially cattlemen, had begun to use barbed wire to enclose their lands, often including public lands they perhaps intended to buy or lease but to which they had no legal claim. They might also cut off farmers or other ranchers from water on public land or from lands they owned within the fenced area. When a drought in 1883 increased the need for grazing land and for water, many cattlemen and farmers resorted to wire cutting. Such activities spread rapidly, occurring most frequently in Frio and Medina counties in Southwest Texas, Navarro and Limestone counties in North Central Texas, Brown and Coleman counties in West Central Texas, and Clay county in Northwest Texas—all along the line where ranching and farming touched and overlapped.

One group of fence cutters posted a note forcefully expressing their grievances which read: "Down with monopolies! They can't exist in Texas and especially in Coleman County. Away with your foreign capitalists! The range and soil of Texas belong to the heroes of the South. No monopolies, and don't tax us to school the nigger. Give us homes as God intended and not gates to churches and towns and schools. Above all, give us water for our stock." Conditions grew worse during 1883 as rustlers took advantage of the situation and gangs developed to carry out extensive raids.[7]

[6] Maggie R. Smith, "The Administration of Governor John Ireland, 1883–1887" (M.A. thesis), pp. 50, 66–99, 126–162.

[7] Wayne Gard, "The Fence-Cutters," *Southwestern Historical Quarterly* 51 (July 1947): 4; Henry D. and Frances T. McCallum, *The Wire That Fenced the West*, pp. 152–163.

Ireland first sent his adjutant general, W. H. King, to inspect the areas of greatest tension, but support for fence cutters proved so pronounced in most places that King accomplished little except to report on conditions. Then the governor ordered out rangers and offered rewards, with little more success. Finally, he called a special session of the Legislature in January 1884. Debates waxed lengthy and often passionate. Many representatives of South and West Texas ranching areas and some few from East Texas opposed as unconstitutional and as destructive of cattle prices bills to prohibit fencing of unowned public or of private lands and to require gates every three miles in fences. One disturbed South Texas senator wrote a rancher near Corpus Christi that "nothing could surprise a man of your conservative mind, more than to see the communistic and agrarian feeling that prevails here in Legislative circles." But the more heavily populated farming areas had majorities in each house, and both bills became part of the compromise solution, which also required that all roads be kept open, made fence cutting a felony, and included the lease of public land and a form of herd law to stop grazing and driving across unowned lands. Even after the session, in the spring of 1884, "free grass" remained an issue in several Democratic county conventions. And Jones opposed Ireland for accepting a compromise agreement which the Independent saw as an aid to large landowners. But the voters favored the compromise solution—at least to the extent of reelecting Ireland governor.[8]

While the fence-cutting war went on in West Texas and in the Legislature, the leasing of public lands also demanded attention. In 1883 the State Land Board had provided that public school, university, and asylum lands might be leased at a minimum of four cents an acre for up to ten years, although the stockmen's convention that year suggested twenty-year leases. When bidding for leases began the board found that the ranchers had agreed in advance who would

[8] McCallum and McCallum, *Wire*, p. 165; *Galveston Daily News*, January 3, 8, 9, February 6, September 12, 1884; N. G. Collins to G. W. Fulton, January 20, 1884, G. W. and James Fulton Papers; Texas, House, *Journal*, 18th Legislature, Called sess., pp. 111, 156, 170; Texas, Senate, *Journal*, 18th Legislature, Called sess., pp. 90, 119–120. See also Chapter 3.

bid which tracts. As a result each bidder paid only the minimum price. To defeat such maneuvers, the board raised the minimum lease price to eight cents an acre. But the ranchers refused to pay more than four cents, and they continued to use the land, despite farmer protests.[9]

To meet the broad differences between ranchers and settlers, Ireland recommended to the Legislature in 1885 that the state leave public agricultural lands open to settlers while it leased other public lands to provide funds for state asylums, schools, and universities. But he vetoed the bill when it reached him because it allowed the leasing of unlimited amounts of land, tended to restrict transit, gave purchasers a leasing advantage over others, and priced watered lands at only two dollars an acre.[10] The Land Board–ranchers dispute simmered throughout 1885 and 1886, with Ireland first suggesting an increase in lease price from five cents an acre to six cents, then a reversal to four cents, in an effort to get some payment from ranchers for the land they continued to use. Antagonism developed between the board and the governor, who came to desire abolition of the board in favor of a land commissioner and appointed land agents to classify lands. Land policy figured in the gubernatorial campaign of 1886, with board member and former comptroller William J. Swain defending the board's actions, and former Confederate general and legislator Lawrence Sullivan "Sul" Ross favoring abolition of the board, sale to settlers only, and short leases. When Ross won the nomination and the election, the ensuing Legislature substantially carried out his aims.[11]

In 1886 Attorney General John D. Templeton had brought suit against several cattlemen for illegal enclosure. In sparsely populated West Texas, juries of their own cowboys and judges whose salaries they supplemented tried and acquitted them. Templeton then ac-

[9] Lang, *Public Lands*, pp. 191–193; Austin, *Texas Farm and Ranch*, May 1, 1884.

[10] Everett Young Seale, "John Ireland and His Times" (M.A. thesis), pp. 100–103; Ernest Wallace, *Charles DeMorse: Pioneer Editor and Statesman*, pp. 226–227.

[11] Wallace, *Charles DeMorse*, pp. 229–230; Seale, "Ireland," pp. 107–110; *Galveston Daily News*, February 4, 25, 1886.

cused Judge Frank Willis of favoritism, and a legislative investigation followed in 1887. Charles Goodnight led a ranchers' lobby against resolutions condemning Willis. The resolutions passed the house but died in the senate.[12]

Public land law in Texas remained unchanged until 1895. A new law then declared forfeit four million acres of previously sold but unpaid-for land and provided for resale at a lower price and interest rate. The school fund lost, at least nominally, from eight to twelve million dollars in the process. Some settlers and corporations, however, may have thus saved their lands in the midst of a depression period. Yet similar acts, passed in 1897 and 1901, caused Land Commissioner Charles Rogan to remark: "While the laws were enacted ostensibly for the benefit of the actual settler, he has derived but little benefit from them. The chief beneficiaries have been land agents, speculators and bonus hunters, and finally the ranch men." His statement may well stand as a summary of Texas land policy for the last two decades of the nineteenth century.[13]

[12] Robert C. Cotner, *James Stephen Hogg*, pp. 106–116; J. Evetts Haley, *Charles Goodnight: Cowman & Plainsman*, pp. 359–392.

[13] McKitrick, *Public Land System*, pp. 100–101; Lang, *Public Lands*, pp. 177–178, 194.

6. PROHIBITION IN THE EIGHTIES

ALONG WITH GREENBACKS and state lands the question of prohibition developed into a major political issue in the 1870's and 1880's in Texas. Temperance agitation before and after the Civil War had been sufficient for Confederate veteran E. L. Dohoney to succeed in having a local option section written into the Constitution of 1876 and to have a law enacted in that same year, providing for local elections to carry out the constitutional provision, thus gaining the title "father of prohibition in Texas." A period of local option struggles followed, with forty elections in the next dozen years, though only three counties adopted prohibition.[1] The president of the United Friends of Temperance commented sadly on liquor and politics in 1878: "The candidate who could make the greatest number of his admirers drunk and furnish the greatest quantity of free whiskey, was the man of success."

[1] H. A. Ivy, *Rum on the Run in Texas*, pp. 19, 24–27; E. L. Dohoney, *An Average American*, pp. 161, 167–169; Glynn Austin Brooks, "A Political Survey of the Prohibition Movement in Texas" (M.A. thesis), p. 13.

The prohibition movement continued, however, to seek a political solution. In 1879 the Legislature passed the "Bell Punch Law," a tax of two cents each on alcoholic drinks and one-half cent each on malt drinks, to be rung up on a cash register; but the tax met widespread opposition followed by repeal. The next year the state Grange added its collective voice to those opposing the sale of liquor. In the legislative session of 1881 a prohibition amendment passed the state senate but failed in the house after considerable debate. That summer in Dallas antiliquor forces organized a State Prohibition Alliance to appeal for the election of legislators pledged to submit a prohibition amendment to popular vote.[2]

At the request of Dohoney, Frances E. Willard, national president of the Women's Christian Temperance Union, spoke at Paris, Texas, in May 1882 and established the first WCTU chapter in Texas. The wife of Senator Maxey became a member. Women in North Texas and in the larger towns soon organized other chapters, and a state organization followed in 1883. The Texas Greenback platform of 1882 attacked the Democrats for refusing to submit the prohibition question to the people despite numerous petitions. That same year the prohibition movement gained one of its strongest advocates in J. B. Cranfill, young Texas-born editor of the *Gatesville Advance*. He took up the cause after two saloon fires threatened the entire town of Gatesville.[3]

In 1883 the Legislature again debated the issue, causing one member to write: "We have had some exciting feelings over the school and prohabition [*sic*] questions in the house for the last week. Some members have rode [*sic*] hobby horses here and they cannot be induced to dismount and stand on the level of justice." As a delegate to the Democratic state convention in 1884, Cranfill offered a resolution favoring prohibition, but saw it tabled on the motion of a

[2] Brooks, "Political Survey," p. 12; Ivy, *Rum on the Run*, pp. 20–21; J. W. Truit to "Dear Friend," February 27, 1881, James W. Truit Papers; Charles K. Chamberlain, "Alexander Watkins Terrell" (Ph.D. diss.), pp. 151–156; *Bastrop Advertiser*, August 20, 1881; Ernest William Winkler, ed., *Platforms of Political Parties in Texas*, p. 194.

[3] Winkler, *Platforms*, p. 207; Dohoney, *Average American*, pp. 209–210; Ivy, *Rum on the Run*, p. 46; J. B. Cranfill, *From Memory*, p. 178.

German delegate. Dohoney, a Greenbacker in the late 1870's and early 1880's, refused to support Ben Butler for president in 1884. Instead he attended the Prohibition party's national convention at Pittsburgh. Having served on the platform committee there, he returned to Texas and called a state Prohibition party convention at Fort Worth for September 8. The meeting selected presidential electors and refused a fusion offer from the state Greenback party. The Prohibitionist nominees received about 3,500 votes in November.[4] Though still almost negligible at the polls, prohibition had captured the imagination of many Texans, and it continued to be a major topic of discussion even in the nonelection year of 1885. Roger Q. Mills in a debate with Cranfill at Crawford in August quoted Jefferson and later Democratic leaders in opposing prohibition as an encroachment on personal liberty and democracy. Cranfill replied with quotations from the Bible, from British prime minister William E. Gladstone, and, quite pointedly, from resolutions in the *Corsicana Prairie Blade* of 1855—written in part by Mills. Senator Coke also spoke against prohibition that month in Waco, arguing that the question was not political and that prohibition would injure commerce and industry and stimulate illegal liquor sales.[5]

In 1886 Cranfill failed to be elected a delegate to the Democratic state convention and failed in his efforts to have a prohibition resolution offered in the convention. The Democrats sought to avoid the issue by means of a plank stating that on local option "every Democrat may indulge his own views without affecting his Democracy." Cranfill, far from satisfied, called a Prohibition party state convention. The delegates, although dominated by ministers, primarily Baptists, included the president of the state WCTU, some lay leaders, at least one Republican, and two former Greenbackers who provided practical political knowledge. They came chiefly from the Anglo Baptist and Methodist majority in North, East, and Central Texas.

[4] J. B. Barry to "Dear Wife," February 24, 1883, James B. Barry Papers; Cranfill, *From Memory*, p. 182; Dohoney, *Average American*, pp. 211, 253; Winkler, *Platforms*, p. 231; Ivy, *Rum on the Run*, p. 53.

[5] Diary, June 22, 1885, Horace Chilton Diaries; Richard Coke, Scrapbook; J. B. Cranfill, *Dr. J. B. Cranfill's Chronicle*, pp. 335–339.

The platform denounced both major parties for refusing to support prohibition, called Democratic gubernatorial nominee L. S. Ross "a saloon stump speaker," demanded that a prohibition amendment be submitted to the people, and appealed for votes through attacks on state policies concerning corporations and public lands. The convention nominated Dohoney for governor and elected Cranfill chairman of the state executive committee. In the fall election Dohoney ran a poor third, with 19,186 votes, behind Democrat Ross with 228,776 votes and Republican A. M. Cochran with 65,236 votes. In Mills's congressional district, where many prohibitionist Democrats had been alienated by his outspoken views, however, he faced a stiff race before defeating former Greenbacker J. D. Rankin.[6]

The Prohibition party's executive committee adopted resolutions in January 1887 asking the Legislature to strengthen the local option law, to submit a prohibition amendment to popular vote, and to institute temperance instruction in the public schools. The Legislature that spring did improve the local option law. What was much more important, it passed a prohibition amendment to prevent the production, sale, or exchange of liquor in Texas. Many of the legislators voted for the amendment only as a means of getting the issue before the electorate in a nonpartisan campaign.[7] A second meeting of the prohibitionists promptly collected $14,000 for an avowedly nonpolitical and nondenominational campaign and created a central committee with headquarters in Waco. The new nonpartisan group included evangelical Protestant ministers among its leaders, but politicians dominated, mostly attorneys, with a sprinkling of bankers and farmers, including the grand master of the state Grange.[8]

[6] Cranfill, *Chronicle*, pp. 304–306; Texas, Legislature, Senate, *Journal*, 20th Legislature, Reg. sess., p. 39; Myrtle Roberts, "Roger Quarles Mills" (M.A. thesis), pp. 44–51; Winkler, *Platforms*, pp. 240, 244–246. Information on Prohibition party leaders is based on a check of the list in Winkler, *Platforms*, against Walter P. Webb and H. Bailey Carroll, eds., *Handbook of Texas*, and the biographical volumes listed in Texas Historical Survey, "Index to Biographical Studies of Texans" (ms.). Some information is available on sixteen of twenty-two persons.

[7] Ivy, *Rum on the Run*, p. 21; Sybal Hazel, "Statewide Prohibition Campaigns in Texas" (M.A. thesis), pp. 19–22.

[8] Winkler, *Platforms*, pp. 247–249. The analysis of prohibitionists is based on a

Antiprohibitionists gathered in Austin on March 28 to organize a state executive committee, headed by George Clark, campaign manager par excellence, and to issue a plea for individual freedom and faith in personal and religious temperance efforts. Former Lieutenant Governor Barnett Gibbs had already begun the campaign in Dallas on March 19. On May 4 a convention in Dallas with Mills as the major speaker formulated a longer statement of the antiprohibition position. The amendment would favor the rich, who could import liquor, unjustly injure local wine makers, destroy a source of revenue, and abuse majority rule by forcing areas which opposed prohibition to conform. Democratic politicians, most of them lawyers, controlled the executive committee and the convention.[9]

The prohibitionist campaign relied primarily on local barbecues, picnics, meetings, and speakers. On June 30 a crowd of 15,000 gathered at Fort Worth to hear Democrats Buck Walton, Thomas R. Bonner, Marion Martin, W. S. Herndon, and Sam Bell Maxey. Herndon emphasized the poverty and crime resulting from the liquor trade, while Maxey attacked antiprohibition Democrats for trying to read prohibitionists out of the party. Others who took the stump on what Congressman Reagan called "the side of virtue, thrift and prosperity . . . right, justice and humanity" included ex-Greenback State Senator W. K. Homan, Democratic Congressmen Culberson and Lanham, young Joseph W. Bailey, a recent arrival from Mississippi, and Henry M. Turner, a Negro Methodist bishop from Georgia. Cranfill moved his paper, one of at least ten supporting prohibition, to Waco, where it became a daily with a campaign circulation of about 50,000. The *Texas Christian Advance*, the Methodist state journal, and the *Texas Baptist and Herald* argued at length with the *Dallas News*. Bells tolled hourly in some towns to emphasize the moral

---

check of the list in Winkler against Webb and Carroll, *Handbook of Texas*, and the biographical volumes listed in Texas Historical Survey, "Index." Information is available on at least thirty-one of fifty-one men.

[9] Hazel, "Prohibition Campaigns," pp. 31–37. Information on antiprohibition leaders is based on a check of the list in Winkler, *Platforms*, p. 249, against Webb and Carroll, *Handbook of Texas*, and the biographical volumes listed in Texas Historical Survey, "Index."

issue involved in the campaign. And Cranfill made a trip to the North and to the East to gain financial support from national temperance organizations.[10]

The antiprohibition campaign resembled in methods that of the prohibitionists. Governor Ross, Judge Gustave Cook, former Congressman Giddings, Senator Coke, former Governor Roberts, Attorney General Hogg, and Congressmen Crain, Throckmorton, and Sayers made public statements against the proposed amendment. In San Antonio the Liquor Dealers Association boycotted businessmen who favored it; prohibition speakers, refused the use of public facilities, finally spoke at Fort Sam Houston under military protection to avoid egg-throwing hecklers. In East Texas antiprohibition speakers conjured up the spectacle of Pinkerton detectives enforcing the law and suggested that it was a railroad scheme to turn attention from transportation regulation. The canvass quickly became bitter and personal enough to be marked by fist fights and shootings.[11]

Roger Mills added to the more common arguments an appeal to Negroes on the grounds that prohibition would deprive them of one of their recently acquired rights. Mills also engaged in the most heated debate of the campaign. At Waco on July 6 before about 7,500 persons he faced B. H. Carroll, a Baptist minister. In his closing comments, Carroll quoted a line of doggerel: "Roger the Dodger . . . wriggled in and he wriggled out, but he finally would not dodge the devil." Mills angrily replied that hell was "full of better preachers" than Carroll, "so full that their legs are hanging out at the windows," and added that Carroll had a whiskey account, listing it on his father's bill as "fruits, candy, etc." With great self-control Carroll quietly said

[10] Ben H. Proctor, *Not Without Honor: Life of John H. Reagan*, pp. 266–269; Hazel, "Prohibition Campaigns," pp. 27–28; Brooks, "Political Survey," pp. 20–21; N. W. Ayer, *American Newspaper Annual*, 1887, pp. 216–230; Ivy, *Rum on the Run*, p. 14; Cranfill, *From Memory*, pp. 205–207; Seth Shepard McKay, *Seven Decades of the Texas Constitution of 1876*, p. 190; Sam Hanna Acheson, *35,000 Days in Texas*, p. 134.

[11] Acheson, *35,000 Days*, pp. 134–135; Juanita O. Webb, "The Administration of Governor L. S. Ross, 1887–1891" (M.A. thesis), p. 151; Chilton Diaries, 1887; George Clark to O. M. Roberts, May 7, 1887, Oran M. Roberts Papers; Robert C. Cotner, *James Stephen Hogg*, pp. 130–133; Hazel, "Prohibition Campaigns," pp. 38–42, 47–50.

that he would charge slander if the accusation were not withdrawn. Supporters of each man pressed forward, ready to defend the honor of their respective heroes, and a riot seemed imminent. But Mills wisely retracted his charge and passions subsided without a brawl.[12]

Republican leaders A. M. Cochran and J. P. Newcomb received financial support from the antiprohibition state executive committee to take the stump against the amendment. Clark, chairman of the committee, circulated an editorial by Cranfill in the *Waco Advance*, attacking the Republican speakers and especially their Negro and German followers and stirring great resentment among those groups. The antiprohibitionists closed their campaign with a huge rally at Fort Worth on July 26 before a crowd estimated as high as 40,000 persons. State Treasurer F. R. Lubbock capped the speeches by reading a letter against prohibition from the former President of the Confederate States, Jefferson Davis.[13]

In the election on August 5 the amendment was defeated by a vote of 220,627 to 129,270. Prohibition carried only thirty-two counties, mainly in North Texas along the Red River and in Northwest Texas below the caprock. A slim majority of Anglo Methodists and Baptists had supported the amendment; a similar majority of Negro Baptists and Methodists had opposed it; Mexican Catholics and German Lutherans and Catholics had offered overwhelming opposition. Surprised and disgusted, prohibition leaders charged that the "wets" had imported Mexicans, Negroes, and Indians from outside the state, that Negro women dressed as men had been allowed to vote, and that repeaters had voted at several different boxes in some counties. But a well-organized campaign against the amendment, with strong Republican support, and the basic appeal of individual control over purely personal morals seem to have been far more effective in creating the considerable margin of defeat for prohibition.[14]

After the election, A. M. Cochran observed that "every Republican

[12] Hazel, "Prohibition Campaigns," p. 37; Roberts, "Mills," p. 59; C. V. Terrell, *The Terrells*, p. 207; Jeff D. Ray, *B. H. Carroll*, p. 122.

[13] George Clark to J. P. Newcomb, May 7, 1887, James P. Newcomb Papers; McKay, *Seven Decades of the Texas Constitution*, p. 191; Acheson, *35,000 Days*, p. 135.

[14] Brooks, "Political Survey," pp. 143–147; Cranfill, *From Memory*, p. 206.

county gave an overwhelming Anti majority. The Republicans voted almost solid against the Pro-Amendt. While on the other hand—the Democracy were almost equally divided. . . . But for the Republican vote," he claimed, "Prohibition would have carried in the State." Yet Negro Republican leader N. W. Cuney correctly predicted that the coalition of antiprohibitionist Democrats and Republicans could be only a temporary one, for most Democrats opposed Republicans even more emotionally than they opposed prohibition.[15]

Bitterness lingered after the campaign, despite appeals for peace from Reagan, Coke, and others who feared a permanent split in the Democratic party. The factional division continued in many places until the Democratic state convention of 1888. At the convention antiprohibitionist leaders caucused and tried to push through a "heart of oak" antiprohibition plank that would virtually have read prohibitionists out of the party. Their effort met strong appeals for party unity, however, and the platform merely accepted the election results without taking a position on the issue.[16] Yet the party ties of thousands of prohibitionists had been loosened by the bitter campaign and its aftermath, and these could be more easily broken when other issues arose in the future. The prohibitionist impulse in Texas followed the pattern of similar ardent but only partially successful efforts throughout the South in the 1870's and 1880's. The movement had not died in Texas, but it would remain quiescent as a major political issue until the Progressive period in the early twentieth century.

[15] A. M. Cochran to J. P. Newcomb, March 7, June 3, August 24, September 1, 1887, Newcomb Papers; Maud Cuney Hare, *Norris Wright Cuney*, p. 77.

[16] Richard Coke to Editor of the *Gazette*, August 23, 1887, clipping, Richard Coke Biographical File, Texas Collection, The University of Texas Library; J. H. Reagan to R. M. Johnson, September 21, 1887, John H. Reagan Papers; Sam A. Willson to J. S. Hogg, August 26, 1887, Letters Received, I, James Stephen Hogg Papers; *Fort Worth Gazette*, August 17, 1887; W. W. Merritt to J. W. Throckmorton, April 1, 1888, James W. Throckmorton Papers; *Galveston Weekly News*, May 24, 1888; Terrell, *Terrells*, pp. 207–208.

7. LABOR AND FARMER DISCONTENT

TWO NEW ORGANIZATIONS, the Knights of Labor and the Farmers' Alliance, appeared on the Texas political scene in the 1880's. The Knights, a national labor organization, had chapters in Texas by 1880 and developed an estimated membership of 12,500 by 1886. In 1885 members of the Knights successfully struck against Jay Gould's railroad system, which extended into Texas. But other members met failure in similar action against the Mallory Steamship Lines at Galveston, because of competition from Negroes organized by Republican leader N. W. Cuney.[1]

In the spring of 1886 the Texas and Pacific, one of Gould's lines, fired a member of the Knights at Marshall for overstaying a leave of absence and refused to reconsider the matter. The union accepted what seemed an obvious challenge by calling another strike against the Gould system. This one came to involve violence and destruction of property, the use of gunmen as marshals, and the hiring of strike-

[1] John S. Spratt, *Road to Spindletop*, pp. 239–241; William Neal Ramey, ed., *Texian (Annual)* 2, no. 17 (1886), p. 230.

breakers to replace the Knights. The attitude of the public varied from area to area according to the effect of the strike on local conditions. Considerable support for the Knights developed in East Texas and in Fort Worth, where militia were used to ensure peace after a gunfight between strikers and strikebreakers resulted in several deaths. But the federal courts favored the railroads, and the Haymarket Riot, which developed from a strike in Chicago, helped turn public opinion against the strikers. The Great Southwest Strike failed.[2]

Groups that expressed support for the Knights included the Farmers' Alliances in Gregg and Upshur counties. Their actions caused little surprise, for the county alliances formed part of a larger organization established to seek "freedom from the onerous and shameful abuses that the industrial classes are now suffering at the hands of arrogant capitalists and powerful corporations." The Farmers' Alliance had been organized in the mid-1870's in Lampasas County to stop cattle thieves and land sharks, and had grown into a state organization by 1878 when it collapsed in political disputes over Greenbackism. Influenced by knowledge of the independently created Farmers' Alliance of New York, a Texas group organized in Parker County in 1879 as the Grand State Alliance. The new organization at first assumed vigilance aspects, but soon turned to the promotion of cooperative credit and sales plans to meet falling farm prices and marketing difficulties. When the growth of the Grange declined in the mid-1880's, many farmers turned to the Alliance. It reached a membership of above seventy thousand by 1886.[3]

At a state meeting in Cleburne during August 1886 the Alliance issued a series of demands which accurately reflected farmer and labor hopes and needs in Texas. They comprehended incorporation of trade unions and cooperative businesses, sale of public school lands

[2] Ruth A. Allen, *The Great Southwest Strike*, pp. 77–128; Diary, March 20, 1886, Horace Chilton Diaries.

[3] *Texas New Era* (Longview), May 8, 1886; *Southern Mercury* (Dallas), August 22, 1895; John D. Hicks, *The Populist Revolt*, pp. 104–111; Spratt, *Road to Spindletop*, pp. 186–198; Ralph A. Smith, "The Farmers' Alliance in Texas, 1875–1900," *Southwestern Historical Quarterly* 48 (January 1945): 346–359; Lee Benson, *Merchants, Farmers, and Railroads*, pp. 110–111; Ernest William Winkler, ed., *Platforms of Political Parties in Texas*, p. 235.

only to settlers, abolition of the convict lease system, a mechanics' lien on products to ensure payment of wages, taxation of corporations, taxation of large landholdings at market value of the land, and taxation of railroads on the value of the stock on which they declared dividends. Nationally the demands called for free coinage of gold and silver to expand the amount of currency in circulation, substitution of treasury notes for national bank notes, regulation of the amount of money in circulation according to the population, creation of a national bureau of labor statistics, and an interstate commerce law to regulate freight rates. Thus the Alliance incorporated most Greenback and some Democratic views and added a call for a national labor conference.

Behind the demands lay a worsening economic situation in Texas. Falling farm prices and the trend toward a one-crop cotton economy interacted to aggravate each problem and to increase rural indebtedness. Cotton remained a favorite crop because of its higher value per acre and its greater dependability in drought years. To remain a subsistence farmer meant renouncing those comforts of civilization which had to be purchased with cash, while the acquisition of machinery and land, a bad crop, or simply falling prices meant debt and possible loss of land. Growing debts and decreasing availability of land made for increasing tenancy. Because of federal restrictions against national bank loans based on land and a Texas law against state banks, farmers facing difficult debt payments could borrow funds only from a limited number of private banks and from out-of-state loan companies. Fewer of these companies operated in Texas than in the northern plains states, and they usually charged higher interest, 10 to 12 per cent, because of the greater risks and the legal complications of their Texas business. Other companies preferred to deal with cattlemen and admitted that "the men who are strictly farmers have scarcely any credit whatever with the banks." The majority of Texas farmers, who owned less than two hundred acres, could acquire a loan only as part of a vendor's lien transaction which allowed the loan company legally to circumvent the state homestead law. If most of the companies dealt fairly, all charged high interest rates, and some agents and a few companies hurt their collective reputations by gouging extra commissions, refusing extensions on loans, and foreclosing rapidly on overdue notes. Railroads controlled freight rates and often discriminated against the farmer. Both railroads and loan companies added to the farmers' irritation by lobbying against all efforts to regulate their activities. Finally, a drought struck Northwest Texas in 1886, accentuating other agricultural problems.[4]

Disputes arose within the Alliance because many members wanted to seek direct political solutions for farm problems, while others preferred to work through the dominant Democratic party. C. W. Macune, the handsome, witty, though at times erratic chairman of the Alliance state executive committee, reunified the members in early 1887 by turning their immediate interests to expansion through the South as a regional as well as a state lobby and to entry into larger cooperative business projects.[5]

That the Knights and the Alliance influenced Texas politics became evident when the five major candidates for the Democratic gubernatorial nomination offered their views in the spring of 1886 on such key issues as labor strikes, railroad regulation, and state land policy. Lawrence Sullivan "Sul" Ross, a slender, balding former state senator known as "the little cavalryman" because of his service as a Confederate brigadier, supported the sale of public agricultural lands to settlers and the short lease of other lands. He also favored taxation of alien-owned lands, felt that the railroads would regulate themselves through competition—though the public interests should be guarded—and hoped that labor problems could be solved without endangering public rights. William J. Swain, a tall, sturdy former

[4] Winkler, *Platforms*, pp. 234–237; Gene M. Gressley, "Broker to the British," *Southwestern Historical Quarterly* 71 (July 1967): 12; Roscoe C. Martin, *The People's Party in Texas,* pp. 18–21; Spratt, *Road to Spindletop*, pp. 68–75, 119–139; C. Richard King, *Wagons East*; Allan G. Bogue, *Money at Interest*, pp. 158–166, 273–276; Charles H. Otken, *The Ills of the South*, p. 145; Thomas E. Watson, *The People's Party Campaign Book, 1892*, p. 338; Martin Leon Edwards,"The Farmers' Movement in Delta County" (M.A. thesis), pp. 29–30; Joseph D. Sayers to William C. Whitney, October 17, 1891, June 11, 1892, William C. Whitney Papers.

[5] C. W. Macune, "The Farmers' Alliance," unpublished memoir; Hicks, *Populist Revolt*, pp. 106–108; Annie L. Diggs, "The Farmers' Alliance and Some of Its Leaders," *Arena* 5 (1891–1892): 592, 600.

legislator and member of the State Land Board, advocated continuation of the existing land policies and the creation of a railroad commission to prevent stock watering and rate discrimination. Marion Martin—a frail-looking farmer, ex-lieutenant governor, and the favorite of many Knights, Alliance men, and prohibitionists—wanted sale of public lands to settlers and opposed leasing; he supported regulation of railroads. San Antonio banker John T. Brackenridge, representing West Texas views, spoke for the sale of public lands in amounts according to use—larger blocks for pasture—and for leasing university lands. He suggested a state court of arbitration for labor disputes, but said little about railroad regulation. Brenham banker D. C. Giddings, a former congressman, held similar views on land sales, avoided the question of railroad regulation, but became "the most outspoken against strikes."[6]

In debate prior to the Democratic convention Ross attacked Swain for saying he would use militia to keep men off public lands and favored constructing the Texas capitol out of limestone instead of Texas granite. Swain charged Ross with seeking the votes of the Knights, the Greenbackers, and the Republicans. Martin called Swain and Ross antiprohibitionists. Ross then said, and Martin denied, that Martin had supported land grants to railroads. The *Waco Examiner*, a highly partisan Ross paper, attacked Brackenridge as a national banker and a Republican, called Giddings an attorney for the Galveston Wharf Company, and hit at Martin and Swain with more personal charges. Rumor spoke of Alliance-prohibitionist efforts to break up the impending convention or force the party to endorse a prohibition amendment.[7]

[6] Myrtle Whiteside, "The Life of Lawrence Sullivan Ross" (M.A. thesis), pp. 75–79; Juanita O. Webb, "Administration of Governor L. S. Ross, 1887–1891" (M.A. thesis), pp. 23–37; Norman G. Kittrell, *Governors Who Have Been*, pp. 95–98; William S. Speer, ed., *The Encyclopedia of the New West*, I, 349, 404; John S. Ford to J. T. Brackenridge, December 1, 1885, John T. Brackenridge Papers; Diary, August 11, 1886, William P. Ballinger Papers; *Galveston Daily News*, February 4, 25, May 9, 15, 19, 29, June 6, 1886.

[7] *Galveston Daily News*, May 9, 19, June 26, July 3, August 7, 1886; R. M. Wynne to O. M. Roberts, May 25, 1886, Oran M. Roberts Papers; [unsigned, unaddressed letter], July 12, 1886, James P. Newcomb Papers.

The convention opened on August 10 amid talk of Swain-Martin combinations against Ross, a conservative swing to Giddings, a Ross plot to get Martin's vote by circulating the story that he planned to bolt, and a plan for Ross men to "hurrah" the convention into nominating their hero by acclamation. At that point George Clark, Ross's seasoned and conservative campaign manager, estimated that Ross would lead with 345 delegates on the first ballot; Martin claimed 180, and Swain and Brackenridge over 100 each. The Ross men lost in balloting for temporary chairman, but elected one of their number permanent chairman. The convention refused seats to contesting delegations of Knights and Alliance men from two North Texas counties. Ross supplemented his considerable support among Confederate veterans and Alliance men in West and Central Texas by votes from East Texas farmers who backed James S. Hogg, a candidate for attorney general. At the end of the first ballot for governor, several delegations, including Knights and Alliance men, switched from Martin to Ross, as agreed earlier, to effect his nomination.[8]

Delegates defeated two minority platform reports, one calling for land sales only to settlers with no leasing provision and another opposing all "secret political societies," and adopted a platform generally in line with Ross's views. It favored sale of land in small blocks to real settlers and temporary lease of grazing lands, protection of corporate property from injury or interference, maintenance of offices and books in Texas by railroads operating therein, forfeiture of land grants by railroads with unfulfilled charters, stockholder liability for corporate debts, and requirement of state charters for land corporations.[9]

In the November election Ross polled 228,776 votes to 65,236 for A. M. Cochran, the Republican, and 19,186 for E. L. Dohoney, the Prohibitionist. But factional fights and new opposition groups appeared at several points on the local level. In May the *Fort Worth*

[8] *Galveston Daily News*, August 7–11, 13, 1886; J. S. Ford to J. T. Brackenridge, June 15, 1886, Brackenridge Papers; George L. ——— to L. S. Ross, August 13, 1886, Lawrence S. Ross Papers; Robert C. Cotner, *James Stephen Hogg*, pp. 102–103.

[9] Winkler, *Platforms*, pp. 237–242.

Gazette denounced a local "Dark Lantern" Alliance-Knights group as representing "war on Democracy." The *Mexia Ledger* feared that Greenbackers were trying to take over the Farmers' Alliance. In Johnson, San Saba, and Lamar counties members of the Alliance, Knights, Grange, and Agricultural Wheel held joint meetings to work within the Democratic party, while in McKinney they made separate nominations. The speaker at a Knights-Alliance picnic at Dallas in July said they could control state politics through the Democratic party, which they already had captured locally. An antimonopoly, laboring man's convention held in Waco, with an ex-Greenbacker for chairman, endorsed Democrats Ross, for governor, and A. W. Terrell, for United States Senator, though it opposed Mills as an antiprohibitionist. H. S. Broiles, the reform mayor of Fort Worth, called a larger antimonopoly convention in September. The delegates, who came from twenty-eight North and Central Texas counties and included several former Greenbackers, decided against submitting a state platform or nominees. In East Texas, Democrat Horace Chilton urged Knights and Alliance men not to leave the party and thus weaken its attempts to regulate railroads and corporations. Ex-Greenbacker W. E. Farmer advocated a people's party to oppose monopolies, and such independent movements sprang up in Bowie and Bell counties. In Travis, Waller, Montgomery, and Harris counties similar groups involved Republicans.[10]

Alliance men led by Thomas Gaines in Comanche County, part of the West Texas drought area, called a convention to oppose banks, railroads, monopolies, high tariffs, and the local political "ring." Their opponents named them the "Human Party" and denounced them as Republicans, Greenbackers, and soreheads; but they carried the county by over two hundred votes. A people's ticket also won in

[10] Winkler, *Platforms*, pp. 246–247, 646; *Austin Evening Call*, September 9, 1886; *Galveston Daily News*, May 18, 29, June 9, 11, 25, 26, July 4, 5, August 4, 31, September 6, 7, 16, 1886; Diary, June 17, 1886, Chilton Diaries; H. D. McDonald to O. M. Roberts, September 16, 1886, Roberts Papers; J. W. Truit to Mrs. Susan E. Morris, October 20, November 11, 1886, James W. Truit Papers; George W. Tyler, *The History of Bell County*, p. 325; Frank M. Spindler, "Concerning Hempstead and Waller County," *Southwestern Historical Quarterly* 59 (April 1956) : 458.

Erath County, and fusion candidates succeeded in Frio and Bexar counties. The "Dark Lantern" party carried Tarrant County outside Fort Worth but lost in the town.[11]

In North Texas a bitter struggle developed between Olin Wellborn and former Lieutenant Governor Barney Gibbs for the Democratic congressional nomination. To Wellborn men, land speculator Gibbs seemed to be angling for the Knights and Alliance vote. Gibbs supporters from Bosque County asserted: "This contest is not a personal one between Wellborn and Gibbs, but between corporations, their attorneys and the people . . . It is peculiar that all the national banks, their attorneys, and all the corporate influence of this district are for Wellborn . . ." Wellborn, the incumbent, admitted representing railroads before his election but denied having done so thereafter; he emphasized lower tariffs as the main issue. Conventions in Ellis and Dallas counties split over the nominees, and the district convention in September deadlocked for 171 ballots before compromising on Judge Jo Abbott. In the fall elections Democrats carried every congressional seat over Republicans in Northeast and in South Texas and former Greenbackers elsewhere. Only two members of the newly elected Legislature identified themselves as Independents, and only two as Republicans, but it included at least fourteen Alliance men, ten Grangers, and two Knights.[12]

When the Legislature met early in 1887, it would elect a United States senator, and the contestants had offered their views to the public for a full year. Potential candidates included Sam Bell Maxey, the incumbent; Governor Ireland; Congressmen Mills and Reagan; former Congressman Hancock, and State Senator A. W. Terrell. (Mills, although interested, never entered the campaign. He found himself too occupied with tariff debates in Washington and a hard congressional race in his home district.)

[11] B. B. Lightfoot, "The Human Party," *West Texas Historical Association Year Book*, 31 (1955): 28–40; Oliver Knight, *Fort Worth*, pp. 146–147; Martin, *People's Party*, pp. 31–34; *Galveston Daily News*, November 3, 1886.

[12] *Dallas Morning News*, August 6, 9, 10, 29, September 3, 4, 1886; W. L. Cabell to S. B. Maxey, May 29, 1886, Sam Bell Maxey Papers; Texas, Secretary of State, *Report*, 1886, pp. 145–151; L. E. Daniell, comp., *Personnel of the Texas State Government*, 1887.

Terrell, a former Confederate colonel considered by friends "a delightful orator" but by opponents "a heavy-handed antimonopolist," entered the race a year in advance. His announcement criticized Maxey's use of patronage to strengthen his political position, President Cleveland's opposition to silver coinage, the existing high tariffs, and large land companies in Texas. Presently he made a stronger attack on corporations—especially railroads—for excesses that forced labor to organize and sometimes to resort to violence, and argued for a railroad commission to solve the problem. Then he opposed Maxey's idea of selling federal lands and distributing the funds to states according to the rate of illiteracy. Terrell conceded the right of labor and farmers to organize but warned against their leaving the Democratic party.[13]

John Hancock did not announce for the Senate race, but the *Dallas News* said late in May 1886 that he was in it. He spoke at Fort Worth on July 5 against "class legislation," an oblique attack on the proposals both for a railroad commission and for federal aid to improve Texas harbors. The *Dallas News* had already accused Terrell of socialistic tendencies for seeking labor votes. In a debate at Mexia, Hancock denied his candidacy and called Terrell a demagogue for stirring up discontent; Terrell replied that corporations backed Hancock. At the suggestion of Ireland, who quietly gathered backers while avoiding the bitter exchanges, Hancock then attacked Terrell for having represented the monopolistic Galveston Wharf Company before the constitutional convention of 1875. Terrell admitted as much, but said he had long ago severed all such connections.[14]

In September, Maxey, an able, energetic man of considerable vanity, returned to Texas for debates with Terrell whom he believed to be seeking Knights and Alliance votes. Maxey defended the constitu-

[13] Kittrell, *Governors Who Have Been*, p. 208; S. B. Maxey to Mrs. Maxey, July 5, 1886, Maxey Papers; *Galveston Daily News*, February 5, 1886; Roger Q. Mills to T. S. Henderson, February 12, 1886, Thomas S. Henderson Papers; Allan Nevins, *Grover Cleveland*, p. 287; Charles K. Chamberlain, "Alexander Watkins Terrell" (Ph.D. diss.), p. 274–291.

[14] Chamberlain, "Terrell," pp. 293–314; John Ireland to W. H. Evans, July 12, 1886, Ireland Copybook; B. M. Baker to J. W. Truit, July 24, October 22, 1886, Truit Papers.

tionality of his education bill, denied that his political strength along the coast rested upon patronage, and defended aid to the Corpus Christi and San Diego Railway as a necessary support for frontier defense. He announced in favor of railroad regulation and against monopolies, strikes, and the entry of the Knights or the Alliance into politics. To a certain extent his speeches sounded like farm oratory, but Maxey ran with the support of many railroad men, coastal commercial interests, and West and South Texas ranchers, including Jim Wells.[15]

The tall, heavyset, square-jawed Reagan, called the "Old Roman" in a comparison with the fifth-century farm-leader Cincinnatus, joined the race in December after seeing through to impending passage an act for federal regulation of interstate commerce, especially railroads, which he had sought for ten years. The imminent passage of the bill with only one adverse vote among Texas congressmen made Reagan tremendously popular in East Texas and other farming areas. His advocacy of silver coinage strengthened his position, and his friends had been busy since summer developing support for the moment that he announced his candidacy.[16]

When the Legislature began to ballot on January 25, Maxey led with forty-five votes, mainly from his home area in North Texas, the coast, and sparsely settled South and West Texas. Reagan stood second with thirty-six votes, mainly from East Texas; Ireland ran third with twenty-nine votes, primarily from South Central Texas. Terrell trailed with twenty-five votes, mainly from Central Texas. Reagan and Ireland gained ground on the second ballot. Then Terrell with-

[15] S. B. Maxey, *Speech delivered at Fort Worth, Texas, September 13, 1886*; S. B. Maxey to Mrs. Maxey, May 9, June 14, October 25, 1886, Maxey Papers; Diary, July 6, 1878, October 27, 28, 1886, Ballinger Papers; T. H. Ball to A. W. Terrell, December 20, 1886, A. W. Terrell Papers, University of Texas Library; R. C. Kerens to S. J. Wright, February 16, 1887, Samuel J. Wright Papers; S. B. Maxey to James Wells, May 6, 1886, Thad M. Rhodes to Wells, July 29, 1886, James B. Wells Papers; Chamberlain, "Terrell," pp. 317–319; David B. Gracy II, ed., *Maxey's Texas*, pp. 7–35.

[16] *Galveston News*, June 28, 1885; R. W. Loughery to J. H. Reagan, July 7, 1886, John H. Reagan Papers; *St. Louis Globe Democrat*, December 1, 1886; U.S., Congress, *Congressional Record*, 49th Cong., 2nd sess., p. 881; Ben H. Procter, *Not Without Honor*, pp. 167–168, 253–256.

drew and most of his supporters went to Reagan, who took the lead. For seven days the balloting continued amid lobbying in person and by letter, newspaper editorials, rumors, and political maneuvering. After twenty-three ballots, supporters withdrew Ireland's name and renominated Terrell. But he withdrew again after the twenty-ninth ballot, having never received more than thirty-nine votes. On the thirty-first ballot, with the count sixty-four for Reagan and sixty for Maxey, a representative announced that he would change his vote, since Reagan needed only one for a majority. Actually he required five votes, but before Maxey supporters could deny the statement others began to switch and Reagan swept in by a wide margin. When Reagan then joined other Texas congressmen in recommending Maxey, unsuccessfully, for the Interstate Commerce Commission, he indicated the limited nature of their political differences.[17]

The state's farm and labor problems remained little changed through 1887. In drought-stricken West Texas J. B. "Buck" Barry, a farmer-rancher of Bosque County and an ex-Confederate colonel, declared he had no fears of "Texas democracy," but "no confidence in national democracy . . . and very little in Cleveland," who had vetoed an appropriation of $10,000 to provide seed for farmers of the area because he opposed government paternalism, "pork-barrel" legislation, and the Department of Agriculture's seed-distribution policy. The conservative *Dallas Morning News* admired the president's philosophy but urged immediate private efforts to fill the obvious need. A convention of farmers, laborers, and stock raisers met in Waco on May 15, 1888. The three hundred delegates from seventy counties, primarily in North and West Texas, included many Knights and Alliance men and a few ex-Greenbackers. Upset by "special privileges granted to favored classes . . . to build up a moneyed aristocracy," they declared their "independence of all political parties, rings, bosses, and cliques . . ." The delegates made no nominations

[17] Procter, *Not Without Honor*, pp. 264–266; J. W. Truit to Mrs. Susan E. Morris, January 27, 1887, John H. Reagan Papers; Chamberlain, "Terrell," pp. 326–328; *Galveston Daily News*, January 26, 27, February 2, 1887; Texas, Legislature, House of Representatives, *Journal*, 20th Legislature, Reg. sess., pp. 160, 166, 168–169, 231; Richard Coke and John H. Reagan to the President, February 14, 1887 (copy), Maxey Papers.

but adopted a platform favoring abolition of national banks; issuance of "legal tender money" for low interest loans based on real estate; government ownership of transportation and communications; direct election of president, vice-president, and United States senators; and a national usury law. They opposed alien landowners and land grants to corporations.[18]

At Fort Worth, on July 2 and 3, disillusioned Democrats, former Greenbackers, and a few Republicans, some members of the Farmers' Alliance, and several of the organizers of the May meeting in Waco held a small non-partisan convention. They adopted the Waco platform, adding new planks in favor of free silver coinage, immediate payment of the national debt at face value, a graduated income tax, better schools, rotation in office, compulsory arbitration laws, and taxation of real estate held for speculation. Then they selected nominees for state offices including Evan Jones, president of the Texas Farmers' Alliance, for governor and H. S. Broiles for lieutenant governor. Two days later 110 delegates from forty-seven counties, many of them the same men, met in Fort Worth to organized a Union Labor party in Texas. Its leaders, among them several ex-Greenbackers and members of the Alliance, endorsed the platform of the new national Union Labor party and the state platform and nominees of the nonpartisan convention. In August Jones refused the gubernatorial nomination, and most other Alliance leaders refused to join the new movement. The nonpartisan and Union Labor executive committees then met to endorse former Lieutenant Governor Marion Martin, already the gubernatorial nominee of a Prohibition convention in April. They also replaced Broiles with German Alliance lecturer W. A. Moers of Harris County to avoid being labeled strictly prohibitionist in view. On September 20 the Republican state convention, under the direction of Cuney, decided to back the nonpartisan–Union Labor ticket. The Republicans apparently feared a split vote, since Baptist minister R. M. Humphrey, a former Confederate officer

[18] William C. Pool, *Bosque Territory*, p. 142; Sam Hanna Acheson, *35,000 Days in Texas*, pp. 141–142; *Galveston Weekly News*, April 19, May 17, 1888; Winkler, *Platforms*, pp. 254–257; King, *Wagons East*, p. 54; John A. Garraty, *The New Commonwealth, 1877–1890*, p. 290.

and organizer of the Colored Farmers' Alliance, had announced for Congress as a Union Labor candidate in East Texas. An Alliance ticket in Colorado County included Negro candidates. Several anti-prohibition German delegates refused to support Martin.[19]

Texas Democrats in 1888 renominated Ross and wrote a platform favoring abolition of national banks, issuance of United States currency, and regulation of freight rates and monopolies. They also endorsed a tariff-reduction bill introduced in Congress through the House Ways and Means Committee chaired by Roger Mills. The authors hoped it would forge a lasting link between western and southern agrarians who sought lower priced manufactured goods and the commercial and manufacturing interests of the Northeast who wanted cheaper raw materials. A week later the state Farmers' Alliance met to express its concern over the "alarming destitution" which constantly drove "the masses of the people . . . nearer a condition of serfdom and tenantry." It reaffirmed its earlier demands in the form of recommended "legislative remedies," adding a call for a state railroad commission. It avoided criticism of the Democratic party or any hint of open opposition. Discontent existed, however, in many areas of East and West Texas, and Ross campaigned actively to combat it. A debate between Ross and Martin on October 13 dealt with tax reduction, improvement of public education, protection of voting rights, and, above all, railroad regulation, with Martin chiding the governor for slow or ineffectual action in each area. In the election that followed, Ross defeated Martin by 250,388 votes to 98,447, losing only the previously Republican and Greenback counties on the coast, along the Brazos River, and in Northeast Texas. The 33,384 presidential votes for the Union Labor party indicated more clearly its own strength apart from Republican fusion support—about 10 per cent of the Texas electorate. If third-party votes offer any index to discontent, however, Texas ranked high, for

[19] Winkler, *Platforms*, pp. 260–263, 272–273; Martin, *People's Party in Texas*, pp. 34–35; *Galveston Weekly News*, July 5, August 30, 1888; Catharine Nugent, ed., *Life Work of Thomas L. Nugent*, p. 279; *Galveston Daily News*, October 14, 31, 1888; Lawrence D. Rice, "The Negro in Texas, 1874–1900" (Ph.D. diss.), p. 132.

it polled 20 per cent of the Union Labor party's national vote, second only to Kansas, with half the party's vote in the former Confederate states.[20]

Mills had received unanimous support from Texans in Congress for his tariff bill, which most southern and western and many eastern Democrats preferred to make the primary issue in the national campaign. Other eastern party leaders, including President Cleveland, developed doubts, however, because the bill lowered duties on most eastern manufactured goods and might lose more votes than it won in those closely contested states. The Democratic National Convention adopted a platform favoring the Mills Bill. But after the selection of Calvin Brice of Ohio and William H. Barnum of Connecticut to manage the Democratic campaign, Reagan indignantly wrote: "What a predicament the party is placed in with revenue reform for its battle cry with a known protectionist and the head of the great copper trust of this country as our chairman and leader . . ." He continued to protest without effect against the negative campaign of the national party. Cleveland carried Texas easily on the basis of Democratic tradition but lost the presidential election to Republican Benjamin Harrison and some standing with many Texans because of the evasive campaign.[21]

Again in the congressional races a combination of Alliance men and former Greenbackers opposed Democratic incumbents in most farming areas, while Republicans ran in South Texas, along the coast, and in one North Texas district. The Democratic candidates emphasized, in most cases, their low-tariff plank as a means of in-

[20] R. T. Milner to J. H. Reagan, August 10, 1888, L. S. Ross to Reagan, October 22, 1888, Reagan Papers; Winkler, *Platforms*, pp. 257–259, 265–271; *Galveston Weekly News*, October 18, 1888; Texas, Legislature, Senate, *Journal*, 21st Legislature, Reg. sess., pp. 45–46; Fred E. Haynes, *Third Party Movements Since the Civil War*, pp. 206, 208, 211–212; W. Dean Burnham, *Presidential Ballots, 1836–1892*, pp. 253–255.

[21] Burnham, *Presidential Ballots*, pp. 765–813; John H. Reagan to Chauncey F. Black, July 7, 1888, as quoted in Festus P. Summers, *William L. Wilson and Tariff Reform*, p. 89; Reagan to Calvin S. Brice, August 19, 1888, Reagan Papers; U.S., Congress, *Congressional Record*, 50th Cong., 1st sess., p. 6660; Horace Samuel Merrill, *Bourbon Leader: Grover Cleveland and the Democratic Party*, pp. 117–134.

creasing agricultural exports and lowering the prices of manufactured goods bought by farmers. Mills met strong opposition in his North Central Texas district from a combination of dissident groups including prohibitionists and woolgrowers. Hogg, Coke, and others went in to help Mills, who spent most of his time speaking for his tariff bill in the East and Midwest during the presidential campaign. Texas Democrats generally won by safe margins, although a Republican candidate pressed W. H. Crain closely in South Texas.[22]

Discontent appeared at the local level in several places. Farmers organized in Lampasas County; Dr. Pat B. Clark, an Alliance leader, helped form a new People's party in Red River County; and similar groups enjoyed at least some success in Navarro, Milam, Tarrant, Bell, Delta, and Harris counties. Few legislators identified themselves with dissident groups, but Senator Coke estimated that as many as seventeen were non-Democrats. More important, the Legislature included the largest number of agriculturists elected since the constitution of 1875—approximately half the body with a clear majority in the house.[23]

When the new Legislature met in January 1889 it had to deal with increased interest in legislation to regulate trusts and railroads. A new postwar generation of Texans had grown up in the late nineteenth-century world of rapidly expanding business and railroad combinations able to control prices or rates in entire areas or industries. To grapple with such problems the Legislature, made up increasingly of these younger Texans, more readily accepted the necessity of compromising their traditonal small-government views. Since the individual Texan could not completely control his own affairs in a more

[22] Texas, Secretary of State, *Report*, 1888, pp. 162–164; Myrtle Roberts, "Roger Quarles Mills" (M.A. thesis), pp. 89–90; Robert C. Cotner, *James Stephen Hogg*, p. 151; *Galveston Weekly News*, October 4, 18, 1888.

[23] *Galveston Weekly News*, November 8, 1888; Richard Coke to G. C. Pendleton, November 19, 1888, J. N. Browning to Pendleton, November 28, 1888, Alexander Dienst Collection; E. G. Sessions to Marion Butler, June 11, 1896, Marion Butler Papers; O. M. Kern to J. H. Reagan, August 28, 1888, Reagan Papers; R. J. Boykin to T. S. Henderson, June 1, 1888, Henderson Papers; Martin, *People's Party*, pp. 32–33; Texas, Legislature, House, *Rules of Order of the House of Representatives of the Twenty-first Legislature*; *Galveston Daily News*, January 5, 1889; Edwards, "The Farmers' Movement," p. 32.

complex world dominated by such concentrations of power, the legislators sought to regulate the power and thus protect the rights of the individual. Texans, like other Southerners, however, applied their greater willingness to adopt sweeping legislation also to the realm of race relations where it took the form of laws to legalize segregation.

Texas farmers and ranchers demanded an antitrust law to regulate business combinations that controlled the price of cotton bagging, beef, and other products to limit competition. Agitation in Congress against trusts, including three bills by Texans, and the existence of large land corporations in West Texas also stimulated action in Texas. Attorney General James S. Hogg met with L. L. Foster, commissioner of insurance, statistics, and history, and Representative A. C. Owsley for several nights to write a bill based on one introduced in Congress by Reagan. Owsley later amended it to exempt farmer and rancher organizations. A Kansas legislative resolution against the "beef combine" arrived to bolster supporters of the bill. Finally in March the Texas Legislature passed a compromise bill, with only one dissenting vote, which outlawed restraint of trade, control of prices, prevention of competition, and combinations to set transportation rates.[24]

In the same Legislature W. H. Pope of Marshall, who would later style himself the "Jim Crow Senator," offered a bill to require railroads to provide separate coaches for Negroes. It met opposition on the grounds that it would be a burden to the railroads. After amending it to "authorize" rather than "require" separate coaches, the Legislature adopted the bill by overwhelming majorities in both houses despite opposition from Negro leaders. East Texans pressed for a plank demanding a stronger separate-coach bill in the Democratic state convention of 1890. Hogg, the gubernatorial candidate, had been a paternalistic moderate in matters of race, but acquiesced rather than lose any of his backing or chance the creation of a strong issue that could be used against him. The subsequent Legislature adopted a new bill requiring separate coaches on railroads.[25]

[24] Tom Finty, Jr., *Anti-Trust Legislation in Texas*, pp. 15–17; Cotner, *Hogg*, pp. 160–165.

[25] M. Looscan to J. S. Hogg, May 18, 1892, Letters Received, XVI, James

Railroad regulation, a more controversial issue than antitrust or segregation laws, would wait until the Hogg administration for a final solution.

Labor discontent faded from public attention in the wake of increasing Alliance activities and the failure of the Great Southwest Strike. Unrest continued, however, and resulted in an "eight hour convention" at Dallas in July 1889. Delegates from thirty-four towns represented thirteen organizations consisting of trade unions, Knights of Labor locals, and the Farmers' Alliance. The leaders included at least two prominent Greenbackers, one nonpartisan leader of 1888, and one Negro Republican spokesman, but generally they held positions in the Knights of Labor. The convention deplored the fact that "thousands of men and women are idle, cut off from natural opportunities by unjust systems" and "commercial despotism." It then adopted resolutions in favor of an eight-hour day, a single tax on land, repeal of the national banking system, and government ownership of railroad, telegraph, and telephone lines. To obliterate "all corruption and the damnable boodle system" the delegates further urged a secret ballot, direct election of all public officials, and a lien on products of labor. Most important, they created a State Federation of Labor to seek the fulfillment of their goals.[26]

Although farmer discontent continued to exist through the late 1880's in Texas, it failed to well into massive protest—because of the passage of antitrust and segregation bills, the creation of the Alliance with its emphasis on efforts within the Democratic party and on co-operative business projects, the increasing Democratic interest in railroad regulation, and the election of reformer Reagan to the Senate. Yet the defeat of Mills's tariff bill and the failure of Cleveland to show real concern for southern and western problems had further

Stephen Hogg Papers; Texas, Senate, *Journal*, 21st Legislature, Reg. sess., pp 15, 750; Texas, House, *Journal*, 21st Legislature, Reg. sess., pp. 856–858; N. W. Cuney to Guy M. Bryan, January 30, 1889, Guy M. Bryan Papers; George E. Hopkins, "The Origin of Jim Crow Laws in Texas," paper presented at the Phi Alpha Theta session of the annual meeting of the Texas State Historical Association, April 30, 1966.

[26] Winkler, *Platforms*, pp. 273–275; Ruth A. Allen, *Chapters in the History of Organized Labor in Texas*, pp. 23, 174.

weakened the affection and faith of many men for the Democratic party. Farmer and labor discontent in Texas more than in any other southern state held together and developed a body of ideas and political and pressure group leaders that the Populists would soon draw upon for inspiration and organizational skills.

8. RAILROAD REGULATION

In the periods immediately before and after the Civil War, Texas had few railroads and a great interest in acquiring more. Under the constitutions of 1845 and 1866 public land had been granted to promote new rail lines, but the Republican-dominated convention of 1868–1869 ended this practice and substituted state bonds instead. Democrats returned to land subsidies in 1873 and the process continued until all the land was gone in 1882. Altogether the state granted 32,153,878 acres in return for 2,928 miles of track. Cities, counties, and local landowners also presented lands to railroads as inducements to extend their lines to various parts of the state. By the early 1880's the state's railroads had laid trackage in Texas slightly in excess of six thousand miles which allowed fairly low cost, rapid transportation that enabled Texas farmers to change from subsistence to commercial agriculture. It also opened the way for development of the lumber industry and various commercial and manufacturing houses in the state.[1]

[1] Robert Lewis Peterson, "State Regulation of Railroads in Texas, 1836–

At the same time Jay Gould acquired control of all Texas railroads running north and east and connecting the state with the nation's major population centers. They included by 1882 the Missouri Pacific; the Texas and Pacific; the International and Great Northern; the Missouri, Kansas, and Texas, and some lesser roads. In addition to eliminating the possibility of expensive rate wars for goods flowing north out of Texas, Gould leased the Missouri, Kansas, and Texas to the Missouri Pacific, through which he drained the resources of the Missouri, Kansas, and Texas after selling his own shares of its stock. He allowed the International and Great Northern to deteriorate when it no longer aided his plans. Those dealings set the general pattern for Gould's operations, for he frequently ignored stockholders and the public, overcapitalized his lines to gain support, and manipulated them for his personal benefit alone. In 1882 Gould and Collis P. Huntington, owner of the Southern Pacific, which connected the Gulf with the West Coast, agreed to a division of state transport between their interests, to avoid costly competition in construction and freight rates. In 1885 they formed the Texas Traffic Association—a pool to establish uniformity and to eliminate competition in rates. When the courts dissolved the association in 1888, the railroad men replaced it with the International Association and later with the Southern Interstate Association. Such activities represented only partially successful efforts at private regulation to reduce rate wars among the major lines, allowing them greater profits and promoting more railroad construction in areas of sparse population. But these arrangements, especially Gould's manipulations, attracted growing criticism because they produced rebates and drawbacks from major shippers, higher short-haul charges, discrimination in rates between places and between persons, poor service with worn-out equipment, and political pressure to avoid state action.[2]

1920" (Ph.D. diss.), pp. 13–18; S. G. Reed, *A History of the Texas Railroads*, pp. 157, 194–195, 517; John S. Spratt, *The Road to Spindletop*, pp. 29–32, 36.

[2] Spratt, *Road to Spindletop*, pp. 34–36; Ira G. Clark, *Then Came the Railroads*, pp. 125–151, 209–221; Vera Lea Dugas, "A Social and Economic History of Texas in the Civil War and Reconstruction Periods" (Ph.D. diss.), pp. 543–565; Julius Grodinsky, *Jay Gould, 1867–1892*, pp. 252, 395–410, 534–570.

An increasing demand resulted, in the late 1870's and early 1880's, for railroad regulation. Railroads had been declared common carriers subject to rate regulation by the Legislature in the Grange-influenced Constitution of 1876. They had been required to have offices, records, and at least one public meeting each year in the state. Parallel or competing lines had been forbidden to consolidate. But without enforcement such articles proved useless, and the Legislature failed to act, despite recommendations by Governor Coke in 1876. Then in 1877 the Grange began to petition for regulation, followed by the Greenback party. Throckmorton, an ardent advocate of land grants to the Texas and Pacific, in which he held stock, believed that a regulatory commission would end public inequities and protect the lines from damaging rate wars. But business groups, such as the Cotton Exchange and the Board of Trade in Houston, the state's railroad center, generally opposed any controls that might limit railroad expansion and thus restrict Houston's trade area. A mild compromise resulted initially in the form of a law which set a maximum freight charge of fifty cents per one hundred pounds each one hundred miles.[3]

Some members of the next Legislature renewed efforts at regulation and concentrated on the establishment of a railroad commission. Many railroad executives and businessmen argued that the Legislature lacked the information to set rates, could not delegate that authority under the state constitution, and could not usefully establish intrastate rates in the absence of power to regulate interstate rates. Jay Gould, making a timely inspection trip into the state, commented that its business future seemed bright unless there should be "injudicious interference by Congresses and State Legislatures with business . . . The peril is legislation. This is the danger always." To reinforce his point, Gould stopped work on an extension of the Missouri, Kansas, and Texas until the Legislature defeated the commission bill.[4]

[3] Spratt, *Road to Spindletop*, p. 157; Peterson, "State Regulation of Railroads," pp. 17–20, 27–36, 76; Roscoe C. Martin, "The Grange as a Political Factor in Texas," *Southwestern Social Science Quarterly* 6 (March 1926): 374–375; J. W. Throckmorton to Ashbel Smith, December 22, 1878, January 19, 1879, G. W. Kidd to Smith, February 8, 1879, Ashbel Smith Papers; Ernest William Winkler, ed., *Platforms of Political Parties in Texas*, p. 189.

[4] Texas, Legislature, Senate, *Journal*, 17th Legislature, Reg. sess., pp. 172–173;

At a called session in 1882, the Seventeenth Legislature did reduce maximum fares from five cents to three cents per mile, despite continued railroad opposition, and did prohibit lines from charging more than the amounts stated on bills of lading. That same year the Democratic party added to its platform a plank favoring railroad regulation. At the urging of Governor Ireland in 1883 the Legislature again considered regulation bills, but southwestern railroads still preferred self-regulation and lobbied successfully to produce a compromise creating only the office of state engineer to investigate railroad practices. The position proved so ineffective that its first occupant recommended its abolition.[5]

Again in 1885 legislators defeated a proposal for a rate-making commission after considerable railroad lobbying. A significant shift of opinion appeared on that occasion, however, for the Galveston and Houston cotton exchanges joined the proponents of state regulation because freight rate discrimination channeled much cotton out of the state by rail instead of through the two ports. In 1886 the Farmers' Alliance added its voice to those demanding regulation, and the state Democratic party reaffirmed its favorable stand. But in 1887 Ross, the new governor, influenced perhaps by his campaign manager, railroad attorney George Clark, expressed his belief that competition would regulate rates. Taking heart, presumably from the governor's views, out-of-state railroads tried but failed to procure an act allowing them to build into Texas and to buy Texas lines without maintaining offices in the state. Despite Ross's statement, legislators introduced several regulation bills. One passed the house but met defeat in the senate after Gould returned to the state to say again that such legislation would drive away investment capital and stop railroad building.[6]

Texas, Legislature, House of Representatives, *Journal*, 17th Legislature, Reg. sess., p. 303; Robert Lewis Peterson, "Jay Gould and the Railroad Commission of Texas," *Southwestern Historical Quarterly* 58 (January 1955): 423; Peterson, "State Regulation of Railroads," pp. 76–78.

[5] Peterson, "State Regulation of Railroads," pp. 37–39; Charles S. Potts, *Railroad Transportation in Texas*, pp. 119–120; Winkler, *Platforms*, p. 210.

[6] Winkler, *Platforms*, pp. 236, 239; Potts, *Railroad Transportation*, pp. 120–121; John O'Day to S. J. Wright, January 31, 1887, Samuel J. Wright Papers;

The movement for railroad regulation in Texas received a tremendous boost in 1887 from the successful fight, led for ten years by John H. Reagan as chairman or as a member of the House Commerce Committee, to establish federal regulation of interstate commerce. Though a member of the state constitutional convention of 1875, which provided for state railroad regulation, and the Grange, which had favored such regulation since 1877, Reagan had shown his first if initially somewhat naive interest in federal regulation during his second term in Congress. There he found support from independent oil men in Pennsylvania who opposed rebates and rate discrimination which favored Standard Oil, merchants in New York and across the country who sought to reduce their shipping costs, and commercial farmers of the Midwest and South who hoped to offset falling prices by forcing rate reductions. Eastern railroad men, unable to so nearly monopolize entire trade areas as did some of their western counterparts, also sought regulation to avoid financially ruinous rate wars. Passage of a bill met delays, however, because of differences between advocates of regulation over the exact content of the bill. Some shippers and railroad men opposed equalization of charges per mile for long and short hauls, and some railroads opposed any antipooling clauses. Reagan himself retarded passage for a time rather than accept a regulatory commission which he feared might be dominated by the railroads. But in December 1886, to assure passage of such an act, he finally agreed to creation of the Interstate Commerce Commission because he felt the cost of enforcement through the courts would be prohibitive for most shippers. He refused to accept an act that did not outlaw pools, however, with short-haul–long-haul charges left to the new commission. Most railroad men saw federal regulation as a means of stabilizing rates to avoid cutthroat competition and hoped it would greatly reduce similar state efforts, but federal action only inspired advocates of regulation in Texas. "All the arguments in favor of the interstate commission apply with greater or less force in favor of a state commission,"

Peterson, "Jay Gould," pp. 423–425; Louis Tuffly Ellis, "The Texas Cotton Compress Industry" (Ph.D. diss.), pp. 123–124.

urged Senator Coke, adding, "State regulation of commerce is a necessary supplement of interstate regulation . . ."[7]

In 1887 and 1888, as the result of complaints by Texas merchants and lumbermen, Attorney General Hogg required railroads to keep their lines in repair or forfeit their charters, broke up the Texas Traffic Association by an antimonopoly suit, and forced lines to return their offices to Texas from out of state, as the law required. The boards of trade in Galveston, Houston, and Fort Worth in the spring of 1888 endorsed lower rates set by the Fort Worth and Denver City Railway Company in the hope of forcing other lines to reduce their rates. Clearly Texas merchants had joined agricultural shippers as important voices for state regulation. These efforts made it easier for regulators to renew the planks in the state Democratic platform condemning pools and trusts and rate discrimination. But the convention did not specifically advocate a railroad commission, although A. W. Terrell, who wrote the antidiscrimination plank, actually had that goal in mind. In private Terrell angrily denounced "*platform hypocracy* [*sic*]" and predicted a political revolt comparable to Houston's defeat of the regular Democratic gubernatorial nominee in 1859 if a commission were not created, because the Alliance quite possibly included a majority of Anglo voters in Texas.[8]

Again in 1889 a railroad commission bill began the tortuous trek through the Legislature. Numerous petitions from local alliances and increased support from businessmen, especially those directly involved with shipping problems, considerably aided its progress. Members of the Galveston Cotton Exchange, because they continued to suffer from northward shipment of the state's cotton by rail as a result of rate discrimination, joined the petitioners. The bill passed the house over railroad opposition, but the senate substituted a regulatory act without a commission for enforcement, which the house refused to

[7] Richard Coke to C. W. Harned, July 26, 1889, in newspaper clipping, Richard Coke, Scrapbook; Ben H. Procter, *Not Without Honor*, pp. 218–263; Lee Benson, *Merchants, Farmers, and Railroads*, pp. 214–238; Gabriel Kolko, *Railroads and Regulations, 1877–1916*, pp. 21–43.

[8] Robert C. Cotner, *James Stephen Hogg*, pp. 100, 117–146, 154–159, 169; A. W. Terrell to Guy M. Bryan, November 25, 1888, Guy M. Bryan Papers; Winkler, *Platforms*, pp. 267, 270; Richard C. Overton, *Gulf to Rockies*, p. 195.

accept. Because senate opponents of a commission continued to offer the argument that the Legislature could not constitutionally delegate its regulatory authority to a commission, advocates pushed through the Legislature a constitutional amendment to be submitted to the voters, authorizing regulation. The amendment gained support from bankers, shippers, lumbermen, and merchants.[9]

The Dallas Manufacturers Association that summer held a freight rate convention attended by merchants, farmers, and legislators, followed by an unsatisfactory conference with railroad representatives who refused to effect a voluntary adjustment in rates. Debates over the influence of the railroad lobby and articles for and against a commission filled the papers. State Senator Thomas J. Brown produced probably the best informed and most effective series in the *Southern Mercury*, the Farmers' Alliance journal in Dallas, showing the success of commissions in other states and the high rates caused by unregulated, watered railroad stock. The *Mercury* also published legislators' votes on the railroad commission bill with the warning "if somebody's name is in the wrong column below somebody will get left."[10] Thus the commission amendment became the major issue in the 1890 campaign, and the gubernatorial nomination a key factor in its success or failure.

As early as May 1889 rumor made James Stephen Hogg, the tall, 250-pound attorney general, a leading candidate for governor. Hogg in a sense marked a new generation, less bound by tradition, for he had not fought in the Civil War himself, but was the son of a Confederate general. His youth as printer's devil, sharecropper, and self-taught lawyer gave perspective to a basically conservative man raised on a small plantation by his family that had come to Texas in the days of the republic. Hogg chose as associates the ambitious sons of other prominent East Texas families and rising young attorneys who shared his interest in politics. But he could still attract the typical

[9] *Galveston Daily News*, February 14, 1889; Texas, House, *Journal*, 21st Legislature, Reg. sess., pp. 456–459, 1122–1123; Peterson, "State Regulation of Railroads," pp. 82–87.

[10] Peterson, "State Regulation of Railroads," pp. 88–114; Winkler, *Platforms*, pp. 275–280; Richard Coke, Scrapbook; *Southern Mercury* (Dallas), February 28, March 14, 1889, January 9, 1890.

Texas farmer by casting aside his coat and dropping his suspenders in the midst of a campaign speech in a rural area. A forceful speaker, with a "tremendous voice," his frankness, "homespun humor," and political experience made him a formidable figure in the open and at times rough debates that characterized Texas politics. He would never rank as a political philosopher, but he was well read, and he reflected on the practical issues of the day. He accepted most traditional southern doubts about federal government action, but showed less reluctance to exercise the full authority of the state to meet public needs as he saw them. He took strong stands on issues, once he had formed an opinion about them, and threw himself wholeheartedly into any campaign once he decided to run. To his opponents such characteristics branded him as "dogmatic and arbitrary and a red republican demagogue." His supporters described him as "a native Texan, a fearless officer, a true democrat." "The fight is on hand [against trusts and illegal railroad activities]," he announced while still attorney general, "and I may get the worst of it, but one thing is certain, somebody else will get a little disfigured in the fray." He could count on extensive support from farmer and labor organizations, businessmen, and aspiring young Democratic politicians like himself. He held back throughout 1889 because of official duties, but in April 1890, in response to pleas from close friends, he replied, ". . . by Gatlins, I'll make the race and I'm in it to stay" as a strong advocate of the commission amendment.

Candidates in the field besides Hogg included Lieutenant Governor Thomas B. Wheeler and ex-Governor Throckmorton, both railroad stockholders who favored only a relatively weak commission, and energetic young H. D. McDonald, who had led senate opposition to a commission in 1889. Jay Gould, again touring Texas for his own health and that of his railroad lines, expressed fear of "the disposition in some quarters to hamper railroads." Most of the state's urban dailies agreed with Gould and threw their support behind Hogg's opponents. George Clark, leading railroad attorney and lobbyist, spoke against Hogg and the commission in April.[11]

[11] Robert C. Cotner, ed., *Addresses and State Papers of James Stephen Hogg*, p. 50 n; *Dallas Morning News*, January 25, 1891; W. M. Walton to John H.

Despite the varied and impressive opposition, Hogg's backing developed steadily throughout the farming regions of North, East, and Central Texas, and even among some West Texas ranchers, after a congressional committee exposed the beef trust and its railroad connections. Hogg spoke widely to emphasize the value of a state regulatory commission to end the rate discrimination in Texas which favored out-of-state competition over local merchants, lumbermen, and manufacturers, as well as cattlemen and farmers. He supplemented his strength by working closely with other candidates for state offices. It soon became evident that upon the broad base of the Texas agricultural majority prepared for him by previous Grange and Alliance efforts, he had built an additional following among business and professional men that would prove insurmountable.[12]

In May, Throckmorton left the race because of poor health. Much of North Texas swung over to Hogg, and McDonald also withdrew. Land Commissioner Richard M. Hall, who had opposed Hogg on several issues during the Ross administration, then entered the contest. But Hall only split Wheeler's West Texas support, forcing Hogg's opposition, led by Clark and sustained by the railroads and some businessmen and cattle raisers, to promote the candidacy of erratic, independent, District Court Judge Gustave Cook of Houston. Clark also sought to stir up Confederate sentiment against Hogg, who concentrated in his speeches upon existing issues rather than upon the past. In June, Cook warned of "communistic and agrarian rapacity," but with little effect. The number of delegates pledged to the attorney general continued to grow. The state Democratic convention overwhelmingly nominated him, on a platform that strongly favored the commission amendment and opposed national banks but avoided the Alliance's subtreasury plan and opposed its suggestion for government ownership of railroads and telegraph companies. The new generation of politicians also appeared in East and North Texas with

---

Reagan, August 12, 1890, John H. Reagan Papers; Cotner, *Hogg*, pp. 3–70, 130, 170–197, 216, 322–323; Peterson, "Jay Gould," pp. 425–428; Roscoe C. Martin, *The People's Party in Texas*, p. 26; Walter Prescott Webb and Terrell Webb, eds., *Washington Wife*, p. 3.

[12] Cotner, *Hogg*, pp. 195–200.

the nominations of C. B. Kilgore and Joseph W. Bailey for Congress over old-line Democrats who avoided the issues of the day. Hogg easily defeated his Republican opponent, Webster Flanagan, by 262,452 votes to 77,742; his campaign ensured the passage of the commission amendment, 181,954 votes to 73,106.[13] Discontent seemed at a minimum, for Democratic congressional nominees handily defeated weak Republican opposition and independents received only a scattering of protest votes. Yet on the local level dissatisfaction still existed in places, hidden beneath the clamor for railroad regulation.[14]

In January 1891 the Legislature met with a clear mandate from the voters to establish a railroad commission. Hogg's message suggested a commission that could set rates, require adequate reports from railroads, inspect their books, call witnesses, and prohibit and punish discrimination and extortion by the companies. A. W. Terrell, T. J. Brown, and M. M. Crane, all experienced legislators who understood the problems facing Texas shippers, led the efforts to create a commission. The speaker of the house supported Hogg, but the lieutenant governor appointed Cone Johnson, an ambitious young man of anticommission views, to head the senate committee that would handle bills relating to the commission. In a change of tactics, opposition leaders argued that the commission should be elective, a position that some commission supporters shared. But Hogg favored appointment to keep the commission from being directly involved in politics. Brown guided an act such as Hogg recommended through the house, but he found it impossible to resolve differences with Johnson's senate bill. Crane suggested a special committee to write a joint bill, but continued railroad lobbying led by Clark resulted in a watered-down measure that Hogg and his supporters found unacceptable.[15] Hogg then called in Terrell, Brown,

[13] Cotner, *Hogg*, pp. 200–219; Norman G. Kittrell, *Governors Who Have Been*, p. 106.

[14] J. W. Truit to "My Dear Little Sister," July 13, 1890, James W. Truit Papers; Sam Hanna Acheson, *Joe Bailey*, pp. 36–43; George W. Tyler, *The History of Bell County*, p. 326; Gillespie County [Texas] Farmers' Alliance, Minutes, July 1890; Texas, Secretary of State, *Report*, 1890, pp. 84–86; Martin, *People's Party*, p. 33.

[15] C. V. Terrell, *The Terrells*, pp. 199–201; Cotner, *Hogg*, pp. 221–238;

Crane, and State Senator E. J. Simkins for night meetings that produced a bill along the lines the governor had suggested earlier. Terrell presented it late in February. The senate defeated efforts by a railroad attorney to weaken it by inserting a clause that would allow mandamus or injunction proceedings against the commission without a trial. It also voted down a motion for an elective commission. The bill did have opponents, mostly from railroad towns or from South and West Texas areas still seeking more railroads, but in its somewhat amended final form, it received overwhelming approval by both houses.[16]

To head the new Railroad Commission, Hogg chose Senator John H. Reagan, Texas's leading advocate of railroad regulation. Reagan accepted out of concern for the people of Texas, a belief that railroad regulation represented the most important issue of the day, and a desire to increase the state's manufactures. Probably his election to the Senate had proven a barren honor, since junior senators had little power, and the chairmanship of the commission seemed both well suited to his abilities and interests and a possible steppingstone to the governorship, which might provide a more attractive conclusion to his lengthy political career. Hogg appointed with him L. L. Foster, a former legislator and state commissioner of insurance, statistics, and history, and William P. McLean, a veteran member of the constitutional convention of 1875, legislator, and district judge. Hogg refused, however, to appoint an Alliance member to the commission; his refusal helped create the split between leaders of the farm organization and the Democratic party which led to the formation of the Populist party in Texas.[17]

Dallas Morning News, February 11, 14, 18, 1891; Texas, House, *Journal*, 22nd Legislature, Reg. sess., pp. 10–21, 322–323.

[16] Texas, House, *Journal*, 22nd Legislature, Reg. sess., pp. 422–429, 478–485; *Dallas Morning News*, February 25, 26, March 4, 6, 12–14, 21, 28, 1891; Cotner, *Hogg*, pp. 239–243; M. M. Crane, "Recollections of the Establishment of the Texas Railroad Commission," *Southwestern Historical Quarterly* 50 (April 1947): 481–485; Charles K. Chamberlain, "Alexander Watkins Terrell" (Ph.D. diss.), pp. 341–348.

[17] Cotner, *Hogg*, pp. 244–249; John H. Reagan to J. S. Hogg, April 23, 1891, Reagan Papers; Gerald Nash, "A Chapter From an Active Life" (M.A. thesis), p. 103.

The new commissioners at first attempted to enforce a system of rates based on mileage, with only a few exceptions. But within three years they returned primarily to the "common point" system of equal rates for broad areas in the state which had been used by the railroads themselves, because of the different conditions that existed for different lines in different regions. Among its early activities the commission built up a staff of experts who had experience as employees of various Texas railroads. Commissioners also sought compromise and cooperation with the railroads, for they generally urged reductions by the Southwestern Freight Rate Association, a pool organized in the 1890's, before taking official action to reduce rates. Protests against these actions by farmer organizations emphasized the commissioners' retreat from their original position to one of limited change, which stimulated less controversy. The commission apparently responded to political pressure by providing Texas shippers an advantage in the form of preferential rates. Thus the commissioners helped funnel goods in and out of the state through Houston and Galveston, the state's major ports, rather than overland by interstate railroads.[18]

Although the commission did not drastically reduce rates, five lines filed an injunction in 1892 to test its constitutionality. Federal Judge A. P. McCormick granted the injunction and a district court sustained him in 1893. But the United States Supreme Court upheld the constitutionality of the commission in 1894 in the case of *Reagan v. Farmers Loan & Trust Co.*, though declaring its rates subject to judicial review. In 1898 McCormick again granted an injunction to eight railroads against a lowering of the cotton rates by the commission. Several meetings between the lines and the commission produced slightly higher rates as a compromise in 1899. The commis-

[18] Cotner, *Hogg*, pp. 374–377; Spratt, *Road to Spindletop*, pp. 224–227; Proctor, *Not Without Honor*, p. 284; Gerald Nash, "The Reformer Reformed," *Business History Review* 29: 189–196; William Z. Ripley, *Railroads: Rates and Regulation*, pp. 393–394; Texas, Railroad Commission, *First Annual Report*, 1892, pp. viii–xxiii; Texas, Railroad Commission, *Fourth Annual Report*, 1895, pp. 5–20; W. M. W. Splawn, "Valuation and Rate Regulation by the Railroad Commission of Texas," *Journal of Political Economy* 31 (October 1923): 690–697.

sion thus successfully surmounted two challenges to its existence at the expense of greater judicial restraints on its powers.

In 1893 Hogg urged the Legislature to strengthen the commission by adopting a stocks and bonds law to end the issuance of watered stock, because it frequently forced lines to set high rates to maintain their dividends. Texas legislators responded with an act which required railroads to list stock with the commission and allowed new issues only when company indebtedness did not exceed the value of company property. In emergencies, however, the commission could authorize new stock up to 50 per cent above the value of railroad property. Some lines complained that the commission placed a strain on them by evaluating their property below the actual cost of construction. On other lines service degenerated because the companies could not go into debt for the purchase of new equipment or the addition of needed facilities. Some Texas lines overcame the strict limitations by issuing stock in other states based on the credit of parent companies. In 1901 the Legislature recognized the problem in part by allowing the commission to authorize the issuance by a line of stocks up to the value of new extensions, regardless of its existing securities. The Legislature acted again in 1907 to allow additional stock for the purchase of new railroad cars. The stocks and bonds law did reduce the direct debt of Texas lines, though it increased their floating debt and probably slowed expansion and modernization.[19]

Texas established a railroad commission a decade later than most southern states because of its frontier condition and need for new lines after the Civil War. The late beginning, however, resulted in a stronger commission than in most states because it developed amid greater criticism of railroad activities. Because the commission could not control interstate rates, failed to cooperate completely with the Interstate Commerce Commission, and did not receive consistent support from the Legislature, it proved less effective than many had hoped. It did help reduce intrastate discrimination and rates to a

[19] Splawn, "Valuation," pp. 675–690; Clark, *Then Came the Railroads*, p. 234; Overton, *Gulf to Rockies*, p. 338; Cotner, *Hogg*, pp. 328–332; Potts, *Railroad Transportation*, pp. 140–153; William Z. Ripley, *Railroads: Finance and Organization*, pp. 156, 247–248, 301–306.

greater extent than in most other areas from 1891 to 1906, though Texas rates remained above the national average.[20] To some degree it served the interests of shippers—especially merchants and farmers—who had strongly supported its creation. Despite early challenges and complaints by Texas railroads, the commission sought to cooperate with them to establish rates and as a result established a workable and increasingly positive relationship with the lines. The existence of the commission did not end all the problems of the state's farmers, however, and controversy surrounding the appointment of the original commissioners helped divide the Texas Democracy.

[20] Peterson, "State Regulation of Railroads," pp. 153–202, 485–498; Spratt, *Road to Spindletop*, pp. 219–226; Potts, *Railroad Transportation*, pp. 164, 174.

9. THE DEMOCRACY DIVIDES

THREE FACTIONS EXISTED within the Democratic party in Texas after the creation of the Railroad Commission in 1891. Most railroad men and many businessmen, bankers, land agents, ranchers, and old-guard professional politicians whose economic or political interests drew them to the side of the railroads, still disliked the commission idea and particularly an appointive commission rather than an elective one that they might hope to control more readily. Instead of attacking the regulatory agency directly, this opposition, led by George Clark, sought to regain leadership of the party and, through it, direction of the commission. A second faction included many members of the Farmers' Alliance who shared the unhappiness of the railroad men over the establishment of an appointive commission because they could not control it directly through elections either. The third faction consisted of the numerous farmers, businessmen, and young professional politicians who continued to support Hogg because they believed his policies best represented their views and interests on the issue.

Speculation about the Alliance's becoming a third party had increased steadily in the late 1880's. Leaders who had successfully overthrown old Democratic politicians in their own counties urged separate action on the state level if their demands were not met. Hogg's nomination and election on a commission platform had limited discontent for a time. Yet even during the campaign of 1890 Senator Coke expressed doubt about "The Farmers' Alliance people" who "seem now to have the sub-treasury system proposed by them, as their main and leading tenet." In 1889 C. W. Macune had presented the subtreasury, which Coke considered "absurd and preposterous." It called for the federal government to increase currency in circulation, stabilize prices, and provide short-term farm credit based on agricultural products stored in government warehouses. Despite warnings from Reagan, who thought "they ought to throw Macune and his set overboard," the Southern Alliance made the subtreasury a major point in its national platform adopted at Ocala, Florida, in December 1890. Clearly the crucial idea of federal action on an issue beyond state control aroused states' rights sentiments among most Texas and southern Democratic politicians, regardless of their pro- or anti-farmer sympathies or their progressive or conservative views on state action. The rift widened in the spring of 1891 when Hogg opposed efforts to create an elective railroad commission. Many Alliance members lost faith in him, and the organization's leadership split over the issue. Hogg's backers among Alliance members of the Legislature issued an "Austin Manifesto" accusing the Alliance legislative committee of promoting a third party by insisting on support of the controversial subtreasury plan.[1]

The subtreasury plan soon became a major issue between Hogg men and Alliance leaders. A Waco Alliance meeting in April 1891 heard a Kansas speaker who invited delegates to a national convention at Cincinnati in May; a resolution favoring a third party failed

[1] Merle Mears Duncan, "An 1890 Richard Coke Letter," *Southwestern Historical Quarterly* 66 (July 1962): 71; Roscoe C. Martin, *The People's Party in Texas*, pp. 33–37; Robert C. Cotner, *James Stephen Hogg*, pp. 247–256; Ben H. Procter, *Not Without Honor*, p. 281; J. H. Reagan to A. J. Rose, January 20, 1891, A. J. Rose Papers; *Southern Mercury* (Dallas), November 27, 1890, April 9, 1891.

by only two votes. The defeated faction, which included some former Greenbackers and leaders of the Union Labor party, then formed a separate Alliance. Hogg refused an appeal to appoint an Alliance man railroad commissioner, whereupon several of the organization's leaders stumped the state presenting their views, sometimes in debates with Democratic officeholders.[2]

At the May convention of the People's party, or Populists, in Cincinnati—a predominantly western, professional-reformer meeting—W. R. Lamb, a leader of the Texas State Federation of Labor and an ex-member of the Union Labor party, became the Texas member of the national executive committee. Upon returning home, he called for a state Populist convention to be held in conjunction with the state Alliance meeting in August 1891. In July, Alliance leaders opposed to the subtreasury held a convention in Fort Worth. They refused to seat supporters of the subtreasury, passed resolutions against a third party, and formed the Grand State Farmers' Alliance, an organization which would help hold many farmers behind Hogg in 1892 before it dwindled away, to be merged with an equally weak state Grange in 1894. Populist Senator W. A. Peffer of Kansas and an Indiana Alliance leader both spoke in Northeast Texas in July 1891 in favor of a People's party. When the state Farmers' Alliance met at Dallas in August, it endorsed the national Populist platform, including the subtreasury. At the same time Thomas Gaines, leader of the independent movement in Comanche County, H. S. P. "Stump" Ashby, former Methodist minister and Alliance lecturer, and Lamb organized the first state Populist convention. The fifty delegates pledged themselves "to enact radical reforms of the abuses and usurpations of power" by the major parties, which they accused of aiding corporations "organized to oppress and enslave the people." They sought to win over other Alliance men with attacks on "the banks and sharks of Wall Street and Lombard Street" and "the United States senate [which] has become a den of millionaires."[3]

[2] Cotner, *Hogg*, pp. 257–258, 262; John D. Hicks, *Populist Revolt*, pp. 140–152, 186–202.

[3] Hicks, *Populist Revolt*, pp. 211–217; John S. Spratt, *The Road to Spindletop*, p. 207; Cotner, *Hogg*, pp. 262–265; Keith Lynn Bryant, Jr., " 'Alfalfa Bill' Mur-

In the spring of 1891 Barnett Gibbs, representing the National League of Democratic Clubs, began organizing clubs in Texas and promoting discussions of possible solutions to farmers' monetary problems, including several proposals similar to the subtreasury plan. But Democratic leaders began in October to take action against subtreasury advocates. The Dallas County Democratic executive committee expelled W. R. Cole, who protested the decision for months to come. On the ground that the subtreasury Alliance men already belonged to a third party, Chairman N. W. Finley of the state Democratic executive committee, supported by Hogg, ruled that they should not be allowed to participate in Democratic conventions. In November subtreasury leaders met to discuss their position in Texas politics and to denounce Finley for "bossism." Former Confederate brigadier Henry E. McCulloch asserted that he had been a Democrat before Finley was born and could not be read out of the party. Evan Jones, state Alliance president, admitted that the organization was involved in politics but denied that it was a party.[4]

A convention of the People's party at Fort Worth in February 1892 attracted about 150 delegates, among them several ex-Greenbackers, various leaders of recent independent movements on the county level, and at least two female advocates of woman's suffrage. Only a week later a state conference of 200 "Jeffersonian" Democrats or "Skunk" Democrats, as Finley supposedly called them, gathered in Dallas in reaction to his ruling against subtreasury men and endorsed the national Alliance demands. That same month Ben Terrell of Texas, former national lecturer of the Southern Alliance and president of the Confederation of Industrial Organizations meeting at St. Louis, still urged that the Alliance-dominated convention confine itself to issues. He lost in the balloting for chairman of the

ray," *East Texas Historical Journal* 3 (October 1965): 106–110; Ernest William Winkler, *Platforms of Political Parties in Texas*, pp. 293–297; Martin, *People's Party*, pp. 38, 40–42.

[4] Martin, *People's Party*, pp. 39–40; *Galveston Weekly News*, June 11, 1891; *National Economist* (Washington, D.C.), June 20, 1891; Theodore Saloutos, *Farmer Movements in the South, 1865–1933*, pp. 136–137; Cotner, *Hogg*, pp. 266–268.

convention, however, to the president of the Southern Alliance, L. L. Polk of North Carolina, who favored a third party. The pressure from third-party advocates and the refusal to compromise by Democratic party leaders soon caused most "Jeffersonian" Democrats to unite with the Populists. Energetically they began to use the Alliance organization to promote a third party across most of the state.[5]

Besides disagreement and drift among his farm supporters, Hogg faced a continued attack from the conservative faction in the state Democratic party. Various combinations defeated his proposals to give more authority to the state superintendent of public schools, to lend permanent school funds to railroads for their expansion, to improve the mechanics' lien law, and to strengthen the antitrust law. An act to end alien land ownership passed but met an immediate challenge in the courts. Criticism of the Railroad Commission persisted in a number of papers representing both disaffected groups, although efforts to bring about cooperation between them collapsed for lack of agreement on the subtreasury and silver-coinage issues.[6]

When Reagan resigned from the United States Senate to assume the chairmanship of the Railroad Commission, Hogg had appointed Horace Chilton to the seat. A boyhood friend of Hogg's, Chilton had been a leading Tyler lawyer and an assistant attorney general of Texas in the early 1880's. Hoping to continue in the Senate, the rather reserved Chilton hit the speaker's trail in mid-1891 to overcome his obscurity on the state scene and end old antagonisms from an unsuccessful trial race for Congress in 1882.[7] Chilton's major rival, heavy-set, ruddy-faced former Confederate colonel Roger Q. Mills, won a seat in Congress on Reconstruction issues in 1872 and espoused inflationist views to combat Greenbackers before becoming one of the

[5] Cotner, *Hogg*, pp. 269–273; H. S. P. Ashby to L. L. Polk, April 1, 1892, Leonidas L. Polk Papers; Carl C. Taylor, *The Farmers' Movement, 1620–1920*, p. 275; Hicks, *Populist Revolt*, pp. 224–226; Martin, *People's Party*, pp. 42–43; Winkler, *Platforms*, pp. 297–301; Alwyn Barr, "Ben Terrell," *West Texas Historical Association Year Book* 45 (1969): 58–71.

[6] Cotner, *Hogg*, pp. 250–251, 267–268, 271.

[7] Horace Chilton to O. B. Colquitt, May 5, August 9, October 6, 1891, Oscar Branch Colquitt Papers; Chilton to J. W. Truit, July 9, November 20, 1891, March 9, 1892, James W. Truit Papers.

Democratic party's tariff experts in the 1880's. The nationally known champion of lower tariffs admitted to a friend early in 1891 that "the Senate has been my ambition for years." Fearful of Hogg's influence, Mills proceeded quietly to gather support. He counted among his backers most of the Clark faction of the party, but also received support from many Hogg men. Lieutenant Governor George C. Pendleton, who wanted Mills's seat in the House, helped him by spreading a story that Hogg said he appointed Chilton "because he was not embarrassed by a Confederate record."[8] Congressman David B. Culberson of Northeast Texas also aspired to the Senate. Since he, like Chilton, stood strongly for free coinage of silver, his candidacy served only to cut into Chilton's strength. Mills, for his part, favored free silver but continued to argue that tariff reform offered a better answer to western and southern economic problems. His views made him the choice of the anti–free silver Cleveland administration.

Hogg's political situation early in 1892 induced him to call the Legislature into special session, which meant an election to the Senate seat that Chilton held by appointment. Stiff contests over who should be senator took place in several county Democratic conventions. Mills, besides being better known than Chilton, enjoyed the role of sentimental favorite because of his defeat for Speaker of the House in 1891 by eastern high-tariff men and western and southern free-silverites. Despite considerable farmer support and the continued personal backing of Hogg, Chilton withdrew just prior to the balloting, and Mills won easily. His victory, more personal than factional, left the main intraparty struggle to follow in the governor's race.[9]

[8] R. Q. Mills to George C. Pendleton, April 30, July 4, 1891, Monta J. Moore to Pendleton, August 8, 1891, Alexander Dienst Collection; R. Q. Mills to George Tyler, December 20, 1891, January 2, 1892, George W. Tyler Papers; undated newspaper clipping, Roger Q. Mills, Scrapbook, University of Texas Library; M. M. Crane to J. S. Hogg, January 8, 20, 1892, Letters Received, XIII, Mr. Pendleton's Explanation, Letters Received, XVI, James Stephen Hogg Papers.

[9] E. C. McLean to J. S. Hogg, January 2, 1892, E. J. Simkins to Hogg, January 12, 1892, Letters Received, XIII, Hogg Papers; Hogg to Horace Chilton, January 5, 26, 1892, Letter Press 9, Hogg Papers; Roger Q. Mills Papers, March, 1892, Hall of State, Dallas; Horace Chilton to J. W. Truit, January 1, 1892, Truit to D. M. Short and P. G. Swearingen, March 23, 1892, James W. Truit Papers; Gillespie County [Texas] Farmers' Alliance, Minutes, April 1892; *Gal-*

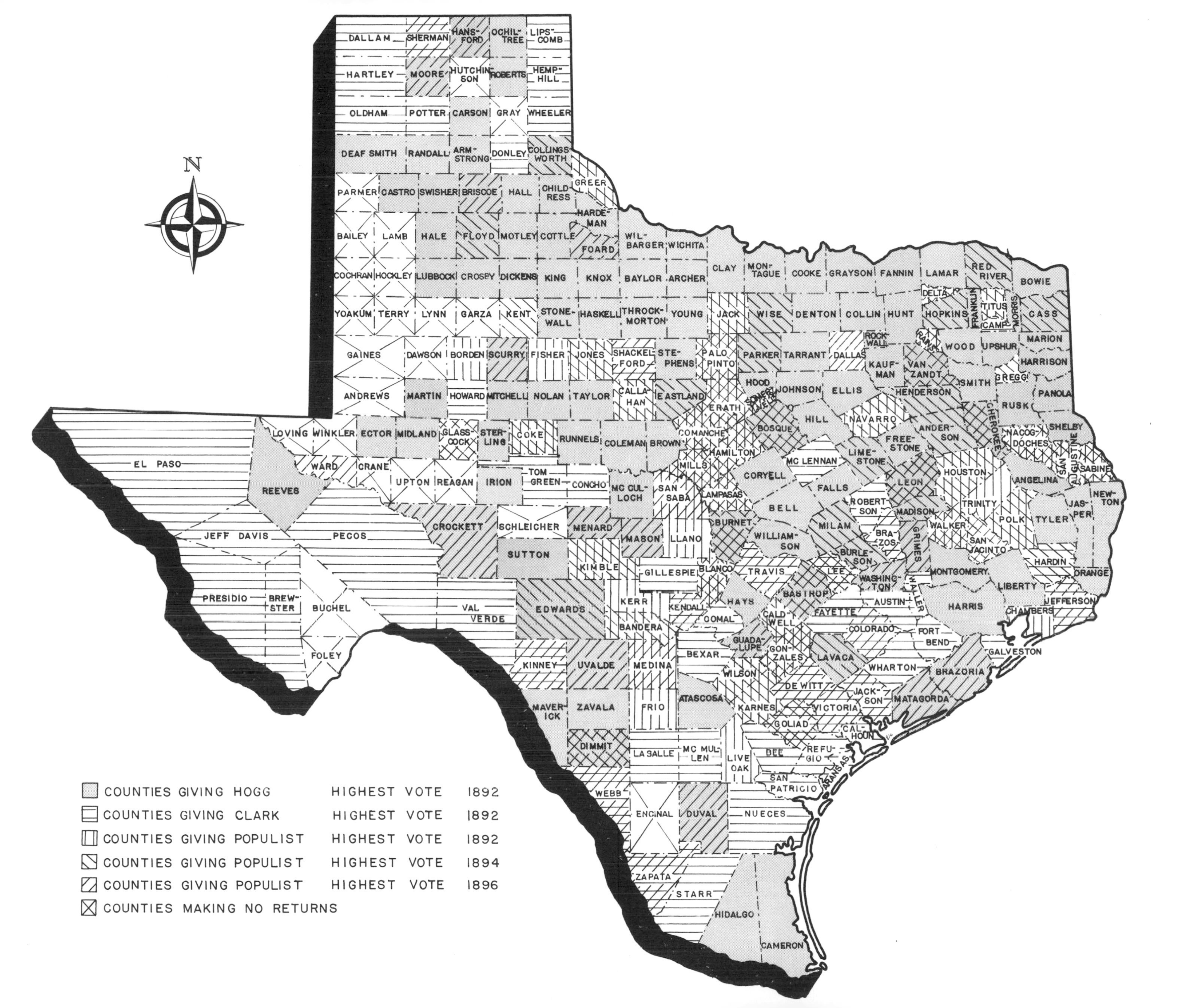
N
DALLAM
SHERMAN
HANS-FORD
OCHIL-TREE
LIPS-COMB
HARTLEY
MOORE
HUTCHIN-SON
ROBERTS
HEMP-HILL
OLDHAM
POTTER
CARSON
GRAY
WHEELER
DEAF SMITH
RANDALL
ARM-STRONG
DONLEY
COLLINGS-WORTH
PARMER
CASTRO
SWISHER
BRISCOE
HALL
CHILD-RESS
GREER
HARDE-MAN
BAILEY
LAMB
HALE
FLOYD
MOTLEY
COTTLE
FOARD
WIL-BARGER
WICHITA
COCHRAN
HOCKLEY
LUBBOCK
CROSBY
DICKENS
KING
KNOX
BAYLOR
ARCHER
CLAY
MON-TAGUE
COOKE
GRAYSON
FANNIN
LAMAR
RED RIVER
BOWIE
YOAKUM
TERRY
LYNN
GARZA
KENT
STONE-WALL
HASKELL
THROCK-MORTON
YOUNG
JACK
WISE
DENTON
COLLIN
HUNT
DELTA
HOPKINS
FRANKLIN
TITUS
MORRIS
CAMP
CASS
GAINES
DAWSON
BORDEN
SCURRY
FISHER
JONES
SHACKEL-FORD
STE-PHENS
PALO PINTO
PARKER
TARRANT
DALLAS
ROCK-WALL
RAINS
WOOD
UPSHUR
MARION
KAUF-MAN
VAN ZANDT
HARRISON
ANDREWS
MARTIN
HOWARD
MITCHELL
NOLAN
TAYLOR
CALLA-HAN
EASTLAND
HOOD
SOMERVELL
JOHNSON
ELLIS
HENDERSON
SMITH
GREGG
PANOLA
RUSK
ERATH
BOSQUE
HILL
NAVARRO
CHEROKEE
LOVING
WINKLER
ECTOR
MIDLAND
GLASS-COCK
STER-LING
COKE
RUNNELS
COLEMAN
BROWN
COMANCHE
HAMILTON
ANDER-SON
FREE-STONE
LIME-STONE
NACOG-DOCHES
SHELBY
SAN AUGUSTINE
SABINE
EL PASO
WARD
CRANE
UPTON
REAGAN
IRION
TOM GREEN
CONCHO
MC CUL-LOCH
MILLS
MC LENNAN
CORYELL
SAN SABA
HOUSTON
LEON
FALLS
ANGELINA
REEVES
LAMPASAS
BELL
ROBERT-SON
MADISON
TRINITY
POLK
TYLER
JAS-PER
NEW-TON
JEFF DAVIS
PECOS
CROCKETT
SCHLEICHER
MENARD
MASON
LLANO
BURNET
WILLIAM-SON
MILAM
BRA-ZOS
GRIMES
WALKER
SAN JACINTO
SUTTON
KIMBLE
GILLESPIE
BLANCO
TRAVIS
BURLE-SON
LEE
WASHING-TON
MONTGOMERY
LIBERTY
HARDIN
ORANGE
PRESIDIO
BREW-STER
BUCHEL
VAL VERDE
EDWARDS
KERR
KENDALL
HAYS
BASTROP
WALLER
AUSTIN
HARRIS
JEFFERSON
CHAMBERS
COMAL
CALD-WELL
FAYETTE
BANDERA
COLORADO
FORT BEND
GUADA-LUPE
GON-ZALES
LAVACA
GALVESTON
FOLEY
KINNEY
UVALDE
MEDINA
BEXAR
WILSON
WHARTON
BRAZORIA
DE WITT
JACK-SON
MATAGORDA
MAVER-ICK
ZAVALA
FRIO
ATASCOSA
KARNES
VICTORIA
GOLIAD
CAL-HOUN
DIMMIT
LA SALLE
MC MUL-LEN
LIVE OAK
BEE
REFU-GIO
ARANSAS
SAN PATRICIO
WEBB
ENCINAL
DUVAL
NUECES
ZAPATA
STARR
HIDALGO
CAMERON
COUNTIES GIVING HOGG HIGHEST VOTE 1892
COUNTIES GIVING CLARK HIGHEST VOTE 1892
COUNTIES GIVING POPULIST HIGHEST VOTE 1892
COUNTIES GIVING POPULIST HIGHEST VOTE 1894
COUNTIES GIVING POPULIST HIGHEST VOTE 1896
COUNTIES MAKING NO RETURNS

George Clark, called the "little Warwick" because of his success as campaign manager for Coke and Ross and the "little giant" because of his short, stocky build, had begun to sound like a gubernatorial candidate in the fall of 1891. A former Confederate officer from Alabama, he had served as secretary of state, attorney general, member of a commission to revise state laws, and judge on the Court of Appeals in the 1870's. He had won a reputation in the 1880's as a railroad attorney and lobbyist for business interests. By September 1891 pro-Clark newspapers predicted "soon or late, the time will come when the reign of King James I will end and his blind followers may stand in need of clemency." Clark opposed Finley's efforts to exclude the Alliance men from the Democatic party and in December made a bid for Alliance support by saying at Denton that most of its demands represented "first-class democracy." Clark announced for governor on February 13, 1892, and in his first speech charged that Hogg's administration drove capital from Texas and damaged its railroads and its economy; he declared an appointive railroad commission unconstitutional. The "little giant" summarized his political philosophy by adopting the campaign slogan "Turn Texas Loose." Although Clark's search for Alliance votes failed because of differences on national finance, Negro Republican leader Cuney suggested the possibility of fusion between his party and anti-Hogg Democrats in February 1892.[10]

Hogg's close backers began as early as January 1892 to discuss the coming gubernatorial race, but the governor delayed his opening speech until after the special legislative session that defeated several of his measures. He then renewed his support for the Railroad Commission and other reform proposals and called for laws to prohibit the issuance of watered stocks and bonds by railroads and excessive bonds by cities and counties, to define perpetuities, and to prohibit land corporations. Strongly endorsed by the *Texas Farmer*, a leading Grange paper, and by Grange leaders A. J. Rose, John B. Long, and

---

veston Weekly News, January 14, February 11, 18, 1892; Myrtle Roberts, "Roger Quarles Mills" (M.A. thesis), pp. 100–104; Festus P. Summers, *William L. Wilson and Tariff Reform*, pp. 122–124; Cotner, Hogg, pp. 271, 315–316.

[10] Cotner, *Hogg*, pp. 266–268, 270–271, 274–276.

A. W. Buchanan, Hogg gained ground rapidly in most farming regions as well as among the labor element in urban areas.[11]

A preliminary test of strength between the Hogg and Clark factions came in the Democratic state convention at Lampasas on June 7 and 8 to elect delegates to the Democratic National Convention. Yet because of the national issues and personalities involved, it provided no clear guide to state politics. Many Texas Democrats had never felt more than lukewarm affection for Grover Cleveland during his first term because of his opposition to silver coinage. By 1892 free coinage of silver had become, in the eyes of most persons in the South and West, an even greater hope for relief of their monetary problems. "In this state nearly all classes want it," Hogg assured Chilton in February, "and *they want Senator* [David B.] *Hill* [of New York] *for President*. . . . let him know that the *kids* in Texas will be on hand at the Convention for him." Coke preferred Senator Arthur P. Gorman of Maryland, or Hill, and believed that "Cleveland is the weakest man we can run." After electing Mills to the Senate, however, the Legislature seemingly accepted his views on national politics and adopted a resolution supporting silver coinage but favoring lower tariffs as the main plank in the Democratic platform. The platform adopted by the state convention took a similar position while opposing the subtreasury. After much debate in committee and on the floor, the convention endorsed Cleveland for a second term, but did not bind the delegates to the national convention to vote for him. Clark men formed a majority of the delegates chosen, and at the national convention H. D. McDonald, an anticommission gubernatorial candidate in 1890, seconded the nomination of Cleveland, who received twenty-three of the thirty Texas votes. Yet even the Clark support stemmed from the fact that Cleveland represented the most conservative candidate with a chance of nomination and victory, for Clark had previously criticized as useless or fraudulent the tariff, bal-

[11] Cotner, *Hogg*, pp. 268, 276, 284–285; Charles K. Chamberlain, "Alexander Watkins Terrell" (Ph.D. diss.), pp. 354–364; George G. Graves to T. S. Henderson, March 16, 1892, Thomas S. Henderson Papers; J. T. Garrison to J. W. Truit, March 20, 1892, Truit Papers; J. W. Spivey to C. P. Estes, April 22, 1892, Letter Press 10, M. Looscan to J. S. Hogg, May 18, 1892, Letters Received, XVI, Hogg Papers.

lot, and civil service reforms Cleveland advocated.[12] Nevertheless the Clark faction achieved its goals on national issues, because it had begun to campaign earlier and because the Hogg "kids" had concentrated more on state issues and races.

Hogg and Clark debated at Cameron and Cleburne on May 3 and 4 before large crowds filled with hot-tempered partisans. Clark described Hogg as "the representative of a government of centralism at the capital." When Clark concluded, Hogg opened by asking: "What is the issue, Judge Clark? I haven't heard you say." Hogg supporters yelled, "Go for him!" Their opponents cried, "Hurrah for Clark!" When a young man in a tree interrupted Hogg later, the governor fired back: "Young man, keep quiet. . . . I did not expect to deal with badgers." The candidates concentrated on the questions of whether the Railroad Commission should be appointive or elective and whether school funds should be lent to railroads, as Hogg suggested or to farmers, as Clark recommended. Then each went his separate way seeking majorities in the county Democratic conventions.

In Houston a circular appeared accusing Hogg of prohibitionist views—actually he favored only temperance—and apparently cost him several German counties. Clark supporters organized Negro Clark clubs in an attempt to influence Democratic county conventions. East Texas lumbermen, unhappy because the Railroad Commission had set a mileage rather than a load basis for lumber rates, closed their mills to let employees attend Clark rallies. Rio Grande Valley political leader Jim Wells and other promoters of railroads into new areas feared the impact of the commission on construction and threw their support to Clark. Yet one railroad man backing Clark warned with remarkable objectivity: "If we can get up some

[12] J. S. Hogg to Horace Chilton, February 10, 1892, Letter Press 9, Hogg Papers; Richard Coke to A. J. Rose, March 22, 1892, Rose Papers; Coke to J. W. Truit, May 13, 1892, Truit Papers; George Clark to George C. Pendleton, January 8, 1890, Dienst Collection; Oran M. Roberts, "Political, Legislative, and Judicial History of Texas," in Dudley G. Wooten, ed., *Comprehensive History of Texas*, II, 294–297; *Galveston Weekly News*, June 9, 30, 1892; Winkler, *Platforms*, pp. 310–313; Richard C. Bain, *Convention Decisions and Voting Records*, pp. 147–148, Appendix D.

scheme to keep the 'horney [*sic*] handed son of toil' at work on his cotton crop while the men who read the papers and are up to the times goes [*sic*] into the primaries we will come out alright[*sic*], but I am afraid that they will come in and swamp us . . ." As he predicted, Hogg's lead continued to grow, reaching in early August an almost certain two-thirds majority of the delegates to the state convention despite contests between rival delegations from a few counties. Some of Hogg's friends, confident of his nomination, began to advise seating doubtful Clark delegations in order to placate the Clark men sufficiently to keep them from bolting the party in November.[13]

Delegates to the state convention poured into Houston in mid-August to seek accommodations as hotels filled their halls and parlors with cots and citizens opened their homes at fifty cents to a dollar a night. Despite brief rains which muddied some streets, the delegates sought relief from the oppressive summer heat under gaily decorated store awnings and in restaurants which offered a variety of thirst-quenching drinks. Clark men at their headquarters in the Hutchins House looked grim and determined. Hogg followers at the Capitol Hotel complained of paying higher railroad fares than those charged their opponents. A Clark caucus developed plans to pack supporters into the streetcar shed where the convention would meet to elect a chairman by voice vote. But during the night Ranger Captain Bill McDonald, who favored Hogg, frustrated the plan by constructing across the open side of the building a fence that kept all nondelegates out. When the time came to elect a temporary chairman, the pre-

[13] C. C. Curtice to Alex Gilmer, May 15, 1892, Gilmer to Z. W. Cannon, August 4, 1891, W. Wiess and L. P. Ogden to Gilmer, May 14, 1892, Alexander Gilmer Papers; Robert C. Cotner, ed., *Addresses and State Papers of James Stephen Hogg*, pp. 233–234; Cotner, *Hogg*, pp. 287–293, 296–297; Grady Stafford St. Clair, "The Hogg-Clark Campaign" (M.A. thesis), pp. 35–59; Democratic Executive Committee, Bexar County, Texas, *The Democratic Situation in Bexar County Explained*; Democratic Executive Committee, Fayette County, Texas, *A Statement of the "Split" in the Fayette County Democracy*; T. S. Henderson to W. S. Baker, July 23, 1892, Henderson to W. C. O'Bryan, August 8, 1892, Letterbook, Henderson Papers; L. M. Strain to A. W. Terrell, April 21, 1892, Letters Received, XV, John W. Spivey to H. C. Randolph, May 28, 1892, Letter Press 10, Hogg Papers; R. B. Parrott to James Wells, June 7, 1892, James B. Wells Papers; *Galveston Weekly News*, August 4, 1892.

Gov. Hogg, since reading of "Jack, the Ripper," in the Statesman, a few days ago, has become much concerned regarding his personal safety, and when he arrived here on Friday's train it was discovered that he had sent ahead for a company of soldiers to escort him past the chile stands. The Governor, however, preferred to walk in the middle of the road, anyway.

The Rolling Stone (Austin), Dec. 21, 1894

siding officer ruled in favor of a roll call by counties instead of a voice vote. The roll call favored the Hogg candidate, but Clark men shouted for their candidate and amid near rioting declared him elected. For a time both men attempted to preside from opposite sides of the same stage. Finally Clark's partisans withdrew to Turner Hall and nominated their favorite with cheers and waving banners, hats, handkerchiefs, canes, and umbrellas. Their platform favored an elective railroad commission and opposed class legislation, "the existing war upon the rights of property in this State," secret political organizations, and the Hogg administration "because it has driven and is keeping capital from the State."

Back in the car shed, the Hogg majority, over some remaining Clark opposition, agreed by a vote of 693 to 168 on the planks presented by the platform committee, John H. Reagan, chairman. The resolutions opposed the subtreasury, government ownership of railroads, protective tariffs, national banks, and Republican efforts to regulate federal elections. They pledged support for free coinage of silver, a graduated income tax, and several of the state laws proposed earlier by Hogg. A compromise on the vexed question of choosing railroad commissioners provided that they should be elected for six-year terms at staggered two-year intervals. After Hogg's renomination his jubilant followers stood on their chairs to cheer his march to the platform.[14]

During the bitter preconvention struggle of the Clark and Hogg factions, the Populists of Texas had energetically recruited on the local level through the farming areas of the state. By May the Democratic state executive committee, fearing that in some regions "so many Hogg democrats are going into the third party organization that he will be left in the primaries," relented on the antisubtreasury test for party fidelity and made quiet conciliatory efforts. But the Populists rejected those belated offers and continued their organizational activity.[15] A state nominating convention in Dallas on June 23 and 24 selected candidates for all state offices. Thomas L. Nugent of

[14] Winkler, *Platforms*, pp. 316–326; Roberts, "Political History of Texas," in Wooten, *Comprehensive History of Texas*, II, 298–300; St. Clair, "Hogg-Clark Campaign," pp. 64–80; Cotner, *Hogg*, pp. 298–302; *Houston Daily Post*, August 15–19, 1892.

[15] Edgar H. Rogan to J. J. Faulk, May 10, 1892, J. J. Faulk Papers; M. S. Park and others to T. S. Henderson, March 9, 1892, A. H. Kerr to Henderson, March 21, 1892, Henderson to T. J. Simmons, July 19, 1892, Henderson Papers; G. C. Pendleton to J. S. Hogg, April 22, 1892, Letters Received, XV, Hogg Papers; Martin, *People's Party*, p. 44.

Fort Worth, a slight, mild-mannered, former Democratic district judge of Confederate background, with strong religious views directed toward social action, accepted the gubernatorial nomination. The meeting also elected delegates to the Populist national convention. When it met at Omaha in early July, James H. "Cyclone" Davis, the tall, humorous Texas orator with a booming voice, helped write the platform, and Ben Terrell not only headed a committee that interviewed W. Q. Gresham about the presidential nomination but also ran a strong second himself for the vice-presidential nomination. "Cyclone" Davis spoke throughout the South in support of the Populist presidential ticket. The *National Economist*, official newspaper of the Southern Alliance, quoted Congressman C. B. Kilgore as saying that "there will be but a mild shower of third party ballots—a slight sprinkle" in Texas, then warned "a buzz-saw is in operation which may even sever his own official head from the broad and manly shoulders . . ." Nugent charged Clark with subordinating "his views to those of the National democracy" and declared, "Hogg's platform is quite meaningless."[16]

Clark's prospects in the gubernatorial race suffered a severe blow soon after the state Democratic convention when Roger Mills, who had preferred Clark's nomination but refused to take sides in the preconvention contest, recognized Hogg as the regular nominee. In another key shift, Jim Wells went over to Hogg to maintain his own position of power within the state party. Yet Clark's newspaper strength remained formidable. In Fort Worth the mayor, a railroad man backed by Texas bankers and out-of-state railroad interests, succeeded after months of work in gaining control of the *Gazette*, which he shifted to Clark. That gave Clark most of the principal newspapers of the state, except the *Houston Post*. Railroad executives offered ad-

[16] *National Economist* (Washington, D.C.), August 20, 1892; *Houston Daily Post*, October 12, 1892; Winkler, *Platforms*, pp. 314–316; *Galveston Weekly News*, June 30, 1892; Emory A. Allen, *The Life and Public Services of James Baird Weaver*, pp. 55–118; George H. Knoles, *The Presidential Campaign and Election of 1892*, pp. 94–121, 187; Wayne Alvord, "T. L. Nugent, Texas Populist," *Southwestern Historical Quarterly* 57 (July 1953): 65–81; Catharine Nugent, ed., *Life Work of Thomas L. Nugent*; Marshall L. Williams, "The Political Career of Cyclone Davis" (M.A. thesis), p. 37.

ditional help by furnishing lists of their employees for use during the campaign. Clark's greatest boost came from the Republicans. Urged on by northern party leaders, National Committeeman Cuney endorsed Clark as a man of Republican principles, guided the delegates at the Republican state convention into forgoing nominations to endorse Clark, and later helped organize additional Clark clubs among Negroes. A. L. Matlock, chairman of Clark's state executive committee, tried to gain recognition from the national Democratic executive committee, claiming with considerable accuracy that he headed the pro-Cleveland faction. He did not succeed. All the while Clark stumped the state describing Hogg as "a false Moses," equating "Hoggism" and "rowdyism," and accusing Hogg men of stealing their platform from the Populists.[17]

Hogg's regional directors and his well-organized campaign committee, which included the adept though enigmatic E. M. House, skillfully met each opposition effort during the fall. Campaign literature and local speakers reached every corner of the state, while local committees raised funds. Senator Coke came home to call for the defeat of the "Three C's—Clark, Cuney, and the Coons." Reagan also warned white Texans against dividing when the Republicans in Congress still favored a "Force Bill" to regulate southern elections and return the state to Negro and Republican rule. At the same time the governor's supporters organized Hogg clubs for Negroes in counties where they might hold the balance of power and sent out black orators to emphasize Hogg's opposition to lynching. Hogg men in other areas refused to allow Populists or Republicans to speak. The governor used his control of state patronage to ensure the active assistance of appointees to state offices. Democratic Alliance speaker

[17] Cotner, *Hogg*, pp. 303–306; Roberts, "Mills," p. 108; Roger Mills to Guy M. Bryan, April 17, 1892, Guy M. Bryan Papers; Virginia Neal Hinze, "Norris Wright Cuney" (M.A. thesis), pp. 104–107; St. Clair, "Hogg-Clark Campaign," pp. 97–99; B. B. Paddock to F. H. Robertson, April 6, 1892, Letterbook, Paddock to George Clark, August 27, 1892, Paddock to R. J. Brown, October 1, 1892, Buckley B. Paddock Papers; A. L. Matlock to A. H. Belo, September 2, 1892, Grover Cleveland Papers, series 2; B. B. Paddock to W. W. Hare, September 5, 1892, Dienst Collection; E. Marks to James Wells, December 2, 1892, Wells Papers; *Houston Daily Post*, October 11, 1892.

Bill Murray interpreted a personal letter from President Cleveland praising Democratic efforts as an endorsement of Hogg until Cleveland publicly proclaimed his neutrality. Hogg spoke often on the main issues; characterized Clark supporters as "calamity howlers," "Copulists," "political guerrillas," and "boltercrats"; and described the Populists as "poisoned from disappointed ambition, mad with the world in general, chimerical in political convictions, shifting in party name."[18]

Hogg won the election by a plurality of 190,486 votes over Clark's 133,395 and Nugent's 108,483. Clark, enjoying considerable business, banking, and railroad backing, led in most of the state's urban areas and did well in the Panhandle, where ranchers controlled. He carried eleven of fourteen largely Mexican Catholic counties along the Rio Grande, where Republican sheepmen and big ranchers dominated, and won two lumbering counties around Beaumont. Clark also led in seven of sixteen counties with Negro Baptist and Methodist majorities that usually voted Republican and fourteen others with black minorities of 20 per cent to 49 per cent. He won eight of eleven counties with heavy German Lutheran and Catholic population that viewed the other candidates as too favorable toward prohibition. Nugent swept the drought-stricken, predominantly Anglo evangelical farming areas of West Central Texas and similar rural counties in East Texas and around San Antonio. He won only one county with a black majority, and eleven others with Negro minorities of 20 per cent to 49 per cent, however, and none with heavy German or Mexican population. Hogg's strength lay primarily in the more economically productive, basically Anglo Baptist and Methodist farming counties of North, East, and Central Texas. About half of the Anglo farmers, influenced by their long-standing ties to the Demo-

[18] Cotner, *Hogg*, pp. 218, 276, 306–310; Rupert N. Richardson, *Colonel Edward M. House*, pp. 46–58; Hinze, "Cuney," pp. 109–111; Harrell Budd, "The Negro in Politics in Texas, 1867–1898" (M.A. thesis), pp. 105–112; R. C. Cotton to T. S. Henderson, October 7, 1892, Henderson Papers; A. B. Watkins to J. J. Faulk, October 11, 1892, J. J. Faulk Papers; A. L. Matlock to "Dear Sir," October 21, 1892, Dienst Collection; J. H. Reagan to H. H. Moore, June 22, 1892, newspaper clipping, Truit Papers; Bryant, " 'Alfalfa Bill' Murray," p. 111; Cotner, *Addresses and State Papers . . . Hogg*, p. 266.

cratic party, their fears of a railroad-Republican victory, their faith in the governor and his program, and the support accorded him by old Grange leaders, had stayed with Hogg. Although Hogg lost some previous business support he retained the support of many merchants and gained the endorsements of W. L. Moody, Galveston banker and director of the Gulf, Colorado, and Santa Fe Railway; that line's chief attorney, State Senator Walter Gresham; and E. P. Hill, attorney for the Southern Pacific Railroad and vice-president of the *Houston Post*, which he swung behind the governor. These railroad men found the commission generally fair and flexible and its rulings a stabilizing factor on freight rates. Such backing combined with labor elements to give Hogg Houston and Fort Worth. Hogg won only three counties with considerable German population and the three heavily Mexican counties in South Texas which Jim Wells controlled. But the governor carried eight of sixteen predominantly black counties and thirty of fifty-five with Negro minorities of 20 per cent to 49 per cent.[19]

Populist strength appeared more ominous at the congressional level. The third party offered candidates in every district and finished second in ten of thirteen races, receiving an aggregate of 131,511 votes to the Democrats' 238,607 and the Republicans' 41,410. Some degree of fusion between Populists and Republicans existed in five districts of East, Central, and North Texas where Populists provided the only candidates. Democratic congressional candidates met the challenge with their own Negro campaigners and could usually count on support from both Hogg men and Clark men. Victories by George C. Pendleton and S. B. Cooper over E. L. Antony and John B. Long in Democratic district conventions gave evidence of a trend toward "silver" candidates in Central and East Texas. Congressman C. B. Kilgore's course provided an interesting example of the problems of politics and principle. He favored Hogg in the gubernatorial race and free coinage of silver, but supported Cleveland for president as

[19] Cotner, *Hogg*, pp. 241–242, 305, 310, 312–315; St. Clair, "Hogg-Clark Campaign," pp. 2–3; Roberts, "Political History of Texas," in Wooten, *Comprehensive History of Texas*, II, 297; *Abilene Reporter*, March 18, 1892.

the best-known Democratic candidate.[20] Cleveland recaptured the White House, but his election only reinforced the three-way split in the Texas Democratic party over the issues of political dominance and economic policy. Despite his handicap as an ex-Union general, Populist presidential candidate James B. Weaver received about 24 per cent of the Texas vote, second for the entire South only to the third-party vote in Alabama.

In 1891 three Democratic factions developed because Clark-led conservatives and Alliance members both opposed Hogg's plan for an appointive state railroad commission and because the state Alliance supported federal implementation of the subtreasury plan of the Southern Alliance. Both dissident factions, like others throughout the South, sought to influence the state organization, while Hogg and most southern Democrats fought to maintain control by reading subtreasury men out of the party. Up to that time most Texas Alliance leaders had exhibited greater reluctance to seek a new political home than western Alliance men and some Southerners, including L. L. Polk and Georgia Congressman Tom Watson. Left without an apparent alternative, about half the members made the transition, first to the "Jeffersonian Democrats" and finally to the new Populist party, originally organized in Texas by consistent dissenters of Greenback or Union Labor party background. Clark and his supporters failed to defeat Hogg for the Democratic nomination but decided to extend their effort to November with the aid of Texas Republicans led by N. W. Cuney. In the three-cornered race that followed, each nominee and organization sought additional support beyond economic attractions to white Baptists and Methodists by appealing to or attempting to control other ethnic and religious groups—Negro Baptists and Methodists, Mexican Catholics, and

[20] L. L. Foster to G. C. Pendleton, November 2, 1892, Dienst Collection; T. S. Henderson to E. Breeding, July 15, 1892, Henderson to Max Weiterberg, September 20, 1892, George C. Pendleton to Henderson, October 4, 1892, Henderson Papers; C. B. Kilgore to Amory Starr, March 31, August 2, 1892, September 10, 1893, Henry Raguet Papers; Sue E. Moore, "The Life of John Benjamin Long" (M.A. thesis), pp. 110–112; *Galveston Weekly News*, September 1, 8, 29, 1892; Texas, Secretary of State, *Report*, 1892, pp. 55–57.

German Lutherans and Catholics—whose votes became quite crucial. For the first time in Texas politics white Democrats organized official Negro political clubs within their party. Clark won most German and Mexican and some Negro votes in addition to those of most white Protestant railroad, lumber, business, cattle, and sheep interests. Nugent carried some black votes along with about half of the Anglo evangelical farm vote. Hogg defeated them by winning some German and Mexican and most Negro votes while retaining the confidence of some merchants and railroad men and the more prosperous Texas agriculturists. Limited reform within traditional political and cultural bounds proved most appealing to a plurality of Texans. Texas Populists ran close races for ten of thirteen congressional seats and polled a higher percentage of presidential votes—24 per cent—than anywhere else in the South except Alabama. The Hogg Democrats had clung to control in Texas, but they seemed sure to face strong challenges if the agricultural depression and factional divisions continued.

10. THE PEAK OF POPULISM

THE PRIMARY STRENGTH of the People's party of Texas, still growing after the elections of 1892, lay in the Farmers' Alliance. The Alliance contained by 1891 over 200,000 members in about 4,000 suballiances which met monthly. Delegates gathered in quarterly county meetings, in semiannual congressional district meetings, and in annual state meetings. Negroes joined the separate but related Colored Farmers' Alliance. When the third-party movement began in 1892, most Alliance lecturers became Populist organizers, and entire local alliances in many areas became Populist clubs. By election time 3,170 clubs had been organized in 213 counties. Members employed a system of conventions to select delegates and make nominations, and executive committees from the precinct through the state level managed efforts between conventions. The new party also established a Young People's League of Texas, a Home Industry Club Association, a Direct Legislation League of Texas, an Industrial Legion, a secret militant Gideon's Band, and glee clubs, which became the most popular.[1]

[1] Roscoe C. Martin, *The People's Party in Texas*, pp. 141–161.

In nonelection years, such as 1893, the Populists continued their appeal by distributing literature, sending out a variety of local and national speakers, holding revivallike camp meetings which combined entertainment, inspiration, and political education, and even established a few schools. They also continued efforts to collect funds from individuals and from local clubs, though voluntary donations from the entire state usually totaled less than $2,000 for a single year.[2]

Populist principles, which had developed as Farmers' Alliance demands in the face of growing economic problems in the late 1880's and early 1890's, aimed basically to provide greater equality of economic opportunity. They called for an end to "the 'sham battle' whose 'clamor' drowns the cry of distress that comes from the farm, the workshop and the factory." It seemed to them "we *dare not* lose, or all human rights and human liberty will go down in the blackness of darkness." Populists urged government regulation of industries affected with a public interest, especially railroads; if regulation proved no more effective than in the first years of the Interstate Commerce Commission, they would seek government ownership. They charged Democrats had "squandered our . . . public domain in donations to corporations and sales . . . to syndicates and land grabbers." Populists called for reserving state lands for settlers and forfeiting to the state any land granted under contracts not fulfilled. Because of the several large British land and cattle companies in West Texas, Populists declared that corporations should own no land beyond their operational needs, and foreign citizens, none at all. To end the deflationary trend of falling farm prices by easing credit restrictions and increasing the amount of money in circulation, in a state with only 346 banks for over 2.5 million people—still well below the national average—the Populists pressed for free and unlimited coinage of silver, issuance of legal tender treasury notes equal to fifty dollars per person, and an end to the inflexible and restrictive national banking system. When cooperative Alliance business exchanges failed in the

[2] *Ibid.*, pp. 162–182.

early 1890's for lack of capital and of managerial experience, Populists brought forward the subtreasury plan for short-term, low-interest government farm loans, secured by land and by agricultural products held in warehouses. The government could sell the stored goods as demand rose, thus avoiding the glutted markets and low prices that usually faced farmers. To the argument that farmers grew too much, Texas Populists offered two responses. Some, with foresight but only limited immediate success, urged voluntary crop reductions. Others took a market view that "overproduction of a thing may seemingly exist in some localities, but the cause is a lack of proper distribution and the ability to purchase on the part of the people." Populists opposed high property taxes, trusts, and monopolies, and they advocated a graduated income tax and economical government.

To improve labor conditions in Texas, Populists advocated an eight-hour day for public employees, improvement in the mechanics' lien law, a state bureau of labor and a board of arbitration, removal of convict labor from competition with free labor, and exemption of the enforced unemployed from prosecution as vagrants. They also urged reform of city governments to end corruption, but took no violently antiurban positions as has been suggested of the national party.

On noneconomic issues Populists proposed to advance education in the state by increasing the school term from four to six months and by providing free textbooks for students. To ensure fair elections they urged adoption of the "Australian ballot." The Populist national platform, which Texas Populists endorsed, sought to make government more responsive to the people by calling for direct election of the president, of United States senators, and of federal judges; limiting all officeholders to two terms; proportional representation; and referendum and recall on specific laws. The Texas Populists debated but refused to support either woman's suffrage or prohibition because of the antagonisms the issues aroused.

Populists could claim as their own innovation only the subtreasury plan. Other portions of the platform represented partially or completely unfulfilled proposals from earlier reform movements or from

Uncle Sam's Advice to the Populists: "Here, take this, get into your cotton patch, and keep off the grass."

The Rolling Stone (Austin), Sept. 8, 1894

the Democrats or the Republicans.[3] The Populists differed from the dominant Democrats basically in their greater willingness to have the federal government attack problems which overlapped state boundaries and seemed beyond the powers of a state government to solve.

"Cyclone" Davis published the most detailed statement of Populist views by a Texan in his *Political Revelation*, a book-length cam-

[3] Norman Pollack, ed., *The Populist Mind*, pp. 44, 287; *National Economist* (Washington, D.C.), May 4, 1889; *Southern Mercury* (Dallas), February 13, 1896; Martin, *People's Party*, pp. 45–57; Ernest William Winkler, ed., *Platforms of Political Parties in Texas*, pp. 293–299, 314–316, 332–334, 379–384, 396–400; Theodore Saloutos, *Farmer Movements in the South, 1865–1933*, p. 99; Avery L. Carlson, *Monetary and Banking History of Texas*, pp. 48, 52; Allyn A. Young, *An Analysis of Bank Statistics for the United States*, p. 3; Milton Friedman and Anna Jacobson Schwartz, *A Monetary History of the United States, 1867–1960*, pp. 89–134.

paign document for 1894. In it Davis discussed the United States Government and the Constitution, the Populist platform, and especially the key issues of transportation and money, quoting at various times Jefferson, Blackstone, Madison, and Governor E. M. Pease of Texas. In an appendix Harry Tracy described the subtreasury plan with quotations from Calhoun, Franklin, and the Bible. Both men drew on their Christian, English, American, and southern heritage to advocate not a utopian past but greater government action in the future.[4]

To spread their ideas by the written word, the Populists relied primarily on the *Southern Mercury*, official organ of the Alliance. A weekly, published in Dallas by Milton Park, it reached a maximum subscription of 40,000 in 1895. The *Texas Advance*, attempted as a daily in Fort Worth in 1892, had failed there and moved to Dallas, where it continued until 1895 as a weekly printed at the *Mercury* office. Smaller Alliance and Populist papers might last only through a campaign; most had circulations under 1,000; and fewer than a fourth of the editors were professional journalists. Probably more than one hundred "reform" weeklies existed in 1895, however, with a total circulation of well over 100,000. Democratic papers outnumbered them six to one, and included fifty-nine dailies.[5]

Populist orators dwelt in their campaign speeches on the depression of the 1890's, with its assorted ill effects; and on Democratic dishonesty, failures, and campaign corruption ranging from bribery to intimidation. They launched verbal broadsides too against "the consecrated money power of Wall Street, New York, and Lombard Street, London, which are to be more dreaded than standing armies." In describing their problems, Texas Populists obviously resorted at times to stereotypes which suggested conspiratorial views of unfavorable events in history. The leaders offered such concepts primarily for effect, though many of the rank and file may have accepted them at face value. In reply they faced equally stereotyped opposition charges that they were "communist nuts" and "Anarchists." If their rhetoric seemed too colorful and expansive at times,

[4] James H. "Cyclone" Davis, *A Political Revelation*.
[5] Martin, *People's Party*, pp. 189–208.

they employed it to arouse interest in their program which aimed at real economic and political problems.[6]

Several ministers and former ministers of evangelical denominations became Populist speakers, and other third party orators, like many Texas politicians of the day, quoted the Bible freely. Though members debated the matter in the *Texas Advance*, the People's party refused all official connection with the American Protective Association, a militant anti-Catholic organization similar to the Know-Nothing party of an earlier day. In an ironic variation, however, at least one anti-Populist Baptist minister charged that "Roman Catholic Power was hid behind the throne in the third party movement." Nativist and anti-Semitic rhetoric crept into a few speeches and letters written to newspapers by both Populists and their political opponents in Texas, but such feelings never developed into any proposals for action against the tiny Jewish minority in the state's urban areas. While the Populists avoided religious connections of all types, the conservative Democratic *Dallas Morning News* said of them with appreciation if not sympathy: "Their earnestness, bordering on religious fanaticism, has a touch of the kind of metal [*sic*] that made Cromwell's round heads [*sic*] so terrible a force in the revolution that ended with bringing the head of Charles I to the block. It would be supreme folly to despise and belittle a movement that is leavened with such moral stuff as this."[7]

Texas Populists seldom mentioned foreign affairs. Their major interest lay in changing domestic policies. But when a dispute between Venezuela and Britain developed in 1895 concerning the boundary

[6] *Advance* (Dallas), February 3, 1894; Norman Pollack, *The Populist Response to Industrial America*, pp. 38–39; Martin, *People's Party*, pp. 183–185; Sam Webb to John F. Sedwick, March 28, 1893, Louis Hamilton Hill Papers. See also Scrapbooks, Samuel J. Wright Papers.

[7] *Dallas Morning News*, June 25, 1892; John T. Garner to L. L. Polk, April 12, 1892, Leonidas L. Polk Papers; *Advance* (Dallas), February 3, March 3, 24, 1894; Thomas J. Pressly and William H. Scofield, *Farm Real Estate Values in the United States by Counties, 1850–1959*, pp. 59–62; Charles A. Cannon, "The Ideology of Texas Populism, 1886–1894" (M.A. thesis), pp. 90–97. David L. Kinzer, *An Episode in Anti-Catholicism: The American Protective Association*, found no connection between the organizations, although C. W. Macune, who had ceased to be a power in the Alliance, was involved.

of British Guiana, Democratic Congressman Thomas M. Paschal of San Antonio urged the Cleveland administration to use the event against its political opponents. "Turn this Venzauelan [*sic*] question up or down, North, South, East or West, and it is a 'winner.' . . . Why . . . just think of how angry the anarchistic, socialistic, and populistic boil appears, on our political surface. . . . One cannon shot across the bow of a British boat in defense of this principle [the Monroe Doctrine] will knock more pus out of it than would suffice to inoculate and corrupt our people for the next two centuries." When Cleveland delivered a strong challenge to the British in his annual message to congress, the *Southern Mercury* and several of its correspondents, who suspected motives such as Paschal had suggested, opposed intervention and charged the president with an attempt to distract the public from internal affairs.[8] They took a similar view of agitation for war against Spain over Cuba.

Farmers provided about half of the Populist leaders—congressional nominees, members of the Legislature, and prominent participants in conventions—attorneys one-fourth, and businessmen, editors, teachers, skilled laborers, ministers, and doctors the remainder. Most had come from the South, few were recent immigrants to the state, and 20 per cent were Texas-born. Only about one-fifth had been Greenbackers, even fewer had been Republicans or had figured in the third parties of the late 1880's. Perhaps one-third had held some offices as Democrats, either in the Legislature or on the county level, but only one in ten had been, like former Lieutenant Governors Marion Martin and Barney Gibbs, a real leader in the Democratic party. Such figures held farmer-oriented views of long standing, though some may have become Populists as a result also of frustrated ambitions within the dominant party. A few Knights of Labor, ex-Grangers, former Prohibitionists, Negroes, and two women participated in party councils. Populist leaders ranged in age from twenty years to seventy-eight, with the average forty-eight. About one-third had attended college.[9] In comparison Texas Democratic leaders ap-

[8] Walter LaFeber, *The New Empire*, p. 264; *Southern Mercury* (Dallas), January 2, 1896.

[9] This analysis is based on a check of leaders listed in Winkler, *Platforms,*

peared to be about 50 per cent attorneys, with somewhat more political experience at the higher levels of state government, and slightly younger, which perhaps explains the fact that about 30 per cent were native Texans.

Anglo evangelical operators of small farms in the broken country of West Central Texas, or on the poor soils of heavily timbered East Texas, or in the less-favored portions of generally more prosperous counties in Central and North Texas formed the majority of the People's party. Many Southwest Texas sheepmen joined the third party when the Cleveland administration lowered the wool duty in 1894. Labor union leaders had been among the early advocates of the People's party and their organizations provided most of the urban support for its efforts. Some Populists took the position that no conflict of interest existed between farmers and laborers, because both were producers. Others argued "the great amount of money in circulation is kept there by the expenditure of consumers. If, therefore, the labor of the man whom you employ on your farm is cut in half, he is only able to consume half as much, and therefore only circulates half as much money." Much of Texas labor remained unorganized, however, and often, especially in deep East Texas lumber camps, strongly influenced by employers. Many Negro laborers as well as foreign and northern immigrant workingmen retained their Republican party ties.[10]

---

against biographical sketches in Walter P. Webb and H. Bailey Carroll, eds., *Handbook of Texas*; the *Galveston News* for the 1890's; Martin, *People's Party*, pp. 113–130; R. L. Polk, *Texas State Gazetteer and Business Directory*, 1891–1892; various city directories; and the biographical volumes listed in Texas Historical Survey, "Index to Biographical Studies of Texans" (ms.). Information was located for 126 of 200.

[10] *National Economist* (Washington, D.C.), December 6, 1890; Martin, *People's Party*, pp. 58–68; Ruth A. Allen, *Chapters in the History of Organized Labor in Texas*, p. 179; James V. Reese, "Early History of Labor Organizations in Texas, 1838–1876," *Southwestern Historical Quarterly* 72 (July 1968): 9; *Texas State Labor Journal* (Dallas), February 29, 1896. This view of labor support for Populism is borne out by a comparison of urban voting by precinct in Austin and Houston, as shown in the *Galveston News*, November 8, 1894, and the *Austin Weekly Statesman*, November 8, 1894, with the occupations of male voters as listed in *Morrison and Fourmy's General Directory of the City of*

Businessmen, resentful of Alliance business activities, seldom became Populists, nor did many professional men enter the party. Their social and professional connections tended to be in urban areas or with the more well-to-do farmers who remained Democratic. At least two-thirds of the Populists had been Democrats, most of them coming by way of the Alliance, whose members in many places joined the People's party in a body. In some areas Populist strength included Republicans and Prohibitionists; in others it represented essentially the Greenbackers of the early 1880's.[11]

A Negro delegate to the first Populist convention argued that "the negro vote will be the balancing vote in Texas." Portly J. B. Rayner, a teacher, an ex-Republican, and the leading black spokesman among the Populists, explained that "if you want the negro to vote a straight people's party ticket you must put men on the precinct or county tickets who he likes. Kind words and just treatment go further with the negro than money or promises." Despite internal opposition, such views caused the People's party to place Negroes on its state executive committee and on many county committees.[12] Platform planks favored black school trustees, "a free vote . . . without regard to nationality," and "equal justice and protection under the law to all citizens, without reference to race, color, or nationality."[13]

Rayner and other black speakers organized numerous Negro Populist clubs, causing a Republican leader to fear as early as 1892 that "most of the colored farming population will vote the third party ticket in the next election, and neither Mr. Cuney, nor anyone else will stop them from it."[14] Nor was it an odd choice for the Negro, in-

---

Austin, 1893–94 and *Morrison and Fourmy's General Directory of the City of Houston, 1889–90*.

[11] Martin, *People's Party*, pp. 69–87; George Mitchell to A. J. Rose, July 12, 1894, A. J. Rose Papers; A. E. Oliver to J. W. Truit, May 24, 1892, James W. Truit Papers; John B. Rushing Papers.

[12] *Dallas Morning News*, August 18, 1891, as quoted in C. Vann Woodward, *Origins of the New South, 1877–1913*, p. 256; Jack Abramowitz, "John B. Rayner—A Grass Roots Leader," *Journal of Negro History* 36 (April 1951): 165; Frederick Kemp Dixon, "A History of Gonzales County" (M.A. thesis), pp. 81, 84–85, 89.

[13] Winkler, *Platforms*, pp. 333, 382–383; Martin, *People's Party*, pp. 89–95.

[14] W. Westhoff to J. P. Newcomb, August 22, 1892, James P. Newcomb Papers.

asmuch as white and Negro tenant farmers and croppers had common interests. As a white Populist put it: "They are in the ditch just like we are."[15] Populists also sought fusion with Republicans and, like their opponents, held all night "Owl Meetings" with food and drink, before accompanying groups of blacks to the polls for their protection. Able Populist sheriffs who could guarantee Negroes safe conduct to the polls and place them on jury rolls proved crucial in some East Texas counties.

Populists exhibited ambivalence in other areas and never suggested social equality. Nugent believed Hogg's proposed antilynching bill to be too strong, as did most Democrats. Citizens of Comanche County, a stronghold of the People's party in West Texas, had driven out all Negroes in 1886 because of the crimes of a few and had erected a sign in DeLeon: "Nigger, don't let the sun go down on you in this town." Elsewhere, Democrats, commanding the greater funds and powers of intimidation, often held off Populist challengers by influencing Negro voters against them.[16]

To appeal to the strong German minority in South Central Texas, Populists employed German nominees and speakers, German-language newspapers, and a local option plank to protect Sunday beer drinking. But Populists developed only limited support among Germans because of alleged connections with the American Protective Association, the prominence within the party of Prohibitionists like E. L. Dohoney, and the greater economic stability of German farmers and sheepmen. For similar reasons the Populists also failed to win over such lesser minorities as the Czechs, Poles, and Swedes.[17]

A Populist leader observed in 1896 that there existed "a large territory south of the Nueces, embracing eight counties and nearly 12,000 voters, uninvaded, where there had never been a populist

[15] *Dallas Morning News*, August 18, 1891, as quoted in Woodward, *Origins of the New South*, p. 257.

[16] Robert Saunders, "Southern Populists and the Negro, 1893–1895," *Journal of Negro History* 54 (July 1969): 246–249, 257; Billy Bob Lightfoot, "The Negro Exodus from Comanche County, Texas," *Southwestern Historical Quarterly* 56 (January 1953): 407–416; Martin, *People's Party*, pp. 96–99; Douglass Geraldyne Perry, "Black Populism" (M.A. thesis).

[17] Martin, *People's Party*, pp. 104–111.

speech or organization except at Corpus Christi and Laredo." His appeal for "Spanish speakers and literature" went largely unanswered, though a Populist Spanish-language newspaper existed in San Antonio for a short period. The failure of the Farmers' Alliance ever to penetrate below the Nueces meant that Populists had no base to build upon in South Texas. Democratic ranchers and Mexican leaders of South Texas controlled the votes of Mexican Catholic vaqueros and laborers and brought in additional "voters" from Mexico as needed. Anglo evangelical Populists, connected in the minds of many Mexicans with prohibition and opposition to alien land ownership, did not stand a chance.[18]

To stem the rising Populist tide in 1893, Governor Hogg and the Democratic Legislature sought to fulfill platform promises. They passed laws to keep the issuance of stocks by a railroad in proportion to the value of its property and to limit city and county bonds in terms of the taxes available to pay them. Another law, which proved ineffectual, attempted to require corporations to sell their landholdings within fifteen years. Nothing of consequence resulted from suggested improvements in taxation.[19]

The pressure of Populist strength obviously made it highly necessary from the Democratic point of view that the Hogg and Clark factions be reconciled. Yet the identification of the Clark faction with the national administration rendered reconciliation more difficult, because Cleveland's desire for repeal of the Sherman Silver Purchase Act tended to drive a wedge between him and most Texas congressmen. Only Mills, in the Senate, and W. H. Crain, Walter Gresham, and Thomas M. Paschal in the House voted for repeal, although G. C. Pendleton and Jo Abbott abstained. All of the Texas delegation—except Crain, who did not vote—backed the Bland silver bill in 1894, only to see the president veto the act. The administration tried to retain its southern support by pushing through a lower tariff. But the Wilson-Gorman bill in much amended form represented such a mild reduction of duties that it received only halfhearted support from the Texas Democrats in Congress.

[18] *Ibid.*, pp. 99–102; *Southern Mercury* (Dallas), May 14, 1896.

[19] Robert C. Cotner, *James Stephen Hogg*, pp. 327–345.

Patronage also proved a stumbling block to ending factionalism. Hogg men felt that the winners should control federal appointments in Texas under the new Cleveland administration, while Clark men pressed claims as the true Cleveland backers in Texas. Mills and several congressmen sought an equal division of offices, knowing that Democratic victory in 1894 might well depend on party unity. Congressmen exercised the major voice on post office appointments in their own districts. Recipients of the more important positions, such as district attorneys, marshals, and customs collectors, frequently received recommendations from both wings of the party, though others received only the backing of Mills and Clark men or identification as Democrats "of the *Cleveland-Mills* stamp." Clearly Cleveland used patronage in an effort to develop support for his legislative program, though it ultimately cut him off from the Texas delegation, with the exception of Mills and Crain. The others faced the greater fear of defeat for reelection at home if they failed to vote for silver coinage. A. W. Terrell of the Hogg faction became the only Texan in a federal position above the state level when he received the appointment as United States minister to Turkey.[20]

In January 1894 former Governors Roberts and Ireland called for Democratic unity, to be achieved in part by separating state and national issues. Later that month leaders of both factions arranged for a meeting in Dallas to establish a truce. Silver advocate John H. Reagan warned that the Clark or "gold" Democrats might require endorsement of the Cleveland administration as the price of unity, which would force silver men to become Populists. Clark men apparently threatened a continued bolt, with former Governor Ross as

[20] U.S., Congress, *Congressional Record*, 53rd Cong., 1st Sess., p. 3067, 2nd Sess., p. 2524; W. A. Kincaid to G. C. Pendleton, February 7, 12, 1893, L. L. Foster to Pendleton, [1893?], William Edwards to Pendleton, April 22, 1894, Alexander Dienst Collection; R. Mills to Guy M. Bryan, March 15, 1893, Guy M. Bryan Papers; D. B. Culberson to Grover Cleveland, March 21, 1893, Grover Cleveland Papers, series 2; Culberson to J. H. Reagan, July 4, 189[3], W. J. Swain to Reagan, July 14, 1893, John H. Reagan Papers; Walter Gresham to T. M. Campbell, March 9, 1894, Walter Gresham Papers; U.S., Department of Justice, Appointment Papers; U.S., Treasury Department, Appointment Papers; Cotner, *Hogg*, pp. 392–393.

a possible nominee for reelection. At the "Harmony Meeting" in Dallas on March 19 and 20, however, both factions put aside old differences and agreed to support the party's national platform as a basis for campaign unity against Republicans and Populists. Reagan and Clark clashed in April, nevertheless, over interpretation of the money plank and whether endorsement of the national platform meant support for Cleveland. To Reagan any stand except one in favor of free silver "would undoubtedly drive thousands of Democrats into the Populist party and prevent a great many others from voting for the party nominees."[21]

Democrats still had to deal with the matter of a gubernatorial nomination. John H. Cochran, speaker of the Texas house, John D. McCall, comptroller, Charles A. Culberson, attorney general, and Congressman S. W. T. Lanham had entered the campaign by April. The early favorite, Culberson, had grown up in East Texas where he became a county attorney soon after receiving a law degree from the University of Virginia in the 1870's. He married the daughter of a Fort Worth banker and moved his law practice to Dallas in the 1880's. At the age of thirty-nine in 1894 Culberson was short, erect, and handsome, with dark, partially curly hair, but more reserved and urbane with less appeal for the rural majority than Hogg. Politically he stood with Hogg on state issues, though less committed to silver coinage or opposed to Cleveland on the national level. His active and adept campaign manager, E. M. House, gathered many former Hogg supporters into an efficient statewide organization and pressed for early primaries in counties where Culberson had majorities. Young Culberson also went to Washington to see his father, Congressman D. B. Culberson, and returned to assure Hogg that the elder Culberson would not seek a United States Senate seat in competition with Hogg's protégé, Chilton.

Because House and Culberson did not emphasize the silver ques-

[21] Ben H. Procter, *Not Without Honor*, pp. 293–294; Cotner, *Hogg*, pp. 394–398; D. A. Nunn to O. M. Roberts, January 5, 1894, Oran M. Roberts Papers; J. H. Reagan to Richard Coke, March 8, 16, 1894, Reagan Papers; T. S. Henderson to C. F. Cohron, February 8, 1894, Letterbook, Thomas S. Henderson Papers.

tion and both seemed indifferent toward Hogg, Reagan presently let it be known that he would accept the nomination if it were offered him. In May, Culberson released Reagan from an earlier pledge of support, and in a speech at Sherman on June 2 the "Old Roman" entered the race. He developed strength in East Texas and in other rural areas, but his late entry cost him many backers who had committed themselves to others. House's effective campaign management kept Culberson in the lead by carrying Dallas County and most of the other urban areas with large delegate strength. Yet early in July one of his campaign managers warned Culberson that "diffidence, timidity [,] want of confidence and underestimate of your powers are not the things to make votes." To avoid hurting Chilton's chances for the Senate seat of the retiring Coke or opening another party split, Hogg remained neutral, despite pleas from his friends in both camps; and in June he left for the East—partly at the urging of House—to explain his reform views there. While Hogg men split between Culberson and Reagan, Clark supporters generally rallied behind Lanham.[22]

At the Democratic state convention in July the Culberson and the Reagan forces combined to repeal the two-thirds rule for nominations. Behind the scenes Hogg tried but failed to mediate the differences between Reagan, who wanted free and unlimited coinage of silver, and Culberson, who favored silver only if parity with gold could be maintained. While they argued, the Clark-led platform committee brought in and after lengthy debate—in which Culberson men resorted to "masterly inactivity"—managed to pass resolutions endorsing the Cleveland administration and silver coinage only at parity with gold. Such a platform forced Reagan to withdraw, and his votes went to Culberson, who defeated Lanham on the first ballot.[23]

[22] Frank Andrews to C. A. Culberson, July 5, 1894, Charles A. Culberson Letterbooks, Executive Correspondence; Procter, *Not Without Honor*, pp. 295–297; Rupert N. Richardson, *Colonel Edward M. House*, pp. 66–85; Cotner, *Hogg*, pp. 398–406; Robert Lancaster Wagner, "The Gubernatorial Career of Charles Allen Culberson" (M.A. thesis), pp. 41–52, 174–175, 199–203.

[23] Cotner, *Hogg*, pp. 413–417; Procter, *Not Without Honor*, p. 298; Richardson, *House*, pp. 87–90; Winkler, *Platforms*, pp. 338–345; Oran M. Roberts,

In the ensuing campaign Culberson felt the pressure of Populism's growing strength and spoke warmly in favor of silver, although Clark had privately assured Cleveland that the Texas Democratic convention repudiated such views. Gold Democrats had no choice but to stay with Culberson, and they probably provided much of his victory margin over Nugent by 216,373 votes to 159,676. "Regular" Republican W. K. Makemson polled 57,147 votes; "Reform" Republican John B. Schmitz, 5,304; and Prohibitionist J. M. Dunn, 21,295. Culberson, like Hogg in his second race, had won with a plurality. Nugent had won over 50,000 votes more than in 1892 and an overall gain of twenty counties, an impressive increase based on several factors. Culberson refused to back Hogg in opposing Cleveland's use of troops in the Pullman strike at Chicago, which cost him organized labor votes, and increased Nugent's urban vote from 10 per cent in 1892 to 25 per cent in 1894. Culberson's shifting views on silver coinage and the worsening drought in West Texas which peaked in the fall of 1894 sent twenty-five East and West Central Texas agricultural counties carried by Hogg in 1892 into the Populist ranks. Populists also gained ground among normally Republican Negroes by carrying three of sixteen counties with black majorities and twenty-four of fifty-four with black minorities of over 20 per cent in East and South Central Texas. But as in 1892 the Populists failed to win any of the counties with considerable Mexican Catholic population. And they carried only two counties with large German minorities—though both contained even larger black minorities.[24]

As often happened, the struggles among and against the Democrats showed up more clearly in the congressional races than in the state contests. Abbott, Pendleton, and Cooper, all silver candidates in North, Central, and East Texas, fought off strong challenges from

"Political, Legislative, and Judicial History of Texas," in Dudley G. Wooten, ed., *Comprehensive History of Texas, 1685–1897,* II, 314–318.

[24] Wagner, "Culberson," pp. 60–69; C. A. Culberson to James G. Dudley, October 23, 1894, Culberson Letterbooks, Executive Correspondence; George Clark to Grover Cleveland, August 16, 1894, Cleveland Papers, series 2; Roy Sylvan Dunn, "Drought in West Texas, 1890–1894," *West Texas Historical Association Year Book,* 37 (1961): 121–136; *Galveston Daily News,* September 30, October 3, 4, 22, 27, November 4, 1894.

even more pronounced silver candidates as well as from gold Democrats to win renomination. Gold Democrats deadlocked the district convention in West Texas and sent their candidate into the November race along with incumbent silverite J. V. Cockrell. In Northeast Texas, Democrats debated the possibility of conceding one district to the Populists and shifting a Democratic county to another district to ensure their success there. Finally they called D. B. Culberson out of retirement to accept renomination after three candidates failed to win a convention majority. In East Texas anti-Cleveland, silver advocate C. H. Yoakum defeated incumbent C. B. Kilgore, who also favored silver but backed the national administration. Cleveland then appointed him a federal judge in the Indian Territory. In South Texas, however, gold Democrat W. H. Crain defeated a silver challenger. In the Hill Country a wool protectionist won nomination over T. M. Paschal, who had voted for the Wilson-Gorman bill to reduce tariffs. In the coastal district, a gold man locked the convention against Walter Gresham, who favored Cleveland but also silver coinage, and the nomination went to a silverite and labor leader, Miles Crowley.[25]

Democratic congressmen faced the strongest opposition Texas Populists had ever offered, and in six districts fusion made the races even closer. Twelve of thirteen Democrats—eleven silver supporters—won, but by margins of five thousand votes or less, and three Democrats only by pluralities. Two Populists came within four hundred votes of success, but both failed in attempts to contest the elections before Congress. In the Hill Country a Populist drew off enough Democratic votes to allow Republican George H. Noonan to win on a wool-tariff platform.

Twenty-two Populists won election to the Texas house, and two

[25] *Galveston Daily News*, April 30, May 20, 23, June 2, 7, 10, 17, 18, July 3, August 3, 9, 10, 22, 24, September 1, 2, 10, 1894; O. B. Colquitt to Jo Abbott, July 17, 1894, Oscar Branch Colquitt Papers; H. C. Ghent to G. C. Pendleton, August 11, 1894, Dienst Collection; C. B. Kilgore to D. F. Clark, May 1, 1895, clipping, V. T. Hart, Scrapbook; D. B. Culberson to J. H. Reagan, July 4, 189[3], Reagan Papers; Fred Cockrell, "Pioneering in Politics on the Plains," *West Texas Historical Association Year Book*, 6 (1930): 107–108.

to the senate, compared to eight and one in 1892, but they still remained too few to greatly affect legislation.[26]

The People's party in Texas developed rapidly from 1892 to 1894 by incorporating most of the Farmers' Alliance organizational structure. Populists also adopted the Alliance state and national platforms with only minor changes. Generally they called for greater government regulation of industries which affected the public and a more flexible monetary system. Populists disagreed over whether to seek voluntary crop reduction or improved distribution of farm surpluses as a solution to overproduction. For its union labor wing the party sought shorter hours, arbitration, and better treatment of the unemployed. Both groups favored more democratic election and legislative procedures. Texas Populists spread their word through books, newspapers, and colorful orators. They used allusions to the past and stereotyped descriptions of opponents to provide a historical foundation and to build support for their views just as all political parties before them had done.

Populist leaders differed from their Democratic opponents only in being slightly older and including fewer attorneys with somewhat less political experience. Anglo evangelical small farmers formed the core of the party with backing from Negro evangelical tenant farmers and union laborers of both ethnic groups. Greater support from all three sources increased the Populist vote from less than 25 per cent in 1892 to over 35 per cent in 1894 as a result of the depression, the drought in West Texas, and Culberson's antilabor views. Yet Texas fell from second among the southern states in Populist strength during 1892 to fifth in 1894, which indicated a slower pace of growth than in most southern or western states because of certain unique limitations.[27] Despite varying degrees of effort the third party found itself unable to develop support in the state's expanding urban busi-

[26] Jo Abbott to O. B. Colquitt, November 16, 1894, Colquitt Papers; Scrapbook, 1894, Joseph D. Sayers Papers; *Galveston Daily News*, September 23, October 25, 26, 1894; Texas, Secretary of State, *Report*, 1894, pp. 245–248; Martin, *People's Party*, pp. 210–229; Oran Jo Pool, "A History of Hamilton County" (M.A. thesis), p. 135; Dixon, "Gonzales County," pp. 86–88.

[27] John D. Hicks, *Populist Revolt*, p. 337.

ness community because of economic differences, among Mexican Catholics because of language and religious differences and local political controls in South Texas, and among German Catholics and Lutherans because of their greater economic stability and fears of inflationist and prohibitionist views in the third party.

Texas Democrats reunited the Hogg and Clark factions, although disputes lingered over national politics. Clark men backed Cleveland, who alienated most of the Texas congressional delegation and the Hogg faction by opposing all silver coinage and by manipulating federal patronage in an attempt to force compliance with his views. Moderate Hogg backer Charles Culberson formed a coalition with Clark men at the Democratic state convention behind a weak silver coinage plank which caused ardent silver supporter John H. Reagan to withdraw from the gubernatorial race. Culberson then won the nomination from Clark's favorite, S. W. T. Lanham, with the aid of former Reagan backers and went on to a plurality victory in November.

In Texas and throughout the South and West the Populists seemed assured of further gains unless the Democrats or Republicans continued to shift ground toward similar positions to maintain their majorities. Yet 1894 proved to be the peak of Populism in Texas, as the silver campaigns of 1896 would surprisingly show.

11. THE SILVER CAMPAIGNS OF 1896

JOHN S. "RIP" FORD, a former Confederate colonel and Democratic state senator, described conditions in Texas to a friend in the summer of 1896: "Times are harder in San Antonio than when you left. Money is almost impossible to get. The drouth gave a back set to everything relating to cash . . . Credit is dead. Confidence between man and man hardly exists. Almost every working man is idle. If these things increase how can common people procure the means of livelihood? How long before the want of bread and meat will cause convulsions, and the use of force to obtain them?"

To solve such problems most southern and western Democrats and Populists by the mid-1890's agreed on at least one major goal—free coinage of silver to expand the amount of money in circulation. The dominant Hogg faction in the Democratic party of Texas had endorsed silver coinage in 1892. Hogg and Reagan continued to be strong advocates, although Culberson, restrained by House, who never believed in silver coinage, remained lukewarm in the silver cause until Populist pressure in the fall of 1894 compelled him to emphasize his prosilver position.[1]

In August 1895 most of the state officials and Democratic party leaders of Texas gathered at a state convention in Fort Worth called by silver Democrats in the Legislature. They heard speeches by Reagan and Attorney General Crane and issued a platform calling for "the free and unlimited coinage of both gold and silver at the ratio of 16 of silver to 1 of gold and that the same be made legal tender for all debts, public and private . . ." The convention created a state executive committee with J. W. Blake, a Mexia banker, as chairman. Blake sent out speakers to offset the argument of the Populists in their camp meetings that silver coinage could not be achieved through the Democratic party. He also arranged for a silver day at the state fair in Dallas at which William Jennings Bryan of Nebraska, the principal speaker, made a good impression among young Democrats. But most Texas silver men felt committed to the presidential candidacy of Congressman Richard Bland of Missouri. In November 1895 the silver executive committee began an attempt to raise $6,000 for the coming campaign.[2]

At the beginning of 1896 O. B. Colquitt, a state senator, reviewed the situation and dourly informed Governor Culberson that "a hard campaign is before us at best. There is no enthusiasm among democrats anywhere." Silver Democratic leaders did start planning early for the crucial campaign that fall. After Chairman James G. Dudley had filled three vacancies on the Democratic state executive committee with silver men, the committee on February 5 decided by a vote of sixteen to fifteen to hold a primary referendum early in June on

[1] John S. Ford to John J. Dix, July 15, 1896, John S. Ford Letters; Appointment to National Bimetallic Convention, August 1, 1893, R. T. Milner Papers; A. J. Warner to J. H. Reagan, August 23, 1893, John H. Reagan Papers; Stanley L. Jones, *The Presidential Election of 1896*, pp. 19–25.

[2] Ernest William Winkler, ed., *Platforms of Political Parties in Texas*, pp. 353–357; J. W. Blake to J. S. Hogg, August 10, 1895, Letters Received, XXXIV, James Stephen Hogg Papers; A. M. Kennedy to ———, November 29, 1895, Alexander Dienst Collection; G. A. Carden to W. J. Bryan, June 8, 1896, William Jennings Bryan Papers; Charles M. Rosser, *The Crusading Commoner*, pp. 19–26; Robert C. Cotner, *James Stephen Hogg*, pp. 460–464.

the question of free coinage of silver. At the same election Texas Democrats would choose delegates to the state conventions that would in turn select delegates to the national convention and nominees for state offices. The state silver committee under Blake continued active in the spring of 1896, distributing thousands of printed speeches, writing letters, and financing speakers. In February, Reagan issued an appeal for Populists to return to the Democratic party, implying that their doing so would guarantee a silver victory in the primary. On the other hand, where silver men felt confident of success in the primary, they worked hard to keep on good enough terms with the gold men to ensure a united Democratic party in the fight against Populists that fall.[3]

Texas silver Democrats also joined in planning for the party's national convention in June. William Jennings Bryan in February asked Hogg to announce for president in order to capture the Texas delegation for silver, adding that he knew Hogg "would not stand in the way of the success of any more available candidate if at the convention you found that you could not be nominated . . ." "Silver Dick" Bland suggested to Congressman Joe Bailey in March that at the national convention silver men should concentrate their efforts first on adopting a favorable platform. In April, Reagan discussed with Arkansas Senator J. K. Jones the possibility of substituting a silver advocate as Texas Democratic national committeeman; Bailey assisted free-coinage efforts in Georgia, West Virginia, and Kentucky during May; and in Dallas "Pitchfork" Ben Tillman of South Carolina denounced the Cleveland administration and called for a bolt if the gold men controlled the Democratic National Convention.[4]

A Texas congressman summarized what were undoubtedly the

[3] O. B. Colquitt to C. A. Culberson, January 7, 1896, Oscar Branch Colquitt Papers; J. W. Blake to J. J. Faulk, February 21, 1896, J. J. Faulk Papers; Blake to ———, May 6, 14, 1896, J. W. Bailey to ———, May 23, 1896, Dienst Collection; T. S. Henderson to N. H. Tracy, May 28, 1896, Thomas S. Henderson Papers; *Galveston Daily News*, February 3, 4, 6, 7, 8, 16, 20, 1896.

[4] Cotner, *Hogg*, p. 465; R. P. Bland to "Joe" Bailey, March 25, 1896, Joseph W. Bailey Papers; James K. Jones to J. H. Reagan, April 14, 1896, Reagan Papers; *Galveston Daily News*, May 16, 1896; Frances B. Purinton, "The Texas Gubernatorial Campaign of 1896" (M.A. thesis), p. 43.

views of many silver Democrats, especially in East Texas, when he admitted that

> the supremacy of the white man and the Democratic party in the southern states is more important to us than the nomination of anybody at Chicago. Not since the war has there ever been before a doubt about how the southern states would vote on state and national candidates, but there is a doubt now. . . . The only chance I see to avert this danger is the nomination of a consistent silver man at Chicago. Then we hold our states in line on the state tickets and on the national. Let the Chicago convention, however, nominate a gold standard man, and the party is irretrievably wrecked for years to come. A number of southern states will elect populist or fusion state tickets, and the democratic party will lose its power, prestige and machinery in the south. The republican party will also come to life, and some of the states may land in that column.[5]

When the Democratic state convention met on June 23 and 24 in Austin, it adopted a platform which Hogg and Blake had approved in advance. It favored free silver, an income tax, and direct election of United States senators. It opposed monopolies and trusts, national banks, presidential use of troops without request from state officials, and the existing tariff policy of free trade in agricultural products while manufactured goods continued to receive protection. The convention chose a strong silver delegation including Bailey, Culberson, Chilton, Hogg, Blake, Dudley, and Reagan for the national convention and instructed it to support Bland for the presidential nomination.

Amid the tension of factional conflict at the national convention in Chicago early in July, Hogg helped organize the silver majority, and Chilton, the Texas member of the Bimetallic Democratic National Committee, moved that the Texans back Bryan for temporary chairman. Bailey, who objected to Bryan as unsound on some issues and a potential bolter, blocked that proposal. John Duncan of Texas then helped lead the fight for John W. Daniel of Virginia as convention chairman over David B. Hill of New York who had become a gold Democrat after 1892. While the convention awaited the report

[5] *Washington Evening Star*, April 27, 1896, as quoted in Jones, *Presidential Election*, pp. 195–196.

of the credentials committee, Hogg lashed the Republican party as a "class-maker and mass-smasher," and he attacked its efforts to centralize power in the national government and monopolies "with unconstitutional writs backed by federal bayonets" in labor disputes. He then called for national instead of international decisions on monetary matters and further tariff reductions. The thirty Texas votes contributed to the adoption of a silver platform. Hogg had a hand in shifting Bryan to be the last speaker in the platform discussion, and, after the wildly enthusiastic reception of his "Cross of Gold" speech, Hogg and others urged Bryan, unsuccessfully, to allow his nomination that night. In the subsequent voting the Texas delegates honored their pledge to Bland, but Bryan gained the nomination on the fifth ballot. Southern and western silver Democrats had won control of the national party from eastern leadership just as they had captured the state organization in Texas.[6]

Texas Populists also divided over silver. Some wished to remain in "the middle of the road" and insisted upon the entire party platform; others preferred to appeal for silver Democratic backing by emphasizing the silver issue, though they considered it only the first step toward reform. Differing views had begun to appear in letters to the *Southern Mercury* by May 1895, although the editors steadfastly supported the whole platform. In August, "Cyclone" Davis called on silver men to unite, explaining, after criticism from the *Mercury*, that he simply wanted to have silver Democrats join the Populists. The debate continued into 1896, when silver Populists gained the upper hand outside Texas and decided to hold the party's national convention after the other parties had met, in the hope of winning over silver men should they be defeated in the Republican and Democratic conventions. Bryan's nomination confronted the Populists with a new decision: should they back him for the sake of silver and possible future reform while risking the future of their

[6] Winkler, *Platforms*, pp. 370–376; *Galveston Daily News*, June 24, 1896; Sam Hanna Acheson, *Joe Bailey*, pp. 70–76; Cotner, Hogg, pp. 466–474; Robert Lancaster Wagner, "The Gubernatorial Career of Charles Allen Culberson" (M.A. thesis), pp. 20–21; Richard C. Bain, *Convention Decisions and Voting Records*, pp. 155–157; William J. Bryan, *The First Battle*, pp. 162–163.

POPULIST CYCLONE.
Southern Mercury (Dallas), June 11, 1896

party, or should they maintain their organization to fight for their broad platform. Despite differences of opinion Texas Populists remained confident: ". . . recruits are coming by 10 scores and 50s," announced one local leader in June. "It looks to me, at this time, that we Pops wil[l] have a walkover in Texas this year."[7]

In the period between the Democratic and Populist national conventions it became apparent that most Texas Populists favored a straight ticket, while national leaders tended to believe that the only chance of achieving Populist goals lay in an endorsement of Bryan. "Cyclone" Davis expressed well the forebodings of the Texans: "If the Populists are swallowed bag and baggage by the Democratic Party the Bourbon Brigadiers will lord it over us Populists in the South more than ever."[8]

In late July at the national convention in St. Louis, where some

[7] E. G. Sessions to Marion Butler, June 11, 1896, Marion Butler Papers; *Southern Mercury* (Dallas), May 23, 30, June 6, September 12, October 3, 1895, April 2, July 9, 1896; *Galveston Daily News,* May 31, June 25, 1896; Jones, *Presidential Election,* pp. 74–90.

[8] *New York Tribune,* July 21, 1896, as quoted in Jones, *Presidential Election,* p. 389.

Populists slept in parks to save money for meals, Davis, "tall, and thin as a southern pine, with eyes kindled with the fire of the prophet, a voice of far reach and pathos, and a vocabulary almost every other word of which seemed drawn from the Gospels or the Denunciatory Psalms, wrestled and prayed with the convention to save the Populists of Texas from the fate that awaited them if they were sent back, unprotected, to their old enemies." The large Texas delegation led the opposition to the nomination of Bryan, although Davis and Jerome Kearby tried to calm the tempers of the more immoderate members, and Barney Gibbs suggested that, as a compromise, the vice-presidential nominee be selected first. The national executive committee rejected that procedure, but the "mid-roaders" succeeded in having it followed in the convention. Texas first backed Frank Burkitt of Mississippi, then swung over to Tom Watson of Georgia, the successful nominee; but on the critical question of the presidential nomination the "mid-roaders" found themselves unable to unite upon a candidate against Bryan. Trying to forestall Bryan's nomination, "Stump" Ashby of Texas jumped onto a chair and asked the chairman about the existence of a telegram from Bryan refusing the nomination, which had been published in several papers but never read to the convention. Twice the Texans caucused on the question of bolting. Finally, when the convention nominated Bryan for president, the Texans refused to join the demonstration and repulsed with drawn pistols an effort to carry their banner into the procession.[9]

After the Texas Populists returned home, rumors flew concerning possible fusion with Republicans or gold Democrats or both. The Populist state convention discussed the possibilities of fusion with the Democrats behind Bryan and Watson, an eight-to-seven division of presidential electors with the Democrats, and fusion with the Republicans. Delegates, however, left actual arrangements to the state executive committee. Texas Democrats refused a Populist offer to divide

[9] Henry D. Lloyd, "The Populists at St. Louis," *Review of Reviews* 14 (September 1896): 299–300; *Galveston Daily News*, August 2, 1896; *Southern Mercury* (Dallas), November 12, 1896; Robert F. Durden, *The Climax of Populism*, pp. 24–49; C. Vann Woodward, *Tom Watson, Agrarian Rebel*, pp. 290–301; Marshall L. Williams, "The Political Career of Cyclone Davis," pp. 39–45; Jones, *Presidential Election*, pp. 244–263.

POPULISTS REFUSE TO ENDORSE BRYAN.
Southern Mercury (Dallas), August 6, 1896

electors. Tom Watson spoke at Dallas in September and staved off fusion with Republicans for a few days. But despite continued opposition from the Populist national chairman, Texas Populist leaders soon promised electoral votes for McKinley in return for Republican support in the state election. As a result, the regular Republican state convention on September 9 and 10 called for "all good citizens irrespective of party to join together in a determined effort to drive the present so-called Democratic party from power in our beloved State." Later that month John Grant, Texas Republican national committeeman, endorsed Populist gubernatorial nominee Jerome Kearby, a handsome, robust Dallas attorney and former Greenbacker with a powerful oratorical style.[10]

[10] Winkler, *Platforms*, pp. 379–384, 392–393; Diary, September 11, 1896, W. B. Wilson Papers; H. W. Reed to Marion Butler, September 7, 1896, Butler

To meet the Populist challenge, the Democratic convention, dominated by the silver wing, renominated all state officeholders. An efficient Culberson campaign committee, again headed by E. M. House, stood ready to manage his race and to expand its control of the party machinery. House played a disingenuous role to a degree, for he and his close friends Jim Wells, T. W. Gregory, and Frank Andrews personally favored a gold standard but stayed with the majority faction to develop influence and power therein.[11]

Culberson opened his campaign in April by defending his administration. He could boast of the passage of a law to punish illegal election practices, a move, though a weak one, toward creation of labor arbitration boards, a revision of the antitrust law to include insurance companies and to exempt labor and farm organizations, and passage of an unimportant but much-publicized law against prize fights. Culberson's bid for reelection moved smoothly ahead although some Democrats felt that "Culberson is a foolish snob and has none of Hogg's . . . sympathy for the poor and oppressed." In the fall, however, Populist-Republican fusion caused Culberson to "think the ticket is in serious danger."[12]

House and the chairman of the state executive committee had managed an active and generally efficient campaign, sending out numerous letters, large quantities of literature, and many speakers. Democrats spent, as they had before, considerable sums on food, drink, and speakers to keep Negro voters from the Populist ranks. Yet, as a local campaigner in Mineola reported, among Negroes the Democrats faced increasing problems of "poverty, dispondency [*sic*], empty corn cribs." From Wharton another Democrat wrote that the

---

to J. S. Bradley, August 25, 26, 1896, to M. D. Harrell, October 1, 1896, to Thomas J. Middleton, October 12, 26, 1896, Letterbook, Butler Papers; *Galveston Daily News*, October 1, 1896; Durden, *Climax of Populism*, pp. 74–76; Purinton, "Gubernatorial Campaign," pp. 49–53, 63–70, 86–88; Wagner, "Culberson," pp. 106–115; Roscoe C. Martin, *The People's Party in Texas*, pp. 118–119.

[11] Rupert N. Richardson, *Colonel Edward M. House*, pp. 103–111.

[12] H. B. Short to J. W. Truit, June 3, 1896, James W. Truit Papers; C. A. Culberson to E. M. House, October 12, 1896, E. M. House Papers; Wagner, "Culberson," pp. 70–105, 122–131.

state ticket had been left off Republican ballots there, for, "we have grabed [*sic*] the goods from Kirby [*sic*]. We are doing all that our *money* and energy can do." "Gooseneck Bill" McDonald, a Negro Republican leader, campaigned for Culberson and did so without having been promised a state appointment as opponents charged. House had a Culberson speech translated into Swedish. Wells spent over one thousand dollars ensuring his usual control over South Texas, where the voters were mostly Mexicans. Joe Lee Jameson, with brewery aid, published circulars depicting Kearby as a prohibitionist; these he distributed, along with ballots containing the Republican national and congressional candidates and the Democratic state ticket, among Texas Germans. On the local level Democrats sought such issues as tax delinquencies to charge against the Populists, though similar failings by their own candidates often negated their efforts. Literature also poured into the state from the Association of National Silver Clubs.[13]

In public the Democrats attacked Kearby as a heavy drinker and an incendiary speaker who was inconsistent on the silver question. Culberson and others hammered on the idea that Populist-Republican fusion might cost Bryan Texas. And Democratic speakers viewed with alarm Populist advocacy of government ownership of railroads as an example of the paternalism to be expected for the third party. Republicans also sent into the state masses of literature. Gold Democrats of the Clark persuasion had met in Waco on August 25 to fulminate against the state and national Democratic planks favoring free silver coinage, but they did not campaign actively. Populists, while offering their reform proposals, charged the Democrats with excessive expenditures and conflicting views on the money question. They brought in such national figures as labor leader Eugene V. Debs, who spoke to workingmen in Dallas and Galveston.[14]

[13] M. M. Giles to E. M. House, October 23, 1896, J. M. Pinckney to House, November 2, 1896, Joe Lee Jameson to House, October 31, 1896, J. W. Blake to House, November 16, 1898, House Papers; George P. Keeney to O. B. Colquitt, October 2, 1896, Nester Morrow to Colquitt, October 1, 1896, Colquitt Papers; Richardson, *House*, pp. 111–117.

[14] *Dallas News*, September 8, 1896; *Galveston Daily News*, September 29,

The election produced a victory for Culberson with 298,528 votes to 238,692 for Kearby. Kearby polled the largest vote ever won by a Texas Populist in capturing 44 per cent of the votes cast. Fusion allowed Kearby to carry eight of the sixteen counties with black majorities, four of the thirteen counties with large Mexican Catholic minorities, and seven of the eleven counties with significant German Catholic and Lutheran minorities. Fusion, hometown appeal, and a further increase in labor support helped him carry Dallas and Austin and win over 40 per cent of the votes in Texas's seven major urban areas. Culberson actually carried a few more counties than he had in 1894, however, running well in ranching areas of West and South Texas and in the more prosperous farming regions of North Texas. In East Texas, where fusion heightened the race issue, he won nineteen counties carried by the Populists two years earlier. Most gold Democrats voted for Culberson as a lesser evil than a Populist. The presidential returns pointed up both the extent of fusion and its partial failure. Democratic electors received 290,526 votes, Republican electors, 163,413, and Populist electors, 79,572. Of the thirty-nine counties that showed Republican majorities in the presidential election, only twenty-four gave Populist majorities in the state election. Some gold Democrats—railroad men, lumbermen, cattlemen, and land dealers—who voted for Culberson supported McKinley for president. Inability to reconcile Populist-Republican differences allowed the Democrats to win twelve counties by pluralities in the state election and twenty-seven in the national election.[15]

1896; Wagner, "Culberson," pp. 136–150; Winkler, *Platforms*, pp. 389–391; Purinton, "Gubernatorial Campaign," pp. 95–115.

[15] Purinton, "Gubernatorial Campaign," pp. 122, 128–138; Edgar Eugene Robinson, *The Presidential Vote, 1896–1932*, pp. 330–350; C. A. John to E. M. House, October 19, 1896, S. Webb to House, October 21, 1896, House Papers. Kearby polled a higher percentage of votes in 1896 than the combined non-Democratic vote of 1894 in twenty-six of thirty-three urban precincts in Houston, Galveston, and Dallas, which suggests an increase in labor support above the effects of fusion. He won fewer votes than the combined non-Democrats of 1894 in all sixteen San Antonio precincts where fusion seems to have failed. *Houston Daily Post*, November 8, 1894, November 7, 1896; *Dallas Morning News*, November 10, 1894, November 8, 1896; *Galveston Daily News*, November 10, 1894, November 7, 1896; *San Antonio Daily Express*, November 18, 1894, November 15, 1896.

In the congressional elections Populists ran strong races on fusion tickets in five districts of East, North, and West Texas but won none of them. Gold Democrats in two of the northern districts and Republicans in six eastern and southern districts split the vote three ways. Four Republicans ran second, and Republican Robert B. Hawley of Galveston won a plurality victory with the support of gold Democrats in a district where commercial interests were powerful. In South Texas two Democrats—James L. Slayden of San Antonio and Rudolph Kleberg, elected in the spring when W. H. Crain died and running with the support of Jim Wells—won close plurality victories over divided opposition. All the Democratic congressmen had run on silver platforms, although their personal views ranged from ardent advocacy by several of the North and East Texans to expedient acceptance by Kleberg.[16]

Partly because of internal disputes, at both state and national levels, the Populist party declined rapidly after 1896, polling not much over 100,000 votes in 1898. Bryan's nomination and the Democratic adoption of several Populist planks enabled many men to go back to the Democrats with the feeling that their third-party venture had accomplished something, at least in principle. Others returned to the Democratic party in order to unite white opposition against Negro majorities in a number of East Texas counties. Improved economic conditions also worked against the Populists as a party of protest. European farm production fell off in 1897 and United States agricultural prices rose, while gold discoveries in Alaska, Australia, and South Africa began to solve the currency shortage. The Spanish-American War in 1898 turned attention away from politics, especially among young men eligible for service. Texas Populists supported the war, but only "in the interest of humanity, and not for conquest." Frustration and bickering within the Texas Populist party increased as membership and hope of success dwindled. Milton Park, editor of the *Mercury*, did manage to hold together a remnant of the

[16] Texas, Secretary of State, *Report*, 1896, pp. 61–64; "To The Democrats of the Eleventh Congressional District of Texas, September 15, 1896," broadside, Scrapbook, Rudolph Kleberg Papers; *Galveston Daily News*, April 5, 17, 28, August 8, 12, September 11, 20, 1896.

"mid-road" faction until well after the turn of the century. But other leaders died or left the party or the state; several of them, including Davis, Tracy, and Gibbs, campaigned for Bryan in 1900.[17]

Some former Populists would be leaders early in the twentieth century of the small Socialist party of Texas. A greater number would help develop the larger and more influential Farmers' Union that expanded from a Texas base into a national pressure group. Politically, most returned to the Democratic party and several served as Democratic legislators.[18] Charles H. Jenkins, Populist congressional candidate, became associate justice of the Court of Civil Appeals for the Third District, 1910–1923; and C. M. Cureton, secretary of the Populist state executive committee in 1896, served as chief justice of the Supreme Court of Texas from 1921 to 1940. "Cyclone" Davis became congressman-at-large, 1915–1917.[19] Thomas P. Gore, the "blind boy orator" defeated for Congress in Texas as a Populist in 1898, would be an active advocate of farm legislation as a Democratic United States senator from Oklahoma, 1907–1921. Joe H. Eagle, another unsuccessful Populist congressional candidate, later won a House seat as a Democrat, 1913–1921 and 1933–1937, forced modification of the Federal Reserve Act, and helped shape the Agricultural Credits Act under President Wilson.[20] Samuel Ealy Johnson, Sr., lecturer and county organizer of the Farmers' Alliance in Gillespie County and member of the Populist state executive committee

[17] Martin, *People's Party*, pp. 242–250, Williams, "Cyclone Davis," pp. 32–33; Harold U. Faulkner, *Politics, Reform, and Expansion, 1890–1900*, p. 269.

[18] Theodore Saloutos, *Farmer Movements in the South, 1865–1933*, pp. 185–188; Winkler, *Platforms*, pp. 442, 470, 484, 513–516, 527, 564, 625; Genevieve Pyle Demme, "Owen Pinkney Pyle, Champion of the Farmer" (M.A. thesis), pp. 61–71, 79, 81–120, 193; J. W. Baird to "Dear Wife," July 28, 1903, James W. Baird Papers; Eugene C. Barker and Ernest William Winkler, eds., *A History of Texas and Texans, by Frank W. Johnson*, III, 1325; B. B. Paddock, ed., *History of Texas*, IV, 570–572, 576.

[19] Walter Prescott Webb and H. Bailey Carroll, eds., *Handbook of Texas*, I, 447, 470, 910.

[20] U.S., Congress, *Biographical Directory of the American Congress, 1774–1961*, pp. 841–842, 960–961; *Galveston Daily News*, August 9, 1896; *Houston Post*, January 11, 1963; Arthur S. Link, *Wilson: The New Freedom*, pp. 218–222; Monroe Billington, "T. P. Gore and Agricultural Legislation," *Agricultural History* 31 (January 1957): 29–40.

in 1891, had a son who became a progressive Democratic state representative. And his grandson, pragmatic but progressive Democratic President Lyndon B. Johnson, acknowledged that "his father and grandfather handed down to him a philosophy of life." Former Populist counties also provided continued support for liberal Democrats of the mid-twentieth century. Thus intellectual and human threads of Populism ran through the fabric of Texas politics even into the 1960's.[21]

The Populists made little personal impact on legislation in Texas or the nation in the 1890's because they failed to elect enough members to the state Legislature or to Congress at any time. Their failure to win control of the state government rested primarily on the economic and ethnic diversity of Texas, for the very reforms and views which brought them a huge following repelled an even larger block of votes. As a party of predominantly Anglo evangelical small farmers and organized laborers the Populists, despite a variety of efforts, could not attract significant support from Mexican Catholics, German Catholics and Lutherans, urban businessmen, West and South Texas cattle and sheep raisers and land dealers, or more prosperous farmers on the better land of North and Central Texas. When the Populists succeeded in developing real fusion with Texas Republicans in 1896, their increased black vote raised the issue of race and cost them thousands of white voters in East Texas. Culture and tradition rivaled economics as influences on Texas voting patterns.

[21] *Austin American Statesman*, August 28, 1966; William C. Pool, Emmie Craddock, and David E. Conrad, *Lyndon Baines Johnson*, pp. 12–45; Winkler, *Platforms*, p. 297; Gillespie County [Texas] Farmers' Alliance, Minutes, 1889–1895; James R. Soukup, Clifton McCleskey, and Harry Holloway, *Party and Factional Division in Texas*, pp. 99–100. Some political scientists have suggested Populism as a possible forerunner of "McCarthyism" and similar movements in the mid-twentieth century. Yet support for Martin Dies, McCarthy's closest counterpart as a Communist-hunter in Texas politics, cannot be traced to a strong Populist heritage. Dies carried only fourteen counties, thirteen in his own congressional district, when he ran fourth in the United States Senate campaign of 1941. Populists had won only six of those fourteen counties at any time and had carried only three more than once. Familiarity with Dies seems to have been the most crucial factor in his majority votes. *Texas Almanac, 1943–1944*, pp. 259–260.

The withdrawal of Populist farmers from the Texas Democratic party opened the way to a reduction in the overall number of agriculturists serving in the state Legislature, though the People's party representatives fell almost entirely in that category. The absence of their influence from the party probably cost Reagan the gubernatorial nomination in 1894 and made possible a series of less reform-oriented state administrations in the late 1890's and early 1900's. Though the Populists clearly influenced southern and western Democrats to seize control of their party from the eastern wing and to demand currency expansion and other reforms in the late 1890's, their major solution—silver coinage—failed to gain a national majority, because it seemed to pose international problems since most other powers had shifted to a gold standard. Populist success in shifting Democratic views, however, created the quandary of backing Bryan and some of their goals, with the hope of immediate victory on the national level, or maintaining their own party to seek all their goals over a longer period of time, with the additional hope of defeating the Democrats on the state level. Both the national and state Populist parties divided on the question and went into decline as a result.

Yet Texas Populists might justly claim that they had offered at least one new proposal and had inspired greater interest in older ones in the 1890's. They then returned to the Democratic party to support and in some cases to provide progressive candidates who, in the early twentieth century, took up with greater success many of the same issues. These included more effective railroad regulation, a graduated national income tax, expanded currency and credit, popular election of United States senators, initiative and referendum, an end to free railroad passes for politicians, reform of the fee system for local officials, the secret ballot, longer school terms, free textbooks, and an improved mechanics' lien law.[22]

[22] Martin, *People's Party*, p. 266; Richard Hofstadter, *The Age of Reform: From Bryan to F. D. R.*, pp. 101–108.

12. REPUBLICAN FACTIONALISM

In the last quarter of the nineteenth century the Republican party in Texas resembled an iceberg in a Democratic ocean, continuously in existence and often in turmoil beneath the surface but holding few elective offices and noticeable only during campaigns. Two factions had developed during Reconstruction. The numerically dominant "radical" wing, led by Governor E. J. Davis, included many ex-Unionists, some Edwards Plateau sheep raisers who favored protective tariffs, and most of the Negro voters, who made up a majority of the party. The smaller "conservative" wing, primarily former Unionists, led by ex-Governor A. J. Hamilton until his death in 1875, had received Democratic support against Davis in 1869, but found itself of no further use to the Democrats once they had won control of the state government in 1874. Many of the Hamilton faction did enjoy federal patronage appointments received through the efforts of United States Senator Morgan C. Hamilton, who had fallen out with Davis during his term as governor. "Carpetbaggers" from the North played only a limited role in either faction, and their mere presence after 1874 indicated a lasting interest in Texas. Davis's defeat for reelection by a two-to-one vote ended any real possibility that Republicans could again control the state in the near future. "Texas is I fear hopelessly Democratic," admitted one sad Republican. Most party leaders retained their Republican views, but they found their chances of political power limited to seeking fusion with third parties and strengthening their position within their own organization, with a particular view to control of federal patronage in Texas.[1]

Before the party convention in May 1875 both factions prepared for a contest over leadership with the federal officeholders hoping to make B. G. Shields, collector of customs at Galveston, or former governor and national banker E. M. Pease chairman of the state executive committee. The convention elected Davis chairman, however, and in the interest of outward harmony took no stand on the constitutional convention that was soon to meet. Chairman Davis, the tall, dignified ex-governor, continued until his death to act as a lightning rod for the criticism of Democrats, who bitterly disagreed with his views but considered him brave and honest. The internal struggle continued, with Davis backing N. W. Cuney, an educated Negro labor organizer, for a position in the Galveston customshouse, while federal appointees refused contributions requested for support of a projected Republican newspaper.[2]

In the state convention of 1876 supporters of Davis controlled the nominations for offices and the election of delegates to the national

[1] W. A. Craft to William E. Chandler, April 18, 1876, William E. Chandler Papers. For background on the party during Reconstruction see Charles W. Ramsdell, *Reconstruction in Texas*; W. C. Nunn, *Texas under the Carpetbaggers*, pp. 4–119; Virginia Neal Hinze, "Norris Wright Cuney" (M.A. thesis), p. 16; Paul Casdorph, *A History of the Republican Party in Texas, 1865–1965*, pp. 1–133. Casdorph's book, pp. 34–89, is almost continuously useful on the subject of the present chapter. It is cited specifically only at points where the information derives mainly from it.

[2] S. A. Hackworth to E. M. Pease, April 27, 1875, George W. Paschal to Pease, May 10, 1875, J. L. Haynes to Pease, May 28, 1875, C. B. Sabin to Pease, October 10, 1875, E. M. Pease Papers; J. L. Haynes to J. P. Newcomb, June 10, 1875, James P. Newcomb Papers; Norman G. Kittrell, *Governors Who Have Been*, p. 52.

convention, with one exception. A. B. Norton, a popular old Unionist and postmaster of Dallas, who was not a Davis man, won election as a delegate. Norton proved the most striking member of the delegation because of his flowing beard, which, in a moment of youthful impetuosity, he had promised not to cut until Henry Clay became president. At the national convention Davis received confirmation as national committeeman for Texas, and most Texas delegates voted initially for Senator Oliver P. Morton of Indiana. Under Norton's influence, however, the Texans went along with others in shifting to the eventual nominee, Rutherford B. Hayes, a college classmate of Norton's and a compromiser interested in building up the Republican party in the South by weaning conservative whites away from the Democrats. Hayes retained most federal officeholders in Texas and, when openings appeared, appointed moderate Democrats, on the advice of former school friend Guy M. Bryan, or "conservative" Republicans, such as Pease. The most obvious effect on the internal struggle came with the removal of Cuney from the customshouse in 1877, despite Davis's opposition to the move. By 1879 Robert H. Taylor, former Unionist and running mate of Davis in 1873, complained, "There are about 1000 P[ost] O[ffice]s in Texas and about 100 Republicans hold them. How can opposition to democracy succeed, with all the state and most federal offices in the hands of the democrats."[3]

In 1878 Davis led the state executive committee in endorsing fusion with the new Greenback party as a potential means of defeating the Democrats and regaining some political power for Texas Republicans. Most federal officeholders felt they could strengthen their relations with the national administration, however, by putting out a Republican ticket in Texas. Their convention nominated Norton and Negro Richard Allen, customs inspector for the port of Houston, for governor and lieutenant governor, with no hope of

[3] Robert H. Taylor to John Sherman, January 5, 1879 [1880], John Sherman Papers; Stanley P. Hirshson, *Farewell to the Bloody Shirt,* p. 36; Vincent P. De Santis, *Republicans Face the Southern Question*, pp. 84, 86, 92; Hinze, "Cuney," pp. 17–20; E. J. Davis to J. P. Newcomb, March 23, 1877, Newcomb Papers; Benjamin H. Miller, "Elisha Marshall Pease: A Biography" (M.A. thesis), p. 166; *Norton's Union Intelligencer* (Dallas), January 13, 1894.

Richard Coke.
(From The University of Texas Library.)

Richard B. Hubbard.
(From The University of Texas Library.)

Oran M. Roberts.
(From The University of Texas Library.)

James W. Throckmorton.
(From the N. H. Rose Collection.)

DEMOCRATS

William H. Hamman.
(*From Hardy and Roberts,* Historical Review of Southeast Texas.)

B. J. Chambers.
(*From* History of Johnson and Hill Counties.)

George W. "Wash" Jones.
(*From Wooten, ed.,* Comprehensive History of Texas.)

Marion Martin.
(*From Love,* History of Navarro County.)

GREENBACKERS AND INDEPENDENTS

John Ireland.
(From The University of Texas Library.)

Lawrence Sullivan "Sul" Ross.
(From The University of Texas Library.)

John H. Reagan.
(From The University of Texas Library.)

Sam Bell Maxey.
(*From Wooten, ed.,* Comprehensive History of Texas.)

DEMOCRATS

James Stephen Hogg.
(From The University of Texas Library.)

George Clark.
(*From Wooten, ed.,* Comprehensive History of Texas.)

Horace Chilton.
(*From Wooten, ed.,* Comprehensive History of Texas.)

Roger Q. Mills.
(From The University of Texas Library.)

DEMOCRATS

Thomas L. Nugent.
(*From Nugent, ed.,* Life Work of Thomas L. Nugent.)

Jerome C. Kearby.
(*From The University of Texas Library.*)

James H. "Cyclone" Davis.
(*From Martin,* People's Party in Texas.)

J. B. Rayner.
(*From Martin,* People's Party in Texas.)

POPULISTS

Edmund J. Davis.
(From The University of Texas Library.)

A. B. Norton.
(From The University of Texas Library.)

Norris Wright Cuney.
(*From M. C. Hare,* Norris Wright Cuney.)

William M. "Gooseneck Bill" McDonald.
(From The University of Texas Library.)

REPUBLICANS

Edward M. House.
(From The University of Texas Library.)

Joseph W. Bailey.
(From The University of Texas Library.)

Charles A. Culberson.
(From The University of Texas Library.)

Jim Wells.
(From the N. H. Rose Collection.)

DEMOCRATS

Joseph D. Sayers.
(From The University of Texas Library.)

S. W. T. Lanham.
(From The University of Texas Library.)

A. W. Terrell.
(From The University of Texas Library.)

Thomas M. Campbell.
(From The University of Texas Library.)

DEMOCRATS

success. They ran far behind Democrat Roberts and Greenbacker Hamman. Hamman received over half the Republican votes.[4]

The following year Davis wrote in despair: "What is the use of our keeping up this war in favor of the Republican party? . . . In the mind of the Republican of the North no Republican here is respectable unless he is nincumpoop [*sic*] enough to curry favor with the Democracy and get their endorsement." Other Republicans also expressed bitterness because Pease, new customs collector at Galveston, had appointed a Democrat and a Greenbacker to positions on his staff. Pease did ease tensions by recommending Cuney for customs inspector.[5]

Early in 1880 the old split still divided Texas Republicans, but they soon compromised and turned their attention to the selection of delegates for the national convention. Most federal appointees favored for the Republican presidential nomination Senator John Sherman of Ohio, who actively sought convention support from Texas. Ulysses S. Grant passed through Texas that spring, however, and won support of the dominant faction, which also instructed its delegates to back Davis for vice-president though he himself termed the idea "popycock [*sic*]." At the national convention most of the Texans stood by Grant through thirty-six ballots, only to see James A. Garfield receive the nomination. The Texans withdrew Davis's name as a vice-presidential nominee and gave nine of fourteen votes to the winner, Chester A. Arthur. In the heated platform debate over civil service reform Webster Flanagan frankly announced the view shared by most party leaders in Texas: "We are not here, sir, for the purpose of providing offices for the Democracy. . . . After we have won the race, as we will, we will give those who are entitled to positions office. What are we up here for . . ."

After the national convention the state executive committee again debated fusion with the Greenbackers, but decided on a separate ticket, to promote harmony in a national election year and to estab-

[4] Casdorph, *Republican Party*, pp. 38–40.

[5] E. J. Davis to J. P. Newcomb, February 8, 1879, Newcomb Papers; H. P. Whittlesey to Secretary of the Treasury, September 12, 1879, E. M. Pease to John Sherman, October 15, 1879, Pease Papers.

lish good relations with a new Republican national administration. Davis succeeded in reuniting the party's vote and ran second, ahead of the Greenback nominee. Garfield's election renewed hope in the Davis faction, which suggested Davis for a cabinet position, though some federal officeholders actively opposed the idea. But James G. Blaine of Maine influenced Garfield to appoint another instead. Davis, hurt, but not surprised, wrote in March: "... our new cabinet and all the other appointments of Mr. Garfield indicate that Southern Republicans need expect nothing."[6]

After Garfield's assassination, however, Texas patronage definitely shifted to the Davis wing of the party. With Arthur's blessing, Davis led the majority of Texas Republicans to join former Greenbackers in the Independent movement behind G. W. "Wash" Jones for governor in 1882. Jones and most other Independents lost, but Davis's friends felt he had done everything possible for the success of the fusion ticket and recommended him for minister to Mexico. After some consideration, Arthur decided to offer Davis the governorship of Washington or Wyoming territory, but Davis died before anything could be done.[7]

At the Republican state convention in April 1884 the delegates divided on the questions of who would replace Davis as party leader and whether to support Arthur or Blaine for the presidential nomination. Negro strength in the convention dictated the selection of Cuney and Richard Allen as two of four delegates-at-large to the national convention. Following the state convention, several of the whites openly protested Negro domination of the party by organizing white Republican clubs in various towns, including Fort Worth, Dallas, and Waco.[8] At the national convention Cuney held a slim major-

[6] E. J. Davis to J. P. Newcomb, March 8, 1881, James A. McKee to Newcomb, March 27, 1880, Newcomb Papers; Davis to "Sir," July 28, 1880, broadside, E. M. Pease to John Sherman, December 10, 1880, Pease Papers.

[7] E. J. Davis to J. P. Newcomb, October 27, November 18, 1881, Newcomb Papers; *Galveston Weekly News*, May 18, 1882; De Santis, *Republicans*, p. 162; Hinze, "Cuney," p. 21.

[8] Maud Cuney Hare, *Norris Wright Cuney*, pp. 55–58; *Dallas Weekly Herald*, May 8, 1884; Harrell Budd, "The Negro in Politics in Texas" (M.A. thesis), pp. 115–117; Walace Hawkins, "Col. Jacob Carl DeGress," Paper.

ity of the delegation for Blaine on the first three ballots, and fifteen out of twenty-three voted for Blaine on the fourth ballot when he received the nomination. With increased prestige and power, Cuney and other former Davis supporters returned to dominate the state convention in September. By a vote of 308 to 80 the delegates again decided to support Independent Jones for governor. A group of federal officeholders and dissident white Republicans nominated Norton for governor, however, to strengthen their own position within the party. Norton ran a poor third. But Blaine's defeat in the presidential contest ended control of federal patronage in Texas by either Republican faction for at least four years. Some black Republicans expressed increased fears about their political and civil status when a Democrat won the presidency for the first time since the Civil War. Others left the Republican party at least briefly because of the anti-Negro sentiments voiced by some of its white members.[9]

The state convention of 1886 produced apparent harmony. Cuney, the tall, thin mulatto who combined organizational ability with the outgoing style of a professional politician, solidified his position as the leading Negro Republican in Texas and the most powerful figure in the party. He won election as national committeeman, and the delegates selected his supporters to be chairman of the state executive committee and chairman of the convention. In complete control of the party, the Cuney men made no effort to oppose the nomination for governor of Dr. A. M. Cochran, former postmaster of Dallas County and chairman of the bolters' convention in 1884. He lost to Ross, 65,236 votes to 228,776.[10]

As Texas Republicans prepared to meet again in April 1888 to select delegates for another national convention, Sherman supporters tried unsuccessfully to smooth over past differences between the dominant Cuney faction which previously had favored Blaine and the pro-Sherman white Republicans of North Texas. The convention

[9] Ernest William Winkler, ed., *Platforms of Political Parties in Texas*, pp. 229–234; Lawrence D. Rice, "The Negro in Texas, 1874–1900" (Ph.D. diss.), pp. 80–83.

[10] Casdorph, *Republican Party*, pp. 50–53; Hinze, "Cuney," pp. 12–15, 57; Hare, *Cuney*, pp. 2–6, 13, 27–28, 60.

decided against instructing its delegation to the national meeting, but Cuney again controlled, he and three of his backers being elected delegates-at-large. To placate the white minority, he did allow Cochran, the convention chairman, to appoint four men from North Texas as alternates.[11]

At the national convention Cuney continued as Texas national committeeman, but sentiment for Blaine had declined. E. H. Terrell, a San Antonio attorney originally from Indiana, gave one of the seconding speeches for his fellow Hoosier Benjamin Harrison, who won the nomination after several ballots in which Texas delegates scattered their votes widely among seven candidates. Some Texas Republicans hoped for new recruits as a result of debates in Congress over the Mills bill to reduce tariffs. "The Tariff question is the only thing that will ever have any effect on the South," one argued. "They care nothing what is said about the suppression of the negro vote, they think they are morally right." Back in Texas in August a committee appointed in the spring convention failed to agree on whether or not to run a state ticket and called a second convention for September. There a fight developed, mainly along racial lines, with white Republicans in favor of a state ticket and the Cuney faction against. Finally the delegates decided on fusion with the Prohibition-Nonpartisan ticket, 256 votes to 130. Several who had opposed fusion announced their support of Democratic Governor Ross.[12]

When Harrison became president, he appointed Terrell ambassador to Belgium and Cuney collector of customs at Galveston. Cuney's appointment at the urging of James S. Clarkson, vice-chairman of the Republican national committee and a long-time friend of Negro Republicans, represented a partial defeat for leaders of the predominantly white minority faction. A compromise seemed to develop, however, with Cuney controlling customs appointments, the white minority leaders dominating justice department appointments

[11] Charles Hedges to John Sherman, April 5, 1888, to "Henry," April 6, 1888, A. B. Norton to Sherman, April 2, 28, 1888, Sherman Papers; De Santis, *Republicans*, p. 186.

[12] J. M. Thornton to John Sherman, January 14, 1888, Sherman Papers; Winkler, *Platforms*, p. 273.

in their North Texas stronghold, and other justice and internal revenue appointments divided between the two factions. Minority leaders still felt disgruntled enough to organize white Republican clubs in North Texas and in most cities as chapters of a newly created national League of Republican Clubs; but most of them still refused to approve efforts made in Houston to create a Lily-white organization outside regular party lines.[13]

Harrison received a variety of advice from Texas Republicans on a major issue facing the national party—whether to attempt legislation for the protection of Negro voting rights. E. H. Terrell wrote: "Regarding the great problem known as the 'Southern question' from the standpoint of a Southern Republican, I sincerely hope you will decide . . . to let it correct itself without any irritating legislation." He foresaw progress because Negroes achieved more education, the press discussed Democratic methods of disfranchisement, and whites divided more frequently over economic and local issues. A. M. Cochran, a former Unionist who preferred harmony but leaned toward the white faction, nevertheless argued: "We need no SouthernPolicy, what we most require is a firm National Policy . . . The certainty of a free ballot and a fair count would quickly solve the so called race problem, and remove the negro nightmare from the political slumbers of the southern people, by forcing both political parties to appeal to the Colored man for aid and support with the assurance that he will be protected in his rights as an American citizen." S. J. Wright, another ex-Unionist and leader of the white faction, urged that the "solution of this southern or negro question . . . is the building up of the republican party in the south with the white man to the front." From these and hundreds of other conflicting recommendations Harrison eventually chose to support the Lodge bill which would allow

[13] De Santis, *Republicans*, pp. 223–224; Hinze, "Cuney," pp. 86–92; *Galveston Daily News*, March 18, 1898; J. C. DeGress to J. P. Newcomb, March 31, April 27, July 27, 1889, S. J. Wright to Newcomb, April 22, November 7, 1889, Newcomb Papers; *Campaign News* (San Antonio), December 15, 1888; U.S., Treasury Department, Appointment Papers; U.S., Department of Justice, Appointment Papers; Edwin H. Terrell to E. W. Halford, December 2, 1889, Benjamin Harrison Papers.

local voters to petition for federal supervisors to judge voter qualifications in national elections.[14]

In 1890 the Republican state convention met in San Antonio. Delegates received copies of the *White Republican*, a newspaper begun by J. P. Newcomb, former secretary of state under Davis, after the local white Republican club lost control of the county convention to federal officeholders with Negro support. The paper suggested that the only hope for the party lay in white leadership to attract new members and at the same time protect the Negroes' civil and political rights. But opposition by white Republicans to the Lodge bill gave Negro Republicans ample cause to question their sincerity. The meeting opened with an appeal for racial harmony and the platform subtly endorsed the Lodge bill. A struggle arose, however, over several contested delegations, with mixed groups from Bexar, Jefferson, Harris, and Travis counties seated over Lily-whites, although an all-white delegation from McLennan County was recognized. Cuney seems to have made no effort to control the ritual of selecting state nominees, though the *Galveston News* felt that "the Negro influence was broken" by the nomination for governor of Webster Flanagan.[15] White Republicans from thirty-five counties, generally in North Texas, held a separate meeting in which Max Urwitz, leader of the unseated Houston delegation, attacked "the federal office holder, who lives on our earnings and is responsible to no one but his political boss in Washington." He called for "war against negro domination." With the authorization of the meeting, Urwitz returned to Houston and as provisional secretary of a "Republican Central Executive Committee" issued an appeal to "Fellow Republicans" to reorganize the party on the basis of segregated primaries. But S. J. Wright of North Texas refused an offer from the committee to be a candidate for governor. In the November election Flanagan lost to Hogg, 77,742 votes to 262,432.[16]

[14] Edwin H. Terrell to Benjamin Harrison, December 31, 1888, A. M. Cochran to Harrison, December 18, 1888, S. J. Wright to Harrison, January 18, 1889, Harrison Papers.

[15] *White Republican* (San Antonio), September 2, 1890; Scrapbook, 1890, Samuel J. Wright Papers.

[16] *San Antonio Daily Express*, September 5, 1890; Scrapbook, Wright Papers; Hinze, "Cuney," pp. 95–96.

At the state convention in April 1892 Cuney remained in complete command. The Lily-whites then called a separate "reform" convention in conjunction with the state League of Republican Clubs and elected S. J. Wright chairman. Henry Cline of Houston asked the delegates: "Do you feel the strong current of your Gothic blood stir in your veins to-day? Are you ready to assert the spirit of white men in this country and govern it?" The delegates roared back, "We are! yes! yes!" Then he called on them to build a respectable party by throwing off Negro domination. In its platform the convention generally adopted his views, condemning the regular Republican leaders as patronage seekers and the Lodge bill as unnecessary. The delegates then nominated A. J. Houston, youngest son of Sam Houston and president of the league, for governor, J. P. Newcomb for lieutenant governor, and for state offices a full slate, including several businessmen who had come to Texas from the North since Reconstruction. They also selected delegates to the national convention.[17]

At the national meeting the regular Texas delegates easily defeated the Lily-whites for the right to represent the state, and Cuney won reelection as national committeeman for another four years. In the fall Cuney threw Republican support behind the conservative Clark Democrats in an attempt to gain greater influence in state affairs. Efforts by both Texas and national Republicans to reach an accord with the Lily-white dissidents failed when they refused to agree on a compromise ticket or to withdraw their candidates, though they polled only 1,322 votes. Clark and Republican President Harrison also lost, however, costing Cuney his control of Texas patronage and any hope of a voice in the state government.[18]

In the spring of 1894 L. P. Goodell of Fort Worth, a Lily-white leader, tried to reach fusion agreements with Populists in the congressional races, especially in the districts around Galveston, Houston, and San Antonio. He also suggested that Republicans encourage Negroes "to organize Colored Clubs in order to educate them to the separate primary business which comes later." At the meeting of the League of Republican Clubs in June members attempted to recon-

[17] Hinze, "Cuney," pp. 97–102; Scrapbook, 1892, Wright Papers.

[18] Lock McDaniel to J. P. Newcomb, September 3, 1892, Newcomb Papers; De Santis, *Republicans*, pp. 244–245.

cile differences between factions. They failed because the Lily-whites insisted on a census plan of convention representation that would create a majority of white delegates, rather than the existing system of representation based on a combination of Republican voting strength and population. Since Negroes formed a considerable majority of the Republican voters, the patent unfairness of the census plan made it an unacceptable Trojan horse to most regular Republican leaders. A Lily-white convention in August nominated John B. Schmitz, a Denton businessman, for governor. A much larger regular Republican convention met two weeks later with Cuney in control and named as its gubernatorial candidate W. K. Makemson, an attorney of Williamson County. In the election both Republicans ran far behind the Democratic and Populist nominees, but the votes they received—57,147 for Makemson to 5,304 for Schmitz—indicated the narrow popular base of the Lily-white faction. Lily-white fusion with Populists failed, but Republicans of the Hill Country–San Antonio district resolved their differences and with increased support from high-tariff woolgrowers elected G. H. Noonan to Congress by a plurality after Populists split the former Democratic majority.[19]

In 1895 Mark Hanna began to line up southern support for the presidential candidacy of William McKinley and asked Cuney to organize McKinley backing in Texas. Cuney declined, because his old friend and political ally, Senator William B. Allison of Iowa, also sought the Republican nomination. Hanna then turned to Webster Flanagan and to Dr. John Grant, energetic young chairman of the state executive committee. At the same time the son of millionairess Hetty Green, E. H. R. Green, railroad president and playboy, and William M. "Gooseneck Bill" McDonald, tall, slender Negro teacher and fraternal leader, agreed to lead the Texas presidential campaign of Speaker of the House Thomas B. Reed of Maine. At the state con-

[19] L. P. Goodell to J. P. Newcomb, May 23, 28, 1894, Newcomb Papers; C. K. Breneman, *In the Republican National Convention, St. Louis, Mo.: Contest From the Twelfth Congressional District of Texas*; "Reform" Republican Party, Texas, *Basis of Representation Adopted by the Republican State Executive Committee for the Texas Republican State Convention to Convene in Dallas, August 6, 1894*; Hinze, "Cuney," pp. 112–115; *San Antonio Daily Express*, November 12, 1894.

vention in March 1896 the Reed and Allison forces united to elect Cuney chairman and Reed men committee chairmen. The credentials committee, with McDonald as chairman, then refused seats to contesting Lily-white and McKinley delegations from some counties. Finally Cuney declared a motion to elect four Reed-Allison men as delegates-at-large adopted by voice vote. McKinley men thereupon rushed the stage, and police had to step in to end the brawl before Cuney could adjourn the convention. Following the adjournment a McKinley meeting selected its own set of delegates to the national convention. And a Lily-white meeting selected yet another set in April.[20]

At the national convention the credentials committee ruled in favor of McKinley men from ten of Texas's thirteen congressional districts. The decision on the state's delegates-at-large went to the convention floor, where the McKinley forces won again. To complete the sweep, they replaced Cuney with Dr. John Grant as Texas national committeeman. When the state convention met in September the McKinleyites defeated Cuney for chairman, but Cuney and McDonald forces, with the aid of money from Green, elected Green chairman of the state executive committee. In Green's absence a plenary committee later voted five to four for fusion with the Populists behind the Republican national ticket and the Populist state ticket. Similar arrangements existed in several congressional districts. McDonald refused to accept the agreement and campaigned for the Democrats. Lily-whites nominated a separate ticket, but withdrew it later, after McKinley leaders in the national party promoted a compromise which gave the Lily-whites some voice in party affairs and seemed to offer "the best means, at the present time, for keeping the Negro Boss [Cuney] turned down."[21] Republicans also drew support for their presidential nominee from gold Democrats and from lumbermen and sheep rais-

[20] Stanley L. Jones, *Presidential Election of 1896*, pp. 129–130, 152, 376; William O. Bundy, *Life of William Madison McDonald*, pp. 113–117; Arthur H. Lewis, *The Day They Shook the Plum Tree*, pp. 74–75; Hinze, "Cuney," pp. 116–121.

[21] Hinze, "Cuney," pp. 126–129; Bundy, *McDonald*, pp. 129–141; Lewis, *The Day They Shook the Plum Tree*, pp. 115–116; J. N. Baker to J. P. Newcomb, July 18, 1896, G. H. Grosvenor to Newcomb, July 6, 1896, H. F. McGregor to Newcomb, August 10, September 12, 1896, Newcomb Papers.

ers who opposed the lower Democratic tariff. Eastern businessmen suggested the expenditure of more funds in Texas. But knowledgeable politicians opposed the idea, for "hoping to carry Texas for McKinley is the biggest rainbow since the deluge." Despite the fusion efforts, all major Populist and Republican candidates lost, except R. B. Hawley of the Galveston congressional district, who won by a plurality when Populists divided the former Democratic vote and gold Democrats backed the Republican. McKinley won, however, which meant that Texas Republicans would again control the state's federal patronage.[22]

Immediately after the election Texas Republicans organized a committee to seek appointment to a cabinet post for Dr. John Grant. By the end of December 1896 they claimed 95,350 signatures on petitions in his behalf. When this improbable effort failed, attention turned to state patronage, where a three-way split soon developed between Grant and Hawley and Green. After Grant refused a compromise proposed by Hanna, the administration consulted Hawley in making further appointments, except for those in Grant's own North Texas judicial district. Former Lily-whites, sensing the shift in leadership, began overtures to Hawley. At the same time H. F. McGregor, a Lily-white leader, admitted frankly that, "the situation . . . depends [upon] whether Cuney lives or dies. . . . if he don't [die] the Negro will still be a factor in politics in Texas [but] with Cuney passing the Negro as a Controlling figure here is Ended . . . If we had money in our hands or Could get $10,000 I would favor resuming business at the old stand."[23]

Prior to the state convention in 1898, McDonald, Negro leader

[22] James S. Clarkson to Samuel Fessenden, October 15, 1896, James S. Clarkson Papers; Cecil A. Lyon to "Dear Sir," September 23, 1896, to Alex Gilmer, September 28, 1896, Alexander Gilmer Papers; N. D. Silsbee to John Henry Kirby, October 1, 1896, John Henry Kirby Papers; Lawson McDonald to R. B. Hawley, February 23, 1898, William McKinley Papers.

[23] H. F. McGregor to J. P. Newcomb, August 25, 29, September 7, 1897, Newcomb Papers; C. B. Dorchester to ———, November 23, 1896, Cecil A. Lyon to "Dear Sir," December 14, 29, 1896, J. C. Stevenson to ———, July 16, 1897, John Grant to "My Dear Sir," September 25, 1897, Alexander Dienst Collection; U.S., Treasury Department, Appointment Papers; U.S., Department of Justice, Appointment Papers; *San Antonio Light*, August 1, 1897.

from Terrell, sent out a circular letter suggesting the reelection of Green as chairman of the state executive committee and calling for better treatment of the Negro majority in the party. Former Lily-whites opposed both ideas as an effort by McDonald to take the place of Cuney, who had died. Hawley and Dr. Grant put aside their differences and, with the aid of Henry Ferguson, a prominent Negro politician from Fort Bend County, defeated the Green-McDonald faction for control of the August state convention; Hawley then compromised with the opposition by promising Green reelection as chairman of the state executive committee. Together Hawley and Green influenced the delegates in favor of fusion with the Populists, though most had originally desired a Republican ticket and some Negroes talked of voting with the Democrats. Republicans then concentrated their efforts on congressional races, including Hawley's bid for reelection. Because of his antagonism toward Hawley, McDonald made an unsuccessful attempt to get Democratic funds for support of an independent Republican in order to split Hawley's vote and cause his defeat.[24]

The three-way struggle for party leadership continued in 1899, with former Lily-whites still hoping for greater influence either as a balance of power between the other groups or by having one of themselves chosen as a compromise leader. The state convention of March 1900 elected McDonald temporary chairman over Ferguson and he harangued the Hawley men for their past actions. The next day Hawley men seized the hall and McDonald led the Green faction out of the meeting. Both groups sent delegates to the national convention, which seated the Hawley men and elected Hawley Texas national committeeman for the next four years. Two separate conventions met in San Antonio during September, and each nominated a state ticket. But a month later the Republican national committee, as expected, recognized the convention held by Hawley with Grant's support. The Green candidates and executive committee then withdrew, after the Hawley men accepted one of the Green nominees

[24] *San Antonio Light,* June 8, 1898; O. B. Colquitt to C. K. Bell, October 19, 22, 1898, Bell to Colquitt, October 21, 29, 1898, Letterbook, Oscar Branch Colquitt Papers.

on their ticket, which was headed by R. E. Hannay for governor and former Lily-white J. B. Schmitz for lieutenant governor. The Hawley executive committee, with Cecil A. Lyon, a Sherman businessman, as chairman, controlled party affairs. Hannay became the first, and for many years the only, Republican candidate to poll over 100,000 votes in Texas. He lost to Sayers, 112,864 votes to 303,586.[25]

After McKinley's death President Theodore Roosevelt selected Cecil Lyon as his manager in Texas, removed some former McKinley men, and forced others who might oppose his nomination for president into a show of unity at the September 1902 state convention. There Hawley became temporary chairman, Green permanent chairman, and Lyon again chairman of the executive committee. The three leaders also agreed on distribution of patronage. The gubernatorial nomination went to George W. Burkett, East Texas railroad builder and banker who had been the candidate of the Green convention in 1900. Lanham swamped him, 219,076 votes to 65,706.[26]

Roosevelt and Lyon used their control of federal and party offices to solidify support for both men during 1903. Early in 1904 McDonald, Burkett, and other opponents of Lyon issued a circular accusing him of using his position to enhance his personal power and to create a "Lily White machine." Rumors spread of a bolt from the state convention by the Green faction, but the March meeting elected Green permanent chairman and selected a compromise slate of delegates to the national convention. Lyon definitely controlled the meeting, however, and decided all contests for delegates as he wished. Lyon admitted to Roosevelt that 80 per cent of the delegates were white, but urged that "the order and general effect of our convention is going to be excellent throughout the State at large. Many of our delegates were young men of Democratic descent, and of the best families." Three members of the executive committee led a bolt because they felt that Negro members of the party were being slighted and in a separate meeting elected their own delegates to the national

[25] H. F. McGregor to J. P. Newcomb, July 26, 1899, January 23, March 21, August 22, 1900, Newcomb Papers.

[26] Cecil Lyon to George H. Noonan, August 6, 1902, Newcomb Papers; John Grant to "the Editor," May 14, 1902, Theodore Roosevelt Papers; R. L. Smith to Booker T. Washington, August 11, 17, 1902, Booker T. Washington Papers.

convention. There the Lyon delegates won seats and Lyon became national committeeman.

During the summer former Lily-white leader H. F. McGregor campaigned against Lyon for the post of chairman of the executive committee, explaining privately that Lyon's candidacy "embarrasses the office holders" and that he hoped to create a sentiment against Lyon's being both national committeeman and chairman of the state committee. But at the August state convention McGregor withdrew to run for Congress, and the delegates reelected Lyon chairman; he then held both of the positions of real power in the Texas party. James G. Lowden of Abilene, a Green supporter, received the gubernatorial nomination, with the usual result—Lanham beat him 206,160 votes to 56,865.[27]

The McDonald-Green faction organized its own executive committee in 1906 and called a convention at Houston in August. There the "reorganized" Republicans, including about twenty-five whites among two hundred delegates, nominated Green for governor and elected Dr. Alex W. Acheson as chairman of their state executive committee. The regular party convention met in El Paso with three hundred delegates, no more than twenty-five of them Negroes. Lyon won reelection as state chairman, and the delegates elected twenty-six new members to the thirty-three–man state executive committee, a wholesale change made necessary by election laws that forbade federal appointees to hold party positions. The convention then nominated Dr. C. A. Gray of Fannin County for governor and heard Lyon condemn the Houston meeting as the work of disappointed office-holders and crooks. Before the November election Acheson replaced the millionaire Green on the "reorganized" Republican ticket, Green having taken himself out of the race for personal reasons. Acheson received only 5,395 votes to Gray's 23,711. Clearly white men's associations, the poll tax, lack of Negro unity, and white opposition to black leadership had dampened Negro interest in voting and brought

[27] H. F. McGregor to J. P. Newcomb, August 2, 9, 1904, Newcomb Papers; Cecil Lyon to "the President," December 3, 1903, February 24, March 12, 15, 24, 1904, circular, Headquarters of the State Central Committee of Roosevelt Clubs of Texas, Terrell [Texas], Roosevelt Papers; Steve D. Gulley, "M. M. Rodgers the Politician, 1877–1909" (M.A. thesis).

about the white Republican majority and white party control that Lily-whites had sought in vain a decade earlier. With the change, however, had come a decline in party strength which made it difficult to contest for even congressional or legislative seats.[28]

Texas Republicans met only frustration and defeat in the thirty-year period after Reconstruction, in a pattern similar to the struggles of most southern Republicans. While retaining their Republican views they found themselves unable to stimulate federal election laws to protect their voting rights from intimidation. All fusion efforts with third parties also ended in failure to produce permanent growth for the Republican party. White Republicans found it virtually impossible to enlarge their party by recruiting white Southerners, because the traditions and emotions which tied them to the Democratic party proved too strong. Negro Republicans, having quite logically joined the party of emancipation, met there an increasing bitterness whenever their majority within the party allowed them to assume leadership and control. Many white Republican immigrants from the North unaccustomed to Negro leadership, found difficulty in accepting it, as did some of the old Texas Unionists who had stood by the party since Reconstruction. Whites eventually gained control of the party because of Negro disfranchisement around the turn of the century and the fact that Booker T. Washington developed only limited influence over Texas Republican patronage in comparison to his power in the Deep South. The accompanying Lily-white movement did the party no good either immediately or in the long run. The federal patronage available when Republican administrations controlled the national government seemed a possible instrument of political success to Texas Republicans. But the number of positions never proved sufficient to provide for all the faithful. Bitter personal and factional battles raged continuously over its dispensation. And McKinley, Roosevelt, and their supporters, national and local, used it to manipulate the state party to their own ends. The party's prospects appeared dim in 1906, with no reason to expect improvement in the predictable future.

[28] Cecil Lyon to "the President," August 30, 1906, Roosevelt Papers.

13. THE RIGHT TO VOTE

AFTER THE CIVIL WAR, Texas Democrats who had fought to protect and perpetuate slavery refused to enfranchise newly freed Negroes in the state constitutional convention of 1866. They denounced and ignored John H. Reagan's warning from Fort Warren prison that only by granting the vote at least to literate freedmen could the state avoid federal action. As Reagan had foreseen, Congress presently required the adoption of a new constitution allowing Negroes to vote and ratification of the Fourteenth and Fifteenth Amendments to protect that right. In 1869 Texas elected a Republican administration with a total of 39,901 votes, about three-fourths cast by Negroes. When the Democrats won back control of the state government in the 1873 election by a two-to-one margin, the Republican vote had grown only to 42,663.

With the Republican defeat most white Texans ceased to worry about Negro domination in politics. Negroes made up a majority of the population in fourteen counties along the Gulf Coast, up the Brazos River, and in Northeast Texas, and at least two-fifths in thirteen other counties. Guy M. Bryan expressed in 1876 the fairly typical white Texan view that Negro voters "can be controlled . . . everywhere by electioneering influences usually resorted to in times of exciting elections, . . . Their intelligence is small and their morals very low. That they may be improved I doubt not but it will be slowly . . ." The *Galveston News* and several of its local correspondents attacked the constitutional convention of 1875, however, for adopting an elective judiciary and permitting voting without a poll tax prerequisite, a combination they feared would create a "Senegambia" ruled by Negroes in the coastal counties. The continuance of any Republican county governments elected by Negro voters and including black officeholders seemed all the more galling to white Texans in those counties, because in the state as a whole the proportion of Negroes in the population fell from 31 per cent in 1870 to 25 per cent in 1880.[1]

Whites in Negro-dominated areas resorted to a variety of devices to eliminate black officials. Negroes frequently could not find whites who would underwrite the often excessively high bonds required of blacks elected to local offices. Some white officials refused to serve with Negroes. Whites often brought charges of fraud or incompetence against black officials with little evidence to support their views. The state Legislature denied seats to at least three Negroes in contested elections, for questionable reasons.[2] None of these efforts kept blacks from voting, however, or removed the possibility of Negro officeholders. For those purposes whites adopted more forceful measures.

The first efforts to upset local Republican rule where Negroes held a decided majority came in Harrison County in Northeast Texas. A citizen's club, including most of the white voters and led by a group of ex-Confederates, reached an agreement with the Republicans

[1] Ernest William Winkler, ed., "The Bryan-Hayes Correspondence," *Southwestern Historical Quarterly* 27 (July 1923): 53–54; Homer Lee Kerr, "Migration Into Texas, 1865–1880" (Ph.D. diss.), p. 26; Vera Lea Dugas, "Social and Economic History of Texas" (Ph.D. diss.), p. 653; W. C. Nunn, *Texas under the Carpetbaggers*, pp. 18, 119; Seth Shepard McKay, *Seven Decades of the Texas Constitution of 1876*, pp. 166, 178.

[2] Lawrence D. Rice, "The Negro in Texas" (Ph.D. diss.), pp. 150–154, 172–173.

whereby in the election of county commissioners the club would select three persons from each beat and the Republicans would then choose one from each beat to run unopposed. For the other county offices the club ran its own candidates, charging that the Republicans had mismanaged county finances. Club leaders requested and received from the Democratic state adjutant general rifles for the local militia —presumably to prevent trouble on election day. The Citizen's party made its ballots similar to Republican ballots in the hope of confusing illiterate Negroes who could not read the names. Despite these stratagems, the Republicans still carried the county.[3] Club leaders then challenged the returns from a key precinct on grounds that the voting box had been improperly situated. A Democratic district judge granted them an injunction, but the Republican county judge refused to recognize it. They then took possession of the sheriff's and county clerk's offices, organized their own court, counted "duplicate" returns for the unchallenged precincts, and issued themselves certificates of election. At the same time the county judge counted the regular ballots and issued certificates of election to the Republican candidates. Both sets of county officials then petitioned the governor for recognition. But outgoing Governor Hubbard and incoming Governor Roberts refused to issue certificates to either side, leaving the citizen's club in control of the offices.[4]

The effect on Harrison County proved permanent. Years later R. L. Jennings, editor of the *Marshall Star*, told a *Dallas News* reporter: "In 1878, by stuffing some boxes, playing tricks on negroes, and partially by force, the county radical ring was overthrown. At first negroes were allowed to vote in the primaries, but so much

[3] Amory Starr to Citizens Club of Harrison County, September 27, 28, 1878, Starr to William Steele, October 24, November 21, 1878, Henry Raguet Papers; *Tri-Weekly Herald* (Marshall), September 26, October 15, November 5, 7, 1878; Sallie M. Lentz, "Highlights of Early Harrison County," *Southwestern Historical Quarterly* 61 (October 1957): 255.

[4] J. B. Williamson to R. B. Hubbard, November 21, 22, 1878, W. L. Coleman to Hubbard, November 22, 1878, George Lane to Hubbard, November 22, 1878, R. E. Coleman to Hubbard, November 24, 1878, Executive Correspondence; *Tri-Weekly Herald* (Marshall), November 19, December 14, 17, 1878; E. M. Pease, *Speech Delivered at Turner Hall, Galveston, Texas, July 12th, 1880*; *Texas Capital* (Austin), March 9, 1879.

fraud was practiced with them that, several years since [in 1888], a resolution was adopted permitting only white men to vote in the primaries." Negroes quit voting because "their votes in state and national matters are never counted." After an election-frauds case in federal court in 1880 cost the political leaders of Harrison County $8,000, they established separate state and federal election boxes. They returned a much larger vote in state elections, where they did not fear prosecution. "In 1892, we gave Jim Hogg 4,500 votes, over 3,000 more than he was entitled to." The voting lists were a joke, containing the names of Jefferson Davis and several national Republican leaders. Club leaders drove ten Negro leaders from the county and fined others for trying to intimidate an election judge when they asked for a public count of ballots.[5] Amory Starr, who had led the citizen's club in 1878, commented in 1882 that instead of running for Congress he would "rather be chairman of a white league, Capt of a rifle club or Mayor of Marshall. *We make congressmen.*"[6]

Harrison County events and similar occurrences in Tyler produced a new election law, passed in 1879. It ruled as illegal any examination of ballots, revelation of votes, or use of ballots with one name pasted over another. It required that all ballots be of white paper with only the party name at the head, which worked a hardship on illiterate voters, and that the ballots be retained in a secure place for one year in case of contested elections.[7]

Sporadic efforts to limit Negro suffrage or nullify its results continued to crop up in Texas during ensuing years. A White Man's party organized at Navasota in 1878–1879 to defeat Negro candidates in local campaigns. In Leon County a Negro elected county commissioner found conditions "so unpleasant for him that he resigned and left the county." White Democrats intimidated black voters in Montgomery, Colorado, and Dewitt counties in the late

[5] *Southern Mercury* (Dallas), October 22, 1896, copied from the *Dallas News*; Rice, "Negro in Texas," pp. 196, 198.

[6] Amory R. Starr to "My Ward," April 20, 1882, Raguet Papers.

[7] *Norton's Intelligencer* (Dallas), November 30, 1878; *Texas Capital* (Austin), April 20, 1879; H. P. N. Gammel, comp., *The Laws of Texas, 1822–1897*, VIII: 1419–1420.

1870's. Masked men carried off a ballot box at Sunny Side in Waller County after the election of 1882. In the fall of 1884 a " 'Thing' which . . . looked as if it was a skeleton dressed in a mother hubbard with the bones shining through" appeared in the Negro section of Houston. The *Evening Journal* suggested that "the appearance of the ghost is but a ruse of the Committee of Twenty-one to force the straight out Republican voters to vote the mongrel ticket for county offices." In Washington County a coffin carrying the names of four Negro leaders went on display in 1879; Democrats threw out Republican ballots because they were diamond shaped; and in 1884 and 1886 masked men seized voting boxes and shot Negro election judges. Negro guards at a voting place shot a white man who burst in on them, and three were lynched. Armed men paraded in Brenham and ordered four Republican leaders out of town within twenty-four hours. Several Negroes died or received wounds in violence directed at black officeholders in Matagorda County during 1887.[8]

In Fort Bend County, where Negroes formed over 80 per cent of the population, several of them had represented the county in the Legislature or had held county offices. Some white citizens charged that the combination of black and white politicians who repeatedly retained majority support in elections practiced varying degrees of neglect, mismanagement, favoritism, and corruption in operating the county government. In July 1888 a social club transformed itself into the Young Men's Democratic club of Richmond. County officeholders, also claiming to be Democrats, countered by organizing a Cleveland-Thurman club. Commonly known as the Jaybirds and the Woodpeckers, the two factions quickly let their differences pass beyond insults to whippings, attempted killings, and murders. About four hundred Jaybirds, bent upon eliminating Negro political leaders

[8] Rayford W. Logan, ed., *The Attitude of the Southern White Press toward Negro Suffrage, 1932–1940*, p. 100; Frances Jane Leathers, *Through the Years*, pp. 53–54; Frank MacD. Spindler, "Concerning Hempstead and Waller County," *Southwestern Historical Quarterly* 59 (April 1956): 458; Work Projects Administration, *Houston*, pp. 93–94; Maud Cuney Hare, *Norris Wright Cuney*, pp. 69–70; *Galveston Daily News*, November 8, 1884, November 18, 1886; *Norton's Union Intelligencer* (Dallas), November 18, December 9, 1886; Rice, "The Negro in Texas," pp. 200–203, 216–218.

who supported the opposition, gathered at the courthouse on September 5 and ordered seven "odious" Negroes to leave the county. All left, including County Clerk C. M. Ferguson, an educated man and a delegate-at-large to the Republican National Convention of 1888. Jaybirds allowed his brother, County Tax Assessor H. C. Ferguson, to remain because he agreed to urge Negro voters to back the Jaybird ticket in the coming county election. But despite those acts of intimidation and coercion the Woodpeckers again carried the county in November. Tension mounted until, on August 16, 1889, the Jaybirds besieged the Woodpeckers in the courthouse. Three men died and several received wounds while three Texas Rangers stood by apparently helpless to stop the fighting. Governor Ross eventually arrived with the militia, but he left the county government lodged in Jaybird hands, most of the Woodpeckers having departed the county. C. M. Ferguson and another Negro who sued in federal court because of their forced eviction finally settled out of court for $14,500. The meetings held to raise that sum resulted in a permanent Jaybird organization, which thereafter held regular primaries, for whites only, on the county level.[9]

In Wharton County, local citizens formed a White Man's Union association in November 1889 which quickly grew to over seven hundred members. Faced with the example of what had happened in neighboring Fort Bend County, Wharton County's Negro officeholders resigned. When a group challenged the association's control of local politics some years later, the opposition candidate was killed.[10] In Colorado County a White Man's Reformation association, organized in April 1894 "to work together toward securing more honesty and less corruption" in county politics, declared that anyone

[9] Pauline Yelderman, "The Jaybird Democratic Association of Fort Bend County" (M.A. thesis), pp. 1–65; Millie L. Kochan, "The Jaybird-Woodpecker Feud" (M.A. thesis); Clarence R. Wharton, *History of Fort Bend County*, pp. 181–221; C. L. Sonnichsen, *I'll Die Before I'll Run*, pp. 232–273. For the court case which ended the segregated primary in the 1950's see Nina Benware Margraves, "The Jaybird Democratic Association of Fort Bend County: A White Man's Union" (M.A. thesis).

[10] Annie Lee Williams, *A History of Wharton County, 1846–1961*, pp. 124, 133–138.

opposing its goals "shall be considered and treated as a social and political outcast." Behind those statements, in part, lay a history of constant feuding among local white politicians, including several killings.[11] In Matagorda County a White Man's association held its first primary election in September 1894. In Brazoria County a month later a "citizen's ticket" of white men announced against the controlling Democratic faction, which had Negro support. Previously members of the opposition had charged corruption and land fraud, but issues of race and Populism were also involved. Whites organized a Tax Payers' Union of Brazoria County in 1895 to recognize "the fact that this is a white man's country and that white supremacy must obtain." The leaders posted notices that Negroes elected to office could not serve and threw armed guards around the courthouse to enforce their edict.[12]

The impulse toward white men's associations or white primaries became statewide in the 1890's when growing Populist strength split the white vote and made it possible for a Negro minority to swing an election. The situation also increased the temptation to election frauds which included attempts to intimidate or influence Negro voters. Scott Field, later a Democratic congressman, described in retrospect events in 1896 in Robertson County, where Populists were active and whites refused to allow an elected Negro to take office as a county commissioner.

> It was then that the white man's primary was established. Few white men went unarmed on election day. The courthouse at Franklin was lined with about forty Winchester rifles, and no Negro votes were cast there. O. D. Cannon was credited with having stood at the election booth room door with his six shooter preventing Negroes from voting.

[11] *Galveston Daily News*, April 28, 1894; John Walter Reese and Lillian Estelle Reese, *Flaming Feuds of Colorado County*.

[12] Juann J. Stieghorst, *Bay City and Matagorda County: A History*, p. 33; *Galveston Daily News*, October 26, 1894; R. M. Chinn to George C. Pendleton, April 13, May 17, 27, June 28, 1891, Alexander Dienst Collection; Chinn to R. M. Johnston, November 15, 1894, E. M. House Papers; Ida Brandon, "The Tax Payers' Union in Brazoria County," *Texas History Teachers' Bulletin* 14 (1926): 86–92. Brandon places the organization in 1885, but other evidence indicates 1895.

In one precinct Negroes were being marched four abreast, but John Taylor and T. B. Jones (who had previously been defeated by Hal Gigger [*sic*] for sheriff) stood at the election room door, one with a gun and the other with a baseball bat, and held them off. O. D. Cannon was county judge from 1890 to 1900 and a staunch Democrat who helped to take control of politics from the radicals and the Negroes. He killed three white men and one Negro and wounded another Negro during his term as county judge. The Negro was Hariel Geiger, member of the legislature in 1881. Geiger was defending an accused man in court and made an insolent remark, whereupon Judge Cannon shot him five times. This was the end of Negro rule in Robertson County. Legislation replaced force, and quiet was restored. White supremacy was back.[13]

Populists with Negro support had carried Grimes County in 1896 and 1898. Then in the spring of 1899, after two Negroes were lynched for a killing and for a church burning, a small group of whites met secretly and organized the White Man's Union of Grimes County. In disputes arising from the first election held by the new organization, three men were killed and the Populist sheriff, wounded, barricaded himself in the jail until militia arrived from Houston to escort him safely from the county.[14] In 1896 white citizens of Cameron in Milam County nominated a ticket for the city election. A vigilance committee, organized in Marion County in 1897, intimidated Negroes who tried to hold political meetings, escorted recalcitrants home personally, and killed two uncooperative Negro politicians. In the spring of 1898 it established a Citizen's White Primary for the avowed purpose of ending corruption in local elections. In March 1898 the Bell County Democratic executive committee adopted a primary pledge which began: "I am a white democratic voter . . ." Dallas County Democrats followed suit in May. The next four years saw white primaries adopted in Hill

[13] Richard Denny Parker, *Historical Recollections of Robertson County, Texas*, Nona Clement Parker, ed., pp. 48–49; Roscoe C. Martin, *People's Party in Texas*, pp. 136–137, 179–180, 236.

[14] E. L. Blair, *Early History of Grimes County*, pp. 197–198; Helen Greenwood, "Anderson, the Rome of Texas," *Texas History Teachers' Bulletin* 13 (1925): 97–103.

County, in Jackson County on the coast, and as far north as Grayson County. Gonzales County Democrats excluded both Negroes and Mexicans from their primaries in 1902.[15]

A Negro newspaper in Houston described the situation at the turn of the century: "Unwise leadership and democratic chicanery have reduced the Negro politicians in the eastern and northern parts of Texas to a very few . . . The whites have driven some Negroes out of politics by the midnight shotgun speeches . . . Those who will not vote the democratic ticket and make democratic speeches are not allowed to teach schools."

By 1902 the white primary trend had run through most of East, Central, and North Texas, where there were appreciable numbers of Negro voters. A few counties such as Van Zandt and Fayette held out, probably restrained by large elements of former Populists and Germans who feared acts aimed at excluding minority groups from voting. When the Legislature began to consider proposals for uniform primaries in 1903, the question arose of whether Negroes could vote in Democratic primaries. Usually progressive Democrat Tom Love of Dallas then offered a successful amendment "that the county executive committee of each party may prescribe further qualifications." In 1904 the state Democratic executive committee gave its approval to the almost statewide practice by suggesting that county committees require primary voters to affirm: "I am a white person and a Democrat." With the Rio Grande Valley vote in mind, "white" was defined to include Mexicans. In July the secretary of the state Democratic executive committee announced: "For the first time under the new election law, the Democrats of Texas have expressed themselves in their primaries . . . It was a white man's primary, the negroes not being permitted to participate."[16]

[15] *Galveston Daily News*, April 1, 1896, March 1, 1898, January 12, June 19, 1902; *Southern Mercury* (Dallas), May 12, 1898; J. A. R. Moseley, "The Citizens White Primary of Marion County," *Southwestern Historical Quarterly* 49 (April 1946): 524–531; Robert Carver to O. B. Colquitt, December 29, 1901, Oscar Branch Colquitt Papers; I. T. Taylor, *The Cavalcade of Jackson County*, pp. 237–243.

[16] *The Western Star* (Houston), January 27, 1900; *Dallas Morning News*, February 10, 1903; *State Topics* (Austin), July 17, 1904; *Galveston Daily News*,

While Negro voting rights were being eroded away in Texas, women's groups began to organize for the purpose of obtaining suffrage for their sex. The constitutional conventions of 1868–1869 and 1875 had considered woman suffrage but had refused to act. Women then became active in the prohibition movement and a woman-suffrage plank came fairly close to inclusion in the Prohibition party platform of 1890. Rebecca Henry Hayes organized the first Texas Equal Rights Association convention at Dallas in the spring of 1893. The association established a woman's congress at the state fair that fall and organized clubs in several of the larger cities and towns. Attempts to induce the three political parties to adopt a woman-suffrage plank and to get a constitutional amendment failed in 1894 and 1895. Then a proposed tour of the state by Susan B. Anthony split the association in 1895, and it expired in 1896 despite the efforts of its officers. In 1903 Annette Finnigan and her sisters Elizabeth and Katherine organized a Woman Suffrage League at Houston, brought in lecturers, and held a convention. A new state association elected Annette president, but it died in 1905 when the sisters moved out of the state. Success was deferred until the end of World War I.[17]

Other methods of trying to improve the Texas electoral system also had been considered from time to time. Voter registration, which had been outlawed in the constitution of 1876, found supporters again in 1887. But the same year Texans defeated a constitutional amendment to provide for registration in towns of ten thousand or more, and in counties designated by the Legislature, by a vote of 148,525 to 81,138, because of the ambiguous second clause. In 1891 the state adopted registration in towns of ten thousand without the county clause. An 1892 law required registration in cities, upon petition of five hundred citizens, and required "official ballots" to avoid

January 22, 1902; F. Lotto, *Fayette County, Her History and Her People*, p. 56; Charles K. Chamberlain, "Alexander Watkins Terrell," p. 472; *Texas Almanac*, 1904, p. 37; Democratic Executive Committee, Texas, *Call for State Democratic Convention, August 14, 1906*.

[17] A. Elizabeth Taylor, "The Woman Suffrage Movement in Texas," *Journal of Southern History* 17 (May 1951): 194–202; Willie D. Bowles, "The History of the Woman Suffrage Movement in Texas" (M.A. thesis), pp. 37–56.

the use of mixed ballots including the names of one party's candidates for some offices and another party's candidates for others.[18]

It is difficult to determine exactly when primary elections began to replace county conventions as a means of selecting local candidates and instructing delegates to state conventions. Certainly they existed in many counties by 1890. The Legislature, moved by the heated factional struggles and numerous illegal election practices among Democrats in the early 1890's, made its first efforts to regulate primaries in 1895. The new law declared it a misdemeanor to vote more than once, to vote outside one's home precinct, to buy a vote, to make a false return, to divulge anyone else's vote, or to attempt to bribe voters or officials in elections.[19]

The same legislators considered acts to stop the common practice of voting Mexican nationals in close elections in South Texas. Jim Wells, Democratic leader in the Rio Grande Valley, immediately warned E. M. House that the bills struck at a source of Democratic strength: ". . . should the Populists and Republicans join hands two years hence we will sorely need *every one of them*," (meaning the Mexican voters.) But the Legislature submitted and the electorate passed 268,262 votes to 51,649 a constitutional amendment requiring foreigners to file for citizenship at least six months prior to voting in an election. Populist leaders in South Texas then went to court to contest the naturalization of Mexicans along the Rio Grande, although with little apparent effect on the campaigns of 1896.[20]

The poll tax, a long-talked-about means of electoral reform, gained new support in the 1890's. Proposals had been offered in the constitutional convention of 1875 to make such a tax a requirement for

[18] Abner V. McCall, "History of Texas Election Laws," in *Vernon's Annotated Revised Civil Statutes of the State of Texas*, IX, xx–xxi; Henry M. Laughlin, "The Election Laws of Texas, 1876 to 1928" (M.A. thesis), p. 45.

[19] G. R. Dunn to T. S. Henderson, May 8, 1890, T. S. Henderson Papers; *Paris* [Texas] *Daily Herald*, February 11, 1892; *Galveston Weekly News*, June 30, 1892; Gammel, *Laws of Texas*, X: 770–771; William Fletcher Garner, "The Primaries in Texas" (M.A. thesis), p. 48.

[20] Laughlin, "Election Laws," pp. 30–31; J. B. Wells to E. M. House, January 24, 1895, E. M. House Papers; House to Wells, January 28, 1895, James B. Wells Papers; *Daily Herald* (Brownsville), August 11, 1896.

voting as a method of eliminating presumably irresponsible non-taxpayers whose votes might be purchasable. Some clearly intended it as a limitation on Negro suffrage. A combination of Republicans and Grangers defeated the proposal, however, partly for fear that a reduction in the electorate might lead to a reduction in congressional representation under the Fourteenth Amendment, and partly from the feeling that it discriminated against the poor, including Negroes, who would nevertheless be eligible for military service in defense of their country.[21]

In 1879 A. W. Terrell introduced in the Legislature a bill to require the poll tax for voting. He said that linking the tax to suffrage would end the high rate of delinquency in its payment. That was not all he had in mind, however, for in November 1878 he had written, "Unless some *flank* movement can be made on the mass of ignorant negro voters, we will soon be at Sea in Texas."[22] And in 1876 he had sponsored an act that created jury commissions to select jurors from among persons who could read and write, thus effectively eliminating most Negroes from jury duty. Later he asserted that "the foremost man of all the world is the Anglo-Saxon American white man." Terrell's poll tax bill passed the senate but failed in the house. Opponents called it an effort "to *deprive the poor man of the suffrage*" and an opening move toward property qualifications for voting.[23]

Poll tax bills disappeared from 1883 to 1889 but reappeared frequently thereafter because of the Populist threat and the success of Mississippi and South Carolina in eliminating Negro voting by a combination of devices, including poll taxes. One East Texan wrote that in his section people "want the Constitutional Convention, for one paramount reason: We now know how to deal with the *race* question." Populists in Texas generally opposed the poll tax as a limi-

[21] McKay, *Seven Decades*, pp. 95–98, 166; Laura Snow, "The Poll Tax in Texas" (M.A. thesis), pp. 28–35.

[22] A. W. Terrell to O. M. Roberts, November 11, 1878, Oran M. Roberts Papers; Chamberlain, "Terrell," p. 142.

[23] *Texas Capital*, March 16, 1879; Chamberlain, "Terrell," pp. 101–105, 143; A. W. Terrell to E. S. C. Robertson, May 24, 1878, in Inez Jarmon, "A Calendar of E. S. C. Robertson Papers, 1842–1879" (M.A. thesis), p. 721; Hare, *Cuney*, pp. 101–102.

tation on suffrage, for they realized its potential effect on their voting strength among poor farmers and laborers, black and white.[24]

Finally in 1902 the Legislature submitted to the Texas electorate a constitutional amendment to allow a poll tax requirement for voting. Opposition came from the *Brownsville Herald*, voice of Jim Wells's political machine, which was based on Mexican votes, from the *Southern Mercury*, still a Populist organ, from the State Federation of Labor, and from the State Brewers Association. The *Amarillo News* said that it would constitute "a property qualification tax" tending "to discourage interest in free government." But most prohibitionists, city newspapers, and advocates of electoral reform among the Democrats favored the amendment as a form of voter registration and as a means of ending various types of political manipulation, especially of poor voters, by the brewers and other moneyed interests. It passed, 200,650 to 107,748. Predominantly Mexican counties along the Rio Grande and strong Populist and labor union counties, mainly in West Central and Northeast Texas, cast the only majorities against the amendment. Because the white primary had already eliminated most Negro voters from the crucial decisions of the dominant Democratic party in the spring, the poll tax simply extended that effect to the less important fall election. But it fell heavily on the poor ex-Populist farmers and laborers who were returning to the Democratic party. Among Democrats who opposed the poll tax, O. B. Colquitt, a future governor, predicted that it would disfranchise many white citizens and, by reducing the electorate, would reduce poll tax revenues as well and would merely set the price of votes, not stop their sale. Colquitt added pointedly that "the man who buys them is not better than the man who sells, from the standpoint of morals."[25] Reform Democrat R. F. Burges of El Paso wrote in 1906

[24] A. B. Watkins to O. B. Colquitt, January 21, 1897, Colquitt Papers; Snow, "Poll Tax," pp. 42–44; C. Vann Woodward, *Origins of the New South*, pp. 321–349; *Southern Mercury* (Dallas), February 7, 1895.

[25] *Southern Mercury*, February 28, 1901, March 20, 1902; O. B. Colquitt to James T. Benton, November 6, 1902, Colquitt Papers; Texas, Secretary of State, *Report*, 1902, pp. 17–18; Laughlin, "Election Laws," pp. 31–33; Snow, "Poll Tax," pp. 47–52; Donald S. Strong, "The Poll Tax: The Case of Texas,"

that the poll tax "serves as an effective registration law and almost entirely disposes of the illegal voter" from Mexico. Yet he bore out the accuracy of Colquitt's prediction by admitting that it also reduced the size of the vote cast by almost half and that ward politicians paid for many poll taxes. Those who wished to influence elections found it possible also to pay poll taxes for tenant farmers and railroad employees.[26]

In 1903 the Legislature enacted a new election law proposed by A. W. Terrell to regulate primaries and elections and thus eliminate voting frauds. It included a requirement that poll taxes be paid between October and February to ensure that only presumably interested, independent voters participated. Proponents of the measure apparently hoped that the poor, especially Negroes and Latin Americans, would either fail to pay so far in advance or lose their receipts. Discussion showed that Terrell's views had changed little since the 1870's. When another legislator offered an amendment to allow one man to pay another's poll tax, Terrell opposed it vigorously, saying that "it would open the flood gates for illegal voting as one person could buy up the Mexican and negro votes."[27] Houston adopted a city poll tax of $2.50 which eliminated 7,500 "irresponsible" voters from a possible electorate of 12,000. Some Democratic leaders wanted to go even further and "disfranchise the negro, not because of illiteracy, not because he owns no property, not because he has not paid a poll tax; but because he is a negro; inferior in intellect, in morals, and in aspirations to the white man, and therefore unfit to have a voice in the government of his superiors."[28]

That statement typified the racial views of most white Texans which remained a constant factor in Texas politics, especially in the

American Political Science Review 38 (August 1944): 693–709; Anti-Saloon League, *The Brewers and Texas Politics*, I, 214–216.

[26] R. F. Burges to Ireland Graves, November 14, 1906, Richard F. Burges Papers; J. H. Kirby to J. A. Mooney, January 25, 1906, John Henry Kirby Papers; George M. Thurmond Memo [January 1904], Colquitt Papers.

[27] *Austin Statesman*, March 5, 1903; Chamberlain, "Terrell," pp. 455–501.

[28] *State Topics*, October 30, 1904; James Weinstein, "Organized Business and the City Commission and Manager Movements," *Journal of Southern History* 28 (May 1962): 177.

development of the white primary and the adoption of the poll tax as a voting requirement. While most white men's associations and poll tax advocates charged corruption as the cause of their activity, the associations without exception resorted to direct, often violent action instead of seeking court decisions. Many counties favored both measures without a hint of local fraud. Supporters of such presumed reforms indiscriminately applied the white primary against all Negroes and the poll tax against all poor persons, including most Negroes and Mexicans, instead of attempting to find individuals who could be proven guilty of fraud or corruption.

Negroes could not, because of their minority status, turn back the course of events which struck so harshly at their voting rights, but they never acquiesced. Through the platforms and newspapers of the Republican and third parties and through appeals to Republican congressmen from other states black Texans repeatedly called for federal action to ensure their right to vote and attacked the various methods used to limit it. They also recognized the possible broader effects of disfranchisement. Former Negro Republican legislator and educator R. L. Smith and others, who publicly took accommodationist positions in the early 1900's similar to that of Booker T. Washington, also followed Washington's path in seeking legal action against segregation and discrimination because "lynch law, peonage, whitecapping and all kindred evils have their root in the rape of the ballot."[29]

Texans did not employ all the disfranchisement devices adopted by other Deep South states, such as literacy tests and the grandfather clause, though a smaller black minority suggests the basic reason. But without doubt the election restrictions effected in the 1890's and early 1900's, including the white primary, the poll tax, and the Terrell election law, substantially changed the makeup of the Texas electorate. Republican leader Cecil Lyon estimated in 1904 that "we

[29] R. L. Smith to Booker T. Washington, November 1905, as quoted in August Meier, *Negro Thought in America, 1880–1915*, p. 253; Ernest William Winkler, ed., *Platforms of Political Parties in Texas*, pp. 179, 196, 200, 213, 217, 234, 260, 272, 275, 291, 297, 329, 382, 408, 435, 457; *Norton's Intelligencer* (Dallas), November 30, 1878, November 18, 1886.

have out of a colored population of some six hundred and fifty thousand not more than twenty-five thousand qualified colored voters." Many poor whites and Mexicans also had been eliminated as potential voters. The result solidified one-party politics in Texas and produced less than 50 per cent voter participation in primary and state elections throughout the first half of the twentieth century.[30]

[30] Cecil A. Lyon to "the President," November 10, 1904, Theodore Roosevelt Papers; V. O. Key, Jr., *Southern Politics in State and Nation*, p. 534.

14. HOUSE AND BAILEY

As Populist opposition faded, Texas political battles shifted primarily to the level of factional fights within the Democratic party. There E. M. House and Joe Bailey formed a loose coalition to promote their rapid rise to dominance. House, the son of wealthy Houston merchant and banker T. W. House, attended several eastern schools before returning to assist in the operation of family enterprises. His business interests expanded to farming and ranching in the 1880's and later to streetcar, railroad, and oil companies. House entered politics as one of several campaign managers for Hogg in 1892 and developed such skill that he became the key figure in organizing Charles Culberson's successful efforts in 1894 and 1896. He approached politics on a personal rather than ideological level, with great calculation and deliberation. A slight, balding, reflective individual, House never ran for elective office, because of his relatively unattractive appearance and poor voice, and because of his questionable health. Yet he sought and enjoyed his position as political adviser, because it provided him an opportunity to manipulate people and events without entering the rough-and-tumble world of stump speaking. While, when necessary, he subordinated his personal views to his search for political power, House in the 1890's privately opposed silver coinage and held business-oriented views in favor of limited regulations which created business stability and reduced demands for further reforms.[1]

Joe Bailey's father, a Confederate veteran and saloonkeeper in Mississippi, sent his son to a number of southern colleges and finally to law school. A strong inclination to anger quickly and to act rashly inspired young Bailey's varied educational career. Joe acquired a law license in Mississippi and entered local politics as a supporter of railroad regulation in the 1880's. He first exhibited characteristic leadership qualities in helping guide Democratic physical intimidation of Republican voters in 1884. The next year he followed friends to Texas in search of greater opportunity and to live down his immediate past. Bailey appeared in Texas politics as an advocate of prohibition in 1887 and won a North Texas congressional seat in 1890 as one of the new political generation who rode growing economic unrest into office. "With smooth face, long hair and longer coat, all at variance with prevailing styles," he attracted followers readily with an outgoing personality, a flair for yarn spinning, and a quick sympathy for the problems and feelings of men from similar backgrounds. He quickly became an able if "impetuous" spokesman for the silver Democrats in congress and a self-proclaimed expert on the Constitution. "The big, handsome, proud, rather arrogant Texan," clearly held personal and political aspirations beyond his attainments, based on a burgeoning popularity that already rivaled Hogg's. Bailey himself probably could not separate his efforts to represent honestly the views of Texas voters from his constant search for issues that would maintain and enhance his popularity with them.[2] A political coalition

[1] Rupert N. Richardson, *Colonel Edward M. House*, pp. 1–6, 19–21, 29–30, 32–34, 44, 199–229, 314, 317; Alexander L. George and Juliette L. George, *Woodrow Wilson and Colonel House*, pp. 76–84.

[2] *Dallas Morning News*, January 25, 1891; Sam Hanna Acheson, *Joe Bailey*, pp. 1–68, 210; Arthur Wallace Dunn, *From Harrison to Harding*, I, 218; Bob Charles Holcomb, "Senator Joe Bailey" (Ph.D. diss.), pp. 1–85.

between Bailey and House with their complementary and effective political styles boded ill for all potential opponents.

Roger Mills's seat in the United States Senate attracted E. M. House and his friends as Mills's term would end in the spring of 1899. John H. Reagan, who enjoyed the backing of many former Hogg men, became the first candidate to announce. Culberson entered the race two weeks later, on August 19, 1897, with the full support of House and his efficient campaign organization. Congressman Bailey let it be known that he preferred to remain in the House where he had just become minority leader. A low-key campaign continued through the fall and winter, until Reagan withdrew in January 1898 because of his age and health. Later that month Mills announced for reelection. His close connections with the Cleveland administration had lost him many of his Texas supporters, however, and Hogg and Bailey soon came out for Culberson. In February the Democratic state executive committee adopted a rule that participants in the party primary must have voted for Bryan and Culberson in 1896. Mills then withdrew, charging that the pledge would eliminate many gold Democrats and that the primaries in several counties were set too early to permit him to campaign. His prospects had been slim at best. House then talked J. W. Blake out of running, leaving Culberson unopposed, and House himself free to concentrate upon managing the governor's race.[3]

In the late summer of 1896 Richard M. Wynne, a Fort Worth attorney and former Reagan supporter, and M. M. Crane, the attorney general and Hogg's favorite, already appeared to be interested in the Democratic gubernatorial nomination to be made in 1898. But neither man felt close to House, nor asked for his support, which went instead to Joseph D. Sayers, a member of Congress and often called the "watchdog of the Treasury." To the wife of a fellow congressman he appeared "a handsome man, heavy and swarthy with fluffy, white hair and a big mustache, but rather careless in dress and carriage." House, the expert organizer, had aided Sayers in 1896

[3] *Galveston Daily News*, February 3, 25, March 7, 1898; Myrtle Roberts, "Roger Quarles Mills" (M.A. thesis), pp. 132–133; Richardson, *House*, pp. 123–126, 317.

and now readily consented to manage his efforts toward the governorship. House first advised Sayers to back the increasingly popular Bailey for minority leader in the United States House of Representatives in return for Bailey's support in the gubernatorial race. Throughout 1897 House worked quietly to line up newspapers behind Sayers. Sayers himself made a speaking tour in August and appointed a railroad commissioner and friend of Reagan's as his official campaign manager.[4]

Crane began to campaign actively in the winter of 1897–1898. He advocated free silver, a federal antitrust law, a vigorous state railroad commission and antitrust laws, and adjustment of freight rates to develop industry. George T. Jester, a banker and state senator, joined the race in mid-January. He set himself apart from Crane by favoring better roads, a state labor bureau, restriction of immigration into the United States, and a just state bankruptcy law. Wynne entered the contest publicly a week later. His distinctive proposals included a tax on banks, an end to free railroad passes, public schools and eleemosynary institutions for West Texas, and minor legal reforms. His opponents began to attack Sayers as a lukewarm advocate of silver and the railroad commission who hoped to win by appealing to former Clark gold Democrats. Sayers's defenders pointed to favorable comments by him on both silver and the commission, and he gained the backing of many former Hogg or silver men, including most Texas congressmen and state officeholders. Yet Sayers's faith in business recovery by individual effort as opposed to government action and his support as early as April 1897 of a compromise on national monetary policy made him acceptable to ex-Clark or gold-standard men.[5]

[4] Walter Prescott Webb and Terrell Webb, eds., *Washington Wife*, p. 6; Richardson, *House*, pp. 127–134; Robert C. Cotner, *James Stephen Hogg*, pp. 478–479; *Galveston Daily News*, August 15, 1896.

[5] *Galveston Daily News*, January 3, 14, 16, 18, 21, 23, 30, 1898; J. D. Sayers to E. M. House, April 14, 24, November 30, 1897, Jonathan Lane to House, July 5, 1898, George F. Burgess to House, August 8, 1898, E. M. House Papers. Former Clark or gold-standard supporters backing Sayers included: Jim Wells, Rudolph Kleberg, John N. Simpson, Thad Thompson, George B. Zimpleman, Jonathan Lane, George F. Burgess, T. M. Harwood, W. B. Sayers, J. F. Miller, T. McNeal, and R. A. John.

In February and March the other candidates elaborated their platforms. Crane spoke for better care for the insane, labor courts, and a franchise tax on corporations. Wynne advocated the use of convicts on roads and an end to convict leases, an industrial school for girls, and abolition of the adjutant general's department. Jester favored liberal land sales in West Texas. Sayers, who stayed in Washington for a session of Congress, issued a brief statement edited by House clarifying his long-standing support of free silver and endorsing better asylums and hospitals, the Confederate home, employment of convicts except in competition with free labor, and fairer tax laws.[6]

House and others organized Sayers headquarters in Austin and Dallas, corresponded widely, and sent out numerous speakers. In areas where Sayers was strong, South and Central Texas, his friends called early primaries to build up an initial lead in delegates to the Democratic state convention. Crane's manager, W. F. Ramsay, tried to follow suit in North Texas, but found it difficult, because of Wynne's candidacy, backed by Bailey specifically to hurt Crane, and because of joint action by Wynne and Sayers men. Jester's backing seemed limited to his home county, Navarro. Discouraged by failure to secure as many delegates as he expected, Crane withdrew, perhaps prematurely, on May 17. Jester left the race soon afterward. Wynne kept doggedly on and unexpectedly carried several counties in North Texas during June.[7] But Sayers's support spread into both West and East Texas, where he picked up backing from Crane men who mistrusted Wynne's friends or his platform pledges, and from lumber-mill owners who controlled the labor vote in certain counties. After Sayers and Wynne men in Dallas had worked out a local compromise, Wynne withdrew from the race on June 28 complaining that unlimited funds had been spent against him. Undoubtedly the bitterness of defeat caused him to exaggerate; but Sayers's campaign

[6] Richardson, *House*, pp. 135–138.

[7] *Ibid.*, pp. 138–142; *Galveston Daily News*, May 10, 15, 17, June 21, 28, 1898; W. F. Ramsey to O. B. Colquitt, March 5, 1898, Oscar Branch Colquitt Papers; E. P. Hill to J. W. Bailey, March 15, 1898, R. M. Wynne to Bailey, January 25, March 29, 1898, W. A. Williams to Bailey, April 12, 1898, Joseph W. Bailey Papers; Cotner, *Hogg*, pp. 478–480.

probably had been the most elaborate and costly one staged in 1898, even though it totaled only a few thousand dollars. And in heated local contests it seemed likely that Sayers's supporters expended money in a questionable manner.[8]

House extended his influence by taking a hand in the successful races of Allison Mayfield for railroad commissioner, of J. N. Browning for lieutenant governor, and of T. H. Ball, Kleberg, and A. S. Burleson for seats in Congress. House men completely controlled the state Democratic convention, although House, as usual in the summer, had gone north for reasons of health. His lieutenant, Frank Andrews, forced Blake to step aside as chairman of the state executive committee while allowing him to be permanent chairman of the convention. House later wrote Sayers that "at the convention we paid a lot of our debts; and I told Jameson to tell our friends that you would reach them in time." The only real fight developed over the platform. Congressmen Bailey, Cooper, Ball, R. L. Henry, and others pressed for a resolution against any territorial expansion as a result of the war with Spain. Hogg, Culberson, Crane, Chilton, and Gregory led in advocating retention of Puerto Rico and annexation of Cuba if its population desired. "We are upon the eve of a radical departure," admitted Sayers. "I do not favor territorial aggrandizement, but can the sentiment be resisted? I fear not." The expansionists prevailed, 721 votes to 334.[9]

The one-sided fall elections indicated that Populism had greatly declined. Sayers defeated Barnett Gibbs, 291,548 votes to 114,955, and Populist congressional candidates lost by wide margins. In South Texas and along the coast Republicans running on platforms calling

[8] L. L. Foster to E. M. House, May 28, 1898, T. M. Campbell to House, May 29, 1898, T. N. Jones to House, June 3, 1898, J. S. Williams to J. D. Sayers, June 5, 1898, Joseph Lipschitz to House, June 7, 1898, John M. Duncan to J. L. Jameson, June 20, 1898, R. E. L. Saner to House, June 27, 1898, House Papers; broadside attacking Wynne, Scrapbook, John B. Long Papers; *Southern Mercury* (Dallas), June 23, 1898; Richardson, *House*, pp. 143–144.

[9] E. M. House to J. D. Sayers, August 14, 1898, Joseph D. Sayers Papers; Sayers to J. H. Robertson, July 12, 1898, James Harvey Robertson Papers; Richardson, *House*, pp. 146–152; Cotner, *Hogg*, pp. 480–482; Acheson, *Bailey*, pp. 114–124; Ernest William Winkler, ed., *Platforms of Political Parties in Texas*, pp. 400–405.

for harbor improvements and tariff protection of wool again challenged Democratic control. Noonan of San Antonio lost votes, however, by a last minute ruling of Attorney General Crane that his name could not appear on ballots along with the Democratic state ticket. Only incumbent Republican R. B. Hawley of Galveston won election.[10]

Before the 1898 campaign ended Bailey had quietly begun to plan a race against Chilton for the Senate in 1901. Bailey emphasized their divergent stands on United States expansion and his own agreement with Bryan, titular leader of the Democratic party, that the national platform in 1900 would oppose territorial acquisitions. He struck responsive chords too when he compared retention of territory to "carpetbagging" and suggested it would result in the immigration of non-white peoples to the United States. Bailey's resignation as minority leader, because the House refused to oust members who left to serve in the war, brought him sympathy in Texas and overshadowed his rather erratic and divisive career as spokesman of the House Democrats. He could be confident of no opposition from House, after supporting Culberson and Sayers in their recent victories. Bailey continued to develop legislative backing, in 1899, and employed his fiery oratory on a summer speaking tour to arouse popular support. Chilton returned to the state to campaign that fall and debated Bailey at Fort Worth. In February 1900 Bailey challenged Chilton to submit their contest to the county Democratic primaries and to continue a public discussion of the issues. With the Senate in session, Chilton, contrary to the advice of close friends, put off the debates until May. Bailey pressed his advantage at home and gained instructed delegations from several counties. When Chilton returned from Washington in April, ill with grippe and discouraged by Bailey's captivating eloquence and growing lead, he, to the anguish of his friends, decided to retire from the race. Thus the second Senate seat went to the dominant House-Bailey coalition in Texas politics.[11]

[10] Texas, Secretary of State, *Report*, 1898, pp. 61–63; C. K. Bell to James Wells, October 19, 1898, James B. Wells Papers; G. H. Noonan to W. W. Mills, September 16, 1898, June 12, 1900, W. W. Mills Papers.

[11] J. W. Bailey to ———, August 14, 1898, James W. Truit Papers; Jesse C.

Although the more progressive Democratic leaders had lost ground in Texas, the reform urge had not entirely died. The Legislature strengthened the antitrust act and recognized the legality of labor unions and peaceful picketing, and Governor Sayers organized a conference of governors in St. Louis to advocate rigid control of monopolies. Sayers vetoed some railroad consolidation bills to the consternation of "the conservative, business element who had been largely instrumental in bringing about his nomination." He also helped organize flood control and relief efforts on the Brazos River and in Galveston after the hurricane of 1900. He failed, however, in an attempt to have the Legislature in a special session pass a new tax law, proposed by the state tax commission. The law, opposed by the conservative urban newspapers and such groups as the Houston Manufacturers Association, would have lowered the tax rate while requiring banks, telephone and telegraph companies, and railroads to render their property at full value for taxation, thus increasing the total revenue.[12]

In national politics Texas Democrats remained Bryan supporters despite the private doubts of House and his personal friends. Bailey and Bryan had agreed on silver coinage and antiexpansion as the major issues as early as 1898. Hogg spoke at Tammany Hall in 1899 to help head off the development of backing for Mayor Augustus Van Wyck of New York as a possible presidential nominee. At the national convention in 1900 Hogg caught the sense of the dominant southern and western wing of his party when he called for silver coinage, an income tax, a revenue tariff, and a United States de-

---

Murrell to Bailey, January 31, 1899, Bailey Papers; Bailey to ———, August 2, 1899, Alexander Dienst Collection; A. G. McIlwaine to O. B. Colquitt, November 7, 1899, Colquitt to Horace Chilton, March 15, 1900, Letterbook, Colquitt Papers; Acheson, *Bailey*, pp. 125–126, 133–139, 210; Cotner, *Hogg*, pp. 489–490; Holcomb, "Bailey," pp. 152–186.

[12] *San Antonio Daily Express*, January 11, 1903; James L. Tenney, "The Public Services of Joseph Draper Sayers" (M.A. thesis), pp. 67–112; Richardson, *House*, pp. 154–165; O. B. Colquitt to C. J. Livsey, March 17, 1900, Colquitt Papers; George P. Huckaby, "Oscar Branch Colquitt" (Ph.D. diss.), pp. 51–60; Robert S. Maxwell, "The Pines of Texas," *East Texas Historical Journal* 2 (October 1964): 82.

veloped isthmian canal. He seemed to speak for most delegates again as he attacked trusts, importation of foreign labor, and any acquisition of territory other than Puerto Rico where constitutional rights should be ensured. In the fall Hogg appeared in the Midwest on behalf of Bryan's second race for president, but to no avail, as McKinley defeated the Nebraskan again and destroyed the South-West alliance of 1896 by recapturing all but four western states for the Republicans.[13]

Congressman Bailey had personally borrowed money in April 1900 from H. Clay Pierce of the Waters-Pierce Oil Company, which had lost its charter in Texas because of connections with the Standard Oil trust. Oblivious to any conflict of interest, Bailey, in May 1900, went to Governor Sayers and Attorney General T. S. Smith on behalf of the oil company, assured them it had severed its ties with Standard Oil, and received their promise of a new charter for Waters-Pierce. Bailey returned to Austin in June to see the Democratic state convention write his views on "colonialism" into the platform and send a majority of Bailey men as delegates to the national convention.[14]

Hogg and several friends had been campaigning that spring for constitutional amendments to require the termination of insolvent corporations, and to prohibit free passes on railroads and the use of corporation money in elections. When he learned that Waters-Pierce had received a new license, Hogg denounced the decision before the Texas Bar Association in July. Bailey defended himelf in the August state convention. After considerable debate, generally between the Hogg and Bailey factions, the convention took no action on the issue. Hogg then tried to speak in favor of the constitutional amendments but was drowned out by jeers. Stubbornly he shouted down the majority and on the strength of the personal respect felt for him won inclusion of his proposals in the platform, though most House men opposed them as unnecessary or wished to water them down. Aside from this Hogg inning the House-Bailey coalition had controlled both state conventions, electing R. M. Johnston, editor of the *Houston Post,* national committeeman and Jim Wells chairman of the state

[13] Acheson, *Bailey*, pp. 125–126; Cotner, *Hogg*, pp. 484–485, 497–499.

[14] Acheson, *Bailey*, pp. 139–145; Holcomb, "Bailey," pp. 191–222.

executive committee. Efforts after the August convention to call new county conventions and reinstruct legislators for someone other than Bailey for United States senator made little headway.[15]

When the Legislature met in January 1901 David McFall of Travis County, a Hogg man, moved for an investigation of the relicensing of the Waters-Pierce Oil Company to determine whether Bailey's relationship thereto disqualified him for a Senate seat. The investigating committee, controlled by Bailey men, read McFall's charges of use of undue influence and a sham dissolution by the corporation, heard Bailey and Smith again defend their actions, and ruled in Bailey's favor. The Legislature accepted the report by 87 votes to 23, an overwhelming majority, but not the unanimous vindication the Bailey forces had made intimidating efforts to secure. Bailey then won election to the Senate almost unanimously, 137 votes to 4, with fifteen members not voting. Later in the session the Legislature politely heard Hogg advocate the amendments written into the Democratic state platform; but railroad and business interests led by B. B. Paddock of Fort Worth, a former leader of the Clark-gold Democrats, lobbied successfully against them.[16]

The trend in Texas politics toward government regulation had slowed in the late 1890's. It reflected in part changes in the state's economy as well as rising farm prices. Manufacturing establishments in Texas increased from 2,996 in 1880 to 12,289 in 1900. In East Texas the lumbering industry had developed to maturity by 1900 and reached peak output in 1907. Oil production began on a permanent basis in the 1890's with the discovery of the Corsicana field and, after the Spindletop gusher in 1901, developed into the state's major industry in the first half of the twentieth century. Several political figures who had gained office and acclaim as advocates of agricultural

[15] Cotner, *Hogg*, pp. 490–511; T. M. Campbell to R. W. Hudson, May 5, 1900, R. W. Hudson Papers; J. D. Sayers to E. M. House, August 14, 1900, House Papers; W. W. Cammack to J. W. Bailey, August 25, 1900, Bailey Papers; Richardson, *House*, pp. 167–170.

[16] Henry Moore to J. W. Bailey, July 26, 1900, Bailey Papers; B. B. Paddock to V. W. Grubbs, January 23, February 4, 1901, Buckley B. Paddock Papers; Acheson, *Bailey*, pp. 148–151; Cotner, *Hogg*, pp. 512–517; Tom Connally and Alfred Steinberg, *My Name is Tom Connally*, pp. 47–48.

reforms now acquired business connections which affected their view of public interest and government action.

Joseph Bailey became a close friend and attorney for Pierce and also for John Henry Kirby, a lumber magnate and the organizer, with eastern financial aid, of the Houston Oil Company. Bailey then took part in intricate dealings which tended to limit competition between the Waters-Pierce and Houston oil companies. James S. Hogg became a partner in the Hogg-Swayne Oil Syndicate, which required financing not available in Texas, and turned to Andrew Mellon of Pittsburgh, a competitor of Standard Oil. Hogg apparently lost no zeal for reform as a result of his new associations, but he did become, perhaps inadvertently, a stumbling block to conservation by suggesting the sale of tiny tracts, or "doormats," for drilling, a practice which led to overproduction and rapid depletion of the state's resources. Hogg and other political figures also seemed oblivious to the extensive dealings in fraudulent stocks that brought Spindletop the nickname "Swindletop." His attacks on corporate influence in politics did lose some of their force when opponents reminded the public that Hogg had been a railroad attorney after his governorship, adding that "he who has done these things should not . . . accuse men who have done no more."[17]

On the occasion of a trip to Texas by the New York Merchants' Association, B. B. Paddock, who had promoted the venture, urged David B. Hill, an eastern conservative presidential hopeful, to accompany the group in order to help bring Texas Democrats "into line on democratic principles and traditions." Paddock boasted that the Legislature "showed its liberality to corporations" by passage of a bill allowing the Houston and Texas Central and the International and Great Northern railroads to consolidate with branch lines, though such action tended to eliminate competition. Although the New Yorkers found public opinion in Texas less suspicious of business

[17] *State Topics*, October 23, 1904; John S. Spratt, *The Road to Spindletop*, pp. 257–260, 272–276; U.S., Census Bureau, *Abstract of the Twelfth Census of the United States, 1900*, p. 333; John O. King, *The Early History of the Houston Oil Company of Texas, 1901–1908*, pp. 73–76; Cotner, *Hogg*, pp. 518–555; Gerald Forbes, *Flush Production*, pp. 19–20, 42–43, 88.

than it had been a short time before, they were still apprehensive over the rate-making power of the Railroad Commission and detected some "prejudiced" or "ignorant" views among legislators. Yet the representative of a cattle and land company asserted: "It is astonishing how much you can do with the legislature if you go about it in the right way. Of course, it takes time and money, but if the object you are after is important enough to warrant the expenditure of time and trouble you can usually accomplish your object." Actually legislative membership had shifted since the mid-1890's from about half farmers and half attorneys and businessmen to a two-thirds majority of the latter.[18]

The visitors correctly assumed that a more favorable atmosphere existed in the state government toward business, for House and his friends who organized and financed so many campaigns were basically business oriented. House, Wells, Andrews, T. W. Gregory, D. F. Houston, and Jonathan Lane stayed with the Democratic party to retain their influence, but they believed in the gold standard in the 1890's. House, Wells, Andrews, Lane, R. H. Baker, E. P. Hill, B. F. Yoakum, and Sayers all held stock in or acted as attorneys for railroads. Lane and T. W. House were bankers. L. L. Foster served as vice-president of the Velasco Terminal Company. Bailey's close friend Jot Gunter was a real estate investor and rancher. The president of the Missouri, Kansas and Texas Railroad recommended Railroad Commissioner Allison Mayfield for the Interstate Commerce Commission. And House, Sayers, and Joe Lee Jameson also dabbled in oil.[19]

[18] B. B. Paddock to David B. Hill, February 6, 1901, Paddock to George D. Cook, March 7, 1901, Paddock Papers; Tenney, "Sayers," pp. 109–112; Merchants' Association of New York, *The Natural Resources and Economic Conditions of the State of Texas*, pp. 107–108, 141–142; Gene M. Gressley, *Bankers and Cattlemen*, pp. 214–215; Texas, Legislature, House, *Rules of Order of the House of Representatives of the Twenty-third Legislature*; *Texas Legislative Manual for 1901*.

[19] H. C. Rouse to E. M. House, October 4, 1900, House to J. D. Sayers, May 30, 1904, House Papers; J. B. Wells to N. A. Stedman, January 27, 1902, Wells Papers; Tenney, "Sayers," p. 123; W. P. Webb and H. Bailey Carroll, eds., *Handbook of Texas*, I, 748; II, 24, 878, 945; Richardson, *House*, pp. 110, 194, 199–229.

House did not, of course, head a formal organization or a political machine; the forces he marshaled and the candidates he managed varied from year to year. His alliance with Bailey rested on expediency. The able political manager preferred not to oppose the popular politician, who held reciprocal views. But by keeping down antagonisms or conflicts as much as possible and by influencing the distribution of state patronage House maintained an inner group whose wide contacts and skill as organizers made them virtually indispensable and gave them considerable power. He used with great success early primaries in counties favorable to his candidates to create an early lead in convention delegates and to stimulate others to climb aboard the bandwagon. House suggested the role of himself and his associates when he remarked to Andrews in October 1901, "While the 'Old Man' [Sayers] has come very near running amuck several times yet in the end we have managed by one way or another to make him do about what we wanted." House exerted his influence at times on the progressive side but on other occasions worked against reform proposals such as the Hogg amendments and progressive candidates such as Crane.[20]

Already in 1901 House cast about for his next gubernatorial candidate. Supreme Court Justice T. J. Brown, his first choice, declined. House considered T. H. Ball, but Culberson disapproved. House feared that Wells might wish to run or that Bailey might press him to do so, in which case Wells's being a Roman Catholic would present difficulties. Finally, in September, House offered his valuable support to Congressman S. W. T. Lanham, "an upright man of fluent speech but limited ability." A former Confederate soldier, Lanham sought the office as a last honor in a long public career. But he had become nervous, sensitive, and often ill in his old age. House picked Lanham because "we could commit him to any line of policy that we thought best."[21] Lanham made W. P. McLean of Fort Worth his campaign manager, but he proved inefficient and House himself ar-

[20] James A. Tinsley, ed., *Letters from the Colonel*, p. 17; R. H. Baker to J. B. Wells, June 12, 1901, Wells Papers; Richardson, *House*, pp. 302–317.

[21] Richardson, *House*, pp. 176–181; Hugh Nugent Fitzgerald, *Governors I Have Known*, pp. 23–24.

ranged for most of the fund raising and publicity. Lanham's only visible rival appeared to be Thomas M. Campbell, a Palestine attorney and a strong supporter of Hogg and Crane in the 1890's, who had been speaking widely as an obvious if unannounced candidate. But he withdrew in January, after an interview with Lanham who expressed his determination to run and mentioned House's blessings. The outcome of several midwinter local primaries held before the campaign had actually begun also influenced Campbell's decision. In a parting blast he denounced both the practice of premature primaries and the dominant political "machine" of the state. With Campbell out House had to do little except approve Lanham's mild speeches calling for abolition of free passes on the railroads, better roads, a better tax system, and conservation of natural resources. House confided to Congressman Burleson that "we could *never stand another such administration* [as Sayers's] and go before the people with any hope of success," and suggested an administration with measures to benefit the people "particularly in a material and economical way." A few weeks later he noted that "Colonel Lanham's speech has been well received. The people want no disturbance just at this time and that is why they like it. He has managed to say nothing in a most convincing and masterly way and the people are pleased."[22]

In 1902 House men offered the Democratic state convention a platform opposing the spoils system and favoring better roads, schools, and colleges, popular election of United States senators, regulation of party primaries, and a "broad and enlightened policy toward capital and corporations." Campbell led a successful move to include a specific plank against the labor of children under twelve years of age. House men received all key positions, among them chairmanship of the state executive committee which went to Wells after something of a contest with Joseph E. Cockrell of Dallas, who won the backing of Blake and Hogg. In congressional races the House "crowd" helped especially to renominate J. L. Slayden of San An-

[22] E. M. House to Albert Burleson, January 26, April 12, 1902, Albert Sidney Burleson Papers; *Galveston Daily News,* January 20, 26, 1902; Richardson, *House,* pp. 181–185.

tonio and R. L. Henry of Waco. Because of weak opposition in the state races that fall, House men concentrated their campaign efforts and funds on the election to Congress of John Nance Garner, a South Texas political ally of Wells, who had worked hard in the Legislature to create a district for himself during the reapportionment of 1901.[23]

The election of T. A. Low, a lumberman, as state representative in November 1902 brought from the *Southern Industrial and Lumber Review of Houston* the comment that "if the practical brains of the country could be induced to give the state the benefit of their services in the legislature for two or three months out of every two years, it would be the best piece of business they could transact during the period, and the country at large would be benefited by sensible and business like laws."[24] A majority of the Legislature and the new administration probably held similar views. The legislators revised the state's antitrust law, despite protests and petitions in opposition, to include labor and agricultural organizations because some believed recent court decisions required it. Later decisions proved them wrong, but Attorney General C. K. Bell soon invoked the law against San Antonio unions in July 1903. The Legislature passed the first, although weak, laws against child labor and the blacklisting of employees. In addition it adopted the first Terrell election law to end voting frauds and to set up binding statewide nominating primaries, which also allowed the exclusion of Negro voters. Federal legislation of a progressive nature also remained limited in the early 1900's, though a majority of the Texas congressmen did support the Newlands Act to provide for federal reclamation projects, a bill to create a department of commerce, and the Elkins Act, which forbade railroad rebates to large companies.[25]

[23] Richardson, *House*, pp. 185–192; Bascom N. Timmons, *Garner of Texas*, pp. 26–31.

[24] *Southern Industrial and Lumber Review* (Houston) 10, no. 4 (November 1902): 19.

[25] Ruby Lee Martin, "The Administration of Governor S. W. T. Lanham, 1903–1907" (M.A. thesis), pp. 32–74; Connally and Steinberg, *Connally*, p. 51; Richardson, *House*, pp. 192–193; Maxwell, "The Pines of Texas," p. 82; U.S., Congress, *Congressional Record*, 57th Cong., 1st sess., p. 6777; 2nd sess., pp. 2008, 2159; *Dallas Morning News*, July 2, 1903.

In the spring of 1904 House and Burleson decided to support Judge Alton B. Parker of New York for the Democratic presidential nomination in preference to William Randolph Hearst, the young journalist, as a means of keeping in check the Hogg men who still favored William Jennings Bryan. Culberson held back, preferring an uninstructed delegation until Parker clarified his views. The state convention, controlled by the House-Bailey coalition, sent a Parker delegation to the national convention. Bailey led efforts in the national convention to compromise between Bryan and the eastern wing of the party, an effort that resulted in a platform making no mention of the dying issue of silver or gold. After Parker's nomination, Burleson, Bailey, and Culberson campaigned for him. House considered but refused a place on the campaign staff. Hogg and many of his old followers, strongly disapproving of Parker as a former "goldbug," felt that "the Democratic party has nestled up as close to the Republican party as possible." Hogg declined an offer of a cabinet post in return for his support, and later denounced Parker while praising Theodore Roosevelt's opposition to trusts. Hogg also spoke out in favor of corporate regulation, similar to the later Clayton Anti-Trust Act, and for a state board of arbitration for labor disputes. When Governor Jeff Davis of Arkansas and Bailey brought the race issue into Texas politics, Hogg criticized such comments. He proved a good judge of national politics, for Roosevelt crushed Parker easily in the fall election.[26]

Before the Democratic nominating convention for state officers met, House made plans to keep his hands on the controls by having Frank Andrews follow Wells as chairman of the state executive committee. Burleson and Bailey opposed the move as politically unwise, because Andrews served as an attorney for the Southern Pacific Railroad. Jeff McLemore, secretary of the state executive committee, warned that it was "a woeful blunder" opening the way "for

[26] John M. Duncan to J. S. Hogg, July 15, 1904, Letters Received, XXXV, James Stephen Hogg Papers; A. S. Burleson to E. M. House, April 8, 1904, House Papers; House to Burleson, June 4, [1904], Crawfordsville, Indiana *Daily News-Review*, October 21, 1904, Burleson Papers; Richardson, *House*, pp. 235–239; Acheson, *Bailey*, p. 170; Cotner, *Hogg*, pp. 557–563.

beginning another anti-corporation crusade." House's close political friends and allies accepted his decision, however, and Andrews won easily over Ben E. Cabell of Dallas and W. L. Radney of Waco. The convention also adopted a platform plank favoring repeal of occupation taxes, advocated by the Federation of Business Organizations of Texas.[27]

McLemore proved an accurate judge of public opinion, for a progressive tide began to rise again in the last years of the Lanham administration. At the same time the loose House-Bailey coalition which had dominated Texas politics for eight years began to weaken. House had talked of growing weary of the game as early as 1899 and refused to run for governor in 1902 with the comment, "In an indirect way I have enjoyed the power of the office sufficiently long for that not to become an object with me." Upon the death in May 1904 of Jameson, his "political right hand," he apparently determined to retire from the field undefeated. His decision may have been influenced also by the limitations placed upon campaign manipulation by the new election law.[28]

Bailey maintained his personal prestige until Attorney General R. V. Davidson and his assistant Jewel P. Lightfoot began a new investigation of the Waters-Pierce Oil Company and its possible connections with Standard Oil. Bailey heard rumors about such activities but denied any wrongdoing and refused to buy supposedly incriminating papers which were offered him. He also failed to take the advice of J. H. Kirby, who suggested he file an antitrust complaint against Waters-Pierce and thus avoid political repercussions. Then in July 1906 D. G. Phillips published a muckraking article in *Cosmopolitan* magazine on the business connections of Senate leaders, including Bailey's dealings with Pierce and Kirby. Bailey denounced the article in the Senate and in Texas as politically instigated by William Randolph Hearst, publisher of the magazine and a possible future candidate for the Democratic presidential nomination.

[27] *State Topics* (Austin), November 13, 1904; S. L. Erwin and others to James Wells, April 20, 1904, Wells Papers; Richardson, *House*, pp. 194–196.

[28] Richardson, *House*, pp. 197–198, 242–251, 271–301; E. M. House to A. S. Burleson, July 22, 1900, Burleson Papers.

In Missouri at about the same time an antitrust suit against Pierce brought out Bailey's business relationship with the oil man, and opposition to Bailey immediately took shape in Texas. Bailey again retorted that he had nothing to hide. But Davidson and Lightfoot brought suit against Waters-Pierce, intimating that political influence had been involved in the relicensing. Bailey offered to provide limited assistance to Davidson, who refused because of the potential restraint upon the investigation, saying that he would prove allegations that had been made. M. M. Crane then debated Bailey on the propriety of a senator's representing corporations subject to government regulation. Bailey replied in bitter and personal terms. When Davidson introduced into evidence damaging papers originally stolen from Pierce's files, Bailey exchanged heated words with the attorney general, and an increasing number of Texans believed him guilty of some wrongdoing. Crane and other anti-Bailey men tried to bring out progressive governor-elect T. M. Campbell as an opponent, in a move aimed at repeating Coke's rapid elections as governor and then senator in 1876. But Campbell apparently accepted the advice of other friends to serve out his terms and then seek a Senate seat rather than face the combined opposition of Bailey men and the supporters of his recently defeated gubernatorial adversaries. Several political leaders, among them G. A. Carden, chairman of the state Democratic executive committee, R. M. Johnston, state Democratic national committeeman, and Congressman S. B. Cooper, rallied to Bailey's defense.

In the legislative investigation that followed, Hogg progressives led the opposition and acted as prosecutors. Numerous witnesses appeared, including J. P. Gruett, Sr., who had stolen the papers from Pierce, and David Francis, who originally had brought Bailey and Pierce together in business matters. Pierce, who was under antitrust indictment at the time did not appear. To Kirby it seemed that "the Socialists have now captured the Democratic Party and Bailey is very much in their way, therefore they seek to destroy him." Only two days after the investigation had begun, however, the Legislature, acting on the results of Bailey's unopposed primary victory, reelected him by a vote of 108 to 39. The state senate then took the investigation out of the hands of its committee, which Bailey supporters felt

The Texas Ventriloquist.
Southern Mercury (Dallas) and *Farmer's Union Passward*, March 3, 1907

was stacked against him, and voted for complete exoneration. The house by 70 votes to 40 adopted the majority report of its committee, which also exonerated him; but the minority report of the committee more accurately held that Bailey, while guilty of nothing illegal, acted in a fashion inconsistent with public policy and failed in candor to the people of Texas. Bailey appeared before the house to castigate the minority as traitors to the Democratic party and swear vengeance on them.[29] Yet the affair had involved primarily questions of personal

[29] J. H. Kirby to J. W. Bailey, July 19, 1905, Bailey to Kirby, August 7, 1905, Kirby to Tom Richardson, October 13, 1906, John Henry Kirby Papers; M. M.

conduct, though fought out in part on a partisan factional level, for the Legislature which exonerated Bailey had been elected in the midst of a growing revival of progressivism.

The Texas trend toward conservatism matched similar shifts throughout the South in the late 1890's as Populists drained off the strength of the Democratic agrarian wing and then collapsed, though the trend lasted slightly longer under the guiding hand of House than in some other states. Like its counterparts the new Texas conservatism did not represent a return to post-Reconstruction politics. Instead House and Bailey combined degrees of reform sentiment with strong ties to new industrial and business interests, especially oil companies. Rather than stand by the gold standard and oppose railroad and business regulation which meant sure defeat, they espoused silver despite some doubts, sought moderate regulation that would not injure railroads or oil companies, and fought further increases in business taxes. Six relatively conservative state administrations and control of both Senate seats, several places in Congress, and numerous lesser state offices attested to their success. They guided the reform movement of the 1890's into paths acceptable to themselves rather than risk open but futile opposition to its general course. But it began to burst the bounds they set for it almost from the moment they gained control.

Crane to T. M. Campbell, January 1, 1906 [1907], R. W. Robertson to Campbell, December 28, 1906, Thomas M. Campbell Papers in possession of William Campbell, Sewanee, Tennessee; Acheson, *Bailey*, pp. 211–240. For more detailed reviews of the case see: Frederick U. Adams, *The Waters-Pierce Case in Texas*; William A. Cocke, *The Bailey Controversy in Texas*; Holcomb, "Bailey," pp. 357–449.

15. THE REVIVAL OF PROGRESSIVISM

AFTER A STEADY DECLINE following the Hogg administrations of the early 1890's, progressivism began to revive as a powerful factor in Texas politics by 1904. The creation of several new organizations helped increase awareness of specific problems and at the same time provided pressure groups to work for amelioration. The State Federation of Labor held its first meeting in 1898 and grew to include 158 unions with 9,171 members by 1906. Its fourth convention, in 1902, established a labor legislative committee, with members from the federation and from the four railway unions, to lobby against child labor, the poll tax, and the use of convict labor in competition with free labor; the committee favored compulsory school attendance, free textbooks, a postal savings bank, and better working conditions and hours. The federation also cooperated actively with the younger but stronger Farmers' Union.[1]

In 1902, at a time when tenants formed almost 50 per cent of Texas

[1] Ruth A. Allen, *Chapters in the History of Organized Labor in Texas*, pp. 123–144, 152.

farm operators, ten of them—three Populists, one Socialist, one Independent, and five Democrats led by Newt Gresham—in Northeast Texas organized the Farmers' Union. It began as a marketing and fraternal group similar to the Farmers' Alliance. Despite internal struggles over leadership and involvement in politics the new movement spread rapidly across Texas and into the surrounding states. By 1906 it claimed 100,000 members and had entered into cooperation with the State Federation of Labor, developed a legislative program, and sent a legislative committee to lobby in the state capital.[2]

At Waco, in 1897, 21 local groups organized the Texas Federation of Women's Clubs. By 1903 it claimed 232 clubs with over five thousand members, including the wives of several prominent politicians. The women took strong stands in favor of a state industrial school for girls; better schools, kindergartens, sanitation, and libraries on the local level; an end to child labor; pure food and drug laws; juvenile courts; and an improved legal position for women in Texas. Although they refused to lobby directly in Austin, the women became "a great, silent force for the enactment and enforcement of good laws" through their male relatives. Women also began to organize local kindergartens in the late 1890's and mothers' clubs in 1902, which eventually resulted in the creation of the Congress of Mothers and Parent-Teacher Associations in 1909.[3]

The Texas Local Option Association represented another new movement with old ties. This prohibitionist group developed in 1903 when calls for a statewide organization by the Grayson County Prohibition executive committee and by Judge C. H. Jenkins of Brownwood, a former Populist, led to meetings at Dallas in October and November. The association found its greatest strength in rural areas, but included an increasing number of teachers, businessmen, and

[2] Samuel Lee Evans, "Texas Agriculture, 1880–1930" (Ph.D. diss.), pp. 311, 319; Robert Lee Hunt, *A History of Farmer Movements in the Southwest, 1873–1925*, pp. 41–84; Charles Simon Barrett, *The Mission, History and Times of the Farmers' Union*, pp. 103–106, 196–202; William P. Tucker, "Populism Up-to-Date," *Agricultural History* 21 (October 1947): 198–208.

[3] Stella L. Christian, *The History of the Texas Federation of Women's Clubs*, pp. 21, 23, 37, 44–46, 49, 55, 81–82, 88, 91, 101, 134–136, 168; Frederick Eby, *The Development of Education in Texas*, pp. 231–236.

professional people. It interested itself in establishing or encouraging local-option campaigns. In 1904 members of the association helped defeat an effort to have the Democratic platform endorse a bill that would have weakened the state's local-option law. Prohibitionist groups also concerned themselves with other issues, for WCTU chapters petitioned Texas congressmen and senators with regard to the problems of labor and agriculture, as well as moral questions of interstate gambling, cigarette sales, prizefights, divorce, and Sunday rest laws.

Alarmed by the prohibitionist revival, the Texas Brewers' Association began in 1903 to assess its members "for the purpose of promoting anti-prohibition matters in Texas." It used part of the money raised to recruit wet voters by paying their poll taxes, part to influence legislation. As the wet-dry conflict grew in intensity, each side anxiously sought to commit candidates to its views. G. C. Rankin, a leading prohibitionist, described the struggle and its effect on politics from his Anglo evangelical point of view. In South Texas

> there is a large mixture of foreign peoples, and the effect upon the customs and usages of the people is marked . . . In North Texas it is vastly different. The population is largely native, and American ideas and customs more largely prevail . . . Protestant Christianity, the public schools and the English language have the right of way. Moral sentiment is in the ascendancy and the saloons have but little influence in politics and social life [illegible] the rural districts are more populated. The cities and the towns do not so much have their way, and the country ideas of morals more than offset the tendency of the city and the town toward vice and the lax enforcement of law. The man who stands for public office in North Texas does not ignore the rural vote, but he respects it very highly.

Clearly ethnic and religious sentiment continued to exercise a strong influence on many persons' views of prohibition and, because of the overlap between prohibitionists and supporters of many progressive ideas, on their views of such proposals. Yet prohibition also served as an important link between the somewhat divergent interests and views of growing urban middle-class progressives and old-line rural reformers. Among these groups only labor took a generally anti-prohibition stand.

Former Congressman Walter Gresham, who represented the brewers in legal matters, expressed fear in May 1905 that "unless there is a bold and aggressive campaign made, Rankin, Davis, and other extreme Prohibitionists will capture the democratic party." The brewers began to pick up as political allies some private bankers, railroad officials, and other corporate businessmen who worried about the effect of new regulatory and tax laws.[4]

Middle-class local businessmen led other phases of the progressive movement, however, aimed at creating more efficient local governments and new services which would benefit business. After the Galveston hurricane in 1900 a businessmen's group for harbor improvement known as the Galveston Deepwater Committee assumed responsibility for developing an effective city government, based on corporate organization, to rebuild the city quickly. Five commissioners heading separate departments and acting together on broader questions replaced an aldermanic system. Similar groups helped bring the commission system to Houston in 1903, to Dallas, Fort Worth, Denison, El Paso, Greenville, and Sherman by 1907, and to other cities across the nation. Behind such developments in some cases lay lengthy factional fights for leadership among local political groups, though they publicly revolved around questions of open gambling and prostitution, public water facilities, and street paving. Commissions which often brought more efficiency and new services to the public frequently resulted, however, in business domination through appointed commissioners or middle-class electorates where

[4] G. C. Rankin, *The Story of My Life*, pp. 334–335; Walter Gresham to George C. Pendleton, May 5, 1905, July 18, 1904, Baker, Botts, Parker & Garwood to Pendleton, December 23, 1905, Alexander Dienst Collection; S. E. Kennedy and others to "Dear Sir," March 17, 1903, William B. Teagarden Papers; H. A. Ivy, *Rum on the Run in Texas*, pp. 55–58; Anti-Saloon League, *The Brewers and Texas Politics*, I, 15, 216–253, 321–418, 511–543; *Southern Industrial and Lumber Review* (Houston) 12, no. 7 (February 1905): 12; U.S., Congress, *Congressional Record*, 54th Cong., 2nd sess., pp. 1717, 1788, 55th Cong., 2nd sess., pp. 716, 1755, 1953–1954.

city poll taxes had been used to eliminate poor voters, especially Mexicans and Negroes. Businessmen also organized local groups that eventually came together in 1903 to create the Federated Commercial Clubs of Texas. They addressed themselves primarily to the development of business and industry, but devoted some time to the support of kindergartens and other public facilities in conjunction with local groups, such as the Civic Improvement League of Dallas. A Good Roads Association of Texas sprang up, too, at the turn of the century under business leadership to coordinate local efforts toward a goal acceptable to farmers and merchants alike.[5]

Professional groups exhibited an increasing interest in specific reforms related to their interests. The Texas Bankers Association strongly endorsed the chartering of state banks, which had been ruled illegal under the constitution of 1876. Hogg had proposed such a change in 1893, but the voters did not open the way with a constitutional amendment until 1904. Members of the Texas State Medical Association had sporadically and unsuccessfully advocated a state board of health and a state board of medical examiners since the 1870's. They stepped up those efforts and also expressed interest in a pure food and drug law after a reorganization in 1903 tied them more closely to the American Medical Association. Their efforts, however, also represented the desires for dominance by some medical schools and branches of the profession who hoped to control such boards. Members of the Texas Bar Association sought a uniform law on the licensing of attorneys and presented papers at their annual meetings on tax reform and corporate land ownership.[6]

Early strains of progressivism appeared in the state Democratic platform of 1904, which called for just rendition of corporate prop-

[5] James Weinstein, "Organized Business and the City Commission and Manager Movements," *Journal of Southern History* 28 (May 1962): 166–182; Harold A. Stone et al., *City Manager Government in Nine Cities*, pp. 270–271, 415; C. L. Sonnichsen, *Pass of the North*, pp. 345–379; Frank H. Bushick, *Glamorous Days*, pp. 69–90; Ralph W. Steen, *Twentieth Century Texas*, pp. 83–84, 126; *Dallas Morning News*, March 13, June 2, July 10, 1903.

[6] Avery L. Carlson, *Monetary and Banking History of Texas*, pp. 49–61; Pat Ireland Nixon, *A History of the Texas Medical Association, 1853–1953*, pp. 64, 71, 222–223, 253–258; *Dallas Morning News*, July 14, 1904, July 13, 1905.

erty for taxes and a law to allow cities to regulate electricity, gas, telephone, and water companies. The movement began to show results in the elections of 1904. M. L. Broocks defeated S. B. Cooper for a congressional seat by capitalizing on the widespread belief that "Cooper is nothing but a tool for J. H. Kirby and his republican corporations." R. V. Davidson, who became attorney general, invigorated the enforcement of the state's antitrust laws. The Legislature considered a variety of reform measures, many of them proposed by Thomas B. Love of Dallas, an energetic young attorney who had come from Missouri in 1899. The *Dallas News* responded with an editorial headed "When in Doubt, Don't." Improvement might be possible and even necessary but "We are doing fairly well in Texas, and common sense and conservatism should guide those who set about to make any material changes." Later the *News* warned against "measures which are . . . radical and revolutionary . . ." Under the pressure of petitions from the heavily populated farming regions and urban areas of North and East Texas, the legislative session of 1905 raised taxes on the intangible assets of corporations, a measure that had failed two years earlier; enacted a tax of 1 per cent on the gross receipts of railroads, proposed by Love; established a tax of 2 per cent on the gross receipts of insurance companies; and created franchise taxes on the stock and profits of corporations. It did not adopt additional corporate taxes suggested by Love. Then in a special session it temporarily increased the ad valorem tax to 20¢ on $100 for 1905–1906, with the provision that it should be 16 2/3¢ thereafter. Legislators raised the gross receipts tax to 2.25 per cent on life insurance companies and to 1.75 per cent on other insurance companies, with a clause reducing the rate in each case to 0.5 per cent if the company invested 25 per cent of its assets in Texas. The new taxes marked a notable step toward better distribution of the tax burden, which had long rested heavily on farmers and other landowners while corporations of comparatively great wealth went virtually untaxed. Finally the Legislature passed a bill that authorized the chartering of state banks.[7]

[7] S. B. Cooper to J. H. Kirby, January 16, June 5, 1904, John Henry Kirby Papers; *Dallas Morning News*, January 22, February 3, 1905; Tom Finty, Jr.,

Bills that Love and a good many other legislators wanted but could not pass, in some cases because of active lobbying against them, would have raised liquor license fees to a prohibitive rate, prevented usurious interest rates on loans to workingmen, placed a punitive occupation tax on persons purchasing the assignment of wages not yet earned, protected household furniture from seizure for debts, created a state pure food and drug law, and allowed the regulation of private banks. Business and industrial interests that had opposed the new antitrust suits and the tax increases felt uneasy about the probable renewal of the unsuccessful progressive proposals and began to look with some apprehension to the next gubernatorial campaign.[8]

The Terrell election law, another progressive measure, brought marked changes in Texas politics. A. W. Terrell had first offered a bill to regulate primaries and elections in 1903. It called for uniform party nominating primaries or conventions to end the practice of "midwinter" primaries that had been used against Crane and Campbell; official ballots for each party to eliminate the mixed or inaccurate ballots used to influence the course of past elections; and the payment of poll taxes between October and February to ensure that only interested independent voters participated. The bill went on to spell out safeguards against frauds of various types that had become common during the heated elections of the 1890's when many voters had followed the admonition to "come early and vote often." After 50 amendments in the house and 101 in the senate the bill had passed into law with backing similar to that given the poll tax.

In 1905 Terrell returned to the Legislature to amend his own law to allow the names of independent candidates on the ballots, to provide for poll watchers and election judges from different parties, and

---

Anti-Trust Legislation in Texas, pp. 49, 63–65; Donna Lee Younker, "Thomas B. Love's Service in the Texas Legislature and in State Government during the Lanham and Campbell Administrations" (M.A. thesis), pp. 1–52; Ruby Lee Martin, "The Administration of Governor S. W. T. Lanham" (M.A. thesis), pp. 94–106; Texas, Legislature, House, *Journal*, 29th Legislature, Reg. sess., pp. 398, 462, 514, 710, 1003–1004; Texas, Legislature, Senate, *Journal*, 29th Legislature, Reg. sess., pp. 320, 690, 833.

[8] Younker, "Love," pp. 48–52; *Southern Industrial and Lumber Review* (Houston) 12, no. 8 (March 1905): 11.

to make the uniform primary mandatory instead of optional for each county. Various delaying tactics led Terrell to accuse Speaker F. W. Seabury, a Jim Wells man from the Rio Grande Valley, of using his position to oppose the bill. Seabury denied the charge and professed support for the bill, which passed the Legislature. Because the bill was incorrectly copied, however, Lanham had to call a special session in 1906 to put it in force.

The electoral system that resulted from the Terrell law included a poll tax and condoned the white primary but produced real improvement in other aspects over previous practices. The key provision—the uniform primary to choose all precinct, county, district, and state officers—became mandatory for parties that polled at least 100,000 votes in the state election. District and state conventions would still be held to ballot on candidates in the event that none received a majority in the primary. After each ballot the candidate with the lowest vote would be eliminated until a nominee was selected. As a result any man who possessed political appeal, ambition, and financial backing could move ahead in the Democratic party without the blessings of established leaders or a party organization. Yet the mandatory primary system placed a financial and administrative burden on small opposition parties, which retarded their growth and perpetuated the developing one-party system. The first opportunity to test the new electoral system would come in 1906.[9]

In the early spring of 1905 Railroad Commissioner O. B. Colquitt wrote a friend that he expected to be the next governor. He then toured North Texas and announced his candidacy on April 22, 1905. M. M. Brooks, judge of the court of criminal appeals, had already announced, and Thomas M. Campbell and former Attorney General C. K. Bell obviously planned to enter the race. The four candidates presented their views at a nonpartisan banquet in Dallas on November 6.

[9] Charles K. Chamberlain, "Alexander Watkins Terrell" (Ph.D. diss.), pp. 455–501; Abner V. McCall, "History of Texas Election Laws," in *Vernon's Annotated Revised Civil Statutes of Texas,* IX, xxii-xxiv; O. Douglas Weeks, "The Direct Primary System," *Southwestern Social Science Quarterly* 13 (September 1932): 95–120.

Bell favored equal taxes and opposed free railroad passes to government officials. He felt that the state's educational, eleemosynary, and penal institutions were in good condition and called the antitrust laws more advanced than those of most states. He believed a constitutional amendment was necessary to tax intangible assets, and doubted corruption in the state government, though he favored an investigation.

Brooks opposed lobbying, railroad consolidation, corporate domination of state affairs, free passes, and occupation taxes. He favored economy, the existing local-option law, and high liquor taxes. He hoped to see reform of the penal system, employment of short-term convicts in work on highways, a blanket primary for both state and local candidates, and a requirement that insurance companies invest 75 per cent of their reserves in Texas.

Campbell opposed corporate control of the state, machine politics, graft, free passes, and railroad consolidation. He proposed the establishment of a state department of agriculture, better pay for teachers, and abolition of the convict lease system. He also urged equalization of property taxes, reduction of the ad valorem tax, a graduated federal income tax, and an increase in the tax on railroad income from 1 per cent to 2 per cent.

Colquitt favored a balanced budget, abolition of certain state offices, exemption of land and personal property from state taxation, taxes on inheritances and corporate stock, and an end to occupation taxes. He noted that the Texas tax level remained the fourth lowest among the states, while corporate power continued to grow and required regulation. Like everyone else he opposed free passes.[10]

In the race that followed, Bell received support from most of the Lanham administration and various other of House's associates, though House himself never took part in the campaign. Bell's strength lay in the vicinity around Fort Worth, his home town, in Jim Wells's domain along the Rio Grande, and among businessmen, especially brewers, since he opposed statewide prohibition. At the end of May 1906 he thought himself ahead: "I do not believe that there is gen-

[10] *Dallas Morning News*, November 7, 1905; George P. Huckaby, "Oscar Branch Colquitt" (Ph.D. diss.), pp. 136–146.

erally a well-settled conviction with reference to the race at this time. People are so prosperous and so busy they are not taking the time to consider political issues."[11]

Brooks, a prohibitionist from North Texas, had the support of Senators Bailey and Culberson. As the oldest of the candidates, he seemed the least likely to become an aspirant for one of their Senate seats.

The handsome, genial Campbell, an East Texas prohibitionist, felt the problem was "a moral question, rather than political." His campaign paper, the *Bagpipe*, carried a front-page photograph of a letter written by Hogg before his death in March 1906 in which he announced himself "unequivocally for Tom Campbell for Governor." Campbell worked through former supporters of Hogg and developed backing among teachers, professional people, workingmen, and small farmers.[12] And at a Prohibition party executive committee meeting, former Populist leader "Cyclone" Davis exhorted his fellow prohibitionists to return to the Democratic party in support of Campbell, "because I think he is the nearest approach to old-time Populism that is now before the country; because he represents the Jim Hogg and Bryan Democracy of Texas."[13]

The stocky, dark-complexioned Colquitt, also a former Hogg man but an antiprohibitionist from North Central Texas, developed support among Texas Germans, saloon owners, and businessmen, while retaining some labor and farmer backing in North Texas. He appeared to be fond of controversy, entering into exchanges and debates with J. F. Wolters, attorney for the Wholesale Liquor Dealers'

[11] C. K. Bell to A. S. Burleson, May 31, 1906, Albert Sidney Burleson Papers; Bell to E. M. House, February 6, 1906, S. W. T. Lanham to House, June 3, 1905, E. M. House Papers; Speech of C. K. Bell, May 3, 1906, broadside, Earl Vandale Collection; Statement, May 19, 1906, Oscar Branch Colquitt Papers; Bell to G. C. Pendleton, May 24, 1906, Dienst Collection.

[12] T. M. Campbell to H. M. Coleman, January 15, 1906, J. S. Hogg to W. F. Cameron, May 16, 1905, Thomas M. Campbell Papers, Archives, University of Texas Library; Campbell to J. H. Robertson, March 17, 1906, James Harvey Robertson Papers; Huckaby, "Colquitt," pp. 145–146; *The Bagpipe* (Palestine, Texas), July 17, 1906.

[13] *Dallas Morning News*, February 28, 1906.

Association, Railroad Commissioner L. J. Storey, and ardent prohibitionists, as well as Bell and Brooks.[14]

In the July primary Campbell polled 90,345 votes. He led in most of East and Southwest Texas and did fairly well across the state. Brooks, who ran first in a majority of North Texas counties, accumulated a total of 70,064 votes. Colquitt received 68,529 votes, primarily in Central and Southeast Texas. And Bell ran first in most counties of West Central Texas and along the Rio Grande to compile a total of 65,168 votes. Each candidate had run best in his own section of the state; no candidate or issue had truly captured the mind of the public. Yet the fact that Bell trailed his three more progressive opponents confirmed the developing trend. Local events indicated that despite the improvements it had wrought the new election law had hardly ended political manipulation in Texas. State and local officials continued to guide the voting of their employees, and, with others, continued to apply pressure on voters through such economic means as rents and property tax reevaluations. The election law did require that the votes of the fourth candidate in each county be prorated among the other three. The prorating process gave Campbell 212.408 convention votes; Colquitt, 169.302; Bell, 164.587; and Brooks, 155.257, because Brooks ran last in the greatest number of counties.[15]

The nominating convention eliminated Brooks on the first ballot. Frank Andrews, who was presiding at the time, then ruled that Brook's supporters had to vote for one of the other candidates by county as they had voted for Brooks. Bailey and other Brooks leaders apparently tried at the last minute to divide Brooks's votes between Campbell and Bell. They aimed to eliminate Colquitt and then reunite their support to nominate Bell, their second choice. But Colquitt, who had hoped to be nominated by getting most of Brooks's

[14] O. B. Colquitt to G. G. Powell, July 12, 1905, Colquitt to A. J. Lamon, April 25, 1906, A. G. McIlwaine to Colquitt, June 8, 1906, Colquitt Papers; Huckaby, "Colquitt," pp. 145–160, 473–474.

[15] *Dallas Morning News*, August 13, 1906; A. E. Masterson to T. M. Campbell, December 27, 1906, E. K. Marrast to Campbell, December 20, 1906, S. P. Wreford to Campbell, December 4, 1906, Thomas M. Campbell Papers in possession of William Campbell, Sewanee, Tennessee.

votes, and later Bell's, defeated their efforts by endorsing Campbell on the second ballot and ensuring his nomination. Bell blamed his defeat on Bailey, however, because the senator had sensed the changing tide in the convention and, in a typically colorful speech, referred to the siege of Lucknow and quoted the famous line "the Campbells are coming." Certainly it stirred enthusiasm for Campbell and at least in appearance placed Bailey on the winning side at the last moment. Campbell probably would have won regardless of the political maneuvering. His backers had organized well, and too much antagonism existed between the groups supporting the other candidates for their leaders to be able to shift votes easily from one to another, especially from Brooks the prohibitionist to either of the antiprohibitionists. And Colquitt's advisers had decided before the convention to throw his strength to Campbell if Colquitt could not win.[16]

The convention outlined the dimensions of progressivism in Texas by adopting several planks not included in the platform of 1904. The delegates called for laws to prohibit lobbying, corporate contributions to political campaigns, continued operation of insolvent corporations, and combinations in restraint of trade. On the positive side the convention added resolutions favoring laws to provide greater protection for creditors and stockholders, a uniform textbook law, and a state department of agriculture; it also endorsed William Jennings Bryan for the Democratic presidential nomination in 1908.[17]

In the fall election Campbell overwhelmed the small fragmented opposition consisting of Republicans and Socialists and a lingering prohibitionist remnant that still clung to a separate party. The Legislature elected with Campbell proved even more progressive than that of 1905–1906, with the strongest support from areas in East and West Central Texas which had backed Hogg and the Populists in the 1890's. In January 1907 Love became speaker of the new house, with support from leaders of the Farmers' Union and the State Federation

[16] O. B. Colquitt to Robert H. Hopkins, August 18, 1906, Colquitt to Thomas D. Gordon, August 20, 1906, Letterbook, Colquitt Papers; C. K. Bell to E. M. House, September 11, 1906, House Papers; Diary, 1909–1918, Horace Chilton Diaries; Huckaby, "Colquitt," pp. 161–170.

[17] Ernest William Winkler, ed., *Platforms of Political Parties in Texas*, pp. 493–496.

of Labor, over opposition from major corporate business interests.[18]

In national politics a majority of the Texas congressional delegation generally supported the progressive trend in legislation. They joined with other representatives of midwestern and southern shippers and many railroad men who favored uniform rates in support of the Hepburn Bill to strengthen the Interstate Commerce Commission by providing it with the power to set railroad rates. Joseph W. Bailey, despite his questionable personal dealings, helped lead an unsuccessful fight in the senate to eliminate court suspension of Interstate Commerce Commission rates, which railroad men opposed, and also backed Robert La Follette's bill to limit the hours of railroad employees involved in interstate commerce, on safety grounds. Senator Charles Culberson spoke for passage of the Employers Liability Act of 1906. Only the Pure Food and Drug Bill received strong opposition from the Texans, not because they disagreed with its goals but because it involved "police regulation" which they believed to be constitutionally reserved to the states.[19]

The elections of 1904 and 1906 as well as the state and federal laws of that period indicated a definite revival of progressivism in Texas, southern, and national politics which would continue into the following decade.[20] To end political manipulation and election abuses and to open the way for enactment of their views, Texas Democratic progressives had adopted a poll tax and a new voting law which to some degree served those purposes but also eliminated many potential

[18] Winkler, *Platforms*, p. 647; Younker, "Love," pp. 59–65; J. H. Kirby to A. D. Hamilton, August 21, 1906, Kirby Papers; Texas, House, *Journal*, 30th Legislature, Reg. sess., pp. 620, 645.

[19] U.S., Congress, *Congressional Record*, 59th Cong., 1st sess., pp. 2766–2767, 2773, 7088, 8969, 9075, 9084–9085; [A. E. DeRicqles] to Joseph Bailey, March 8, 1906, Cattle Association Letters, Matador Land and Cattle Co. Papers; Anne Firor Scott, "A Progressive Wind from the South, 1906–1913," *Journal of Southern History* 29 (February 1963): 56–57; Sam Hanna Acheson, *Joe Bailey*, pp. 185–210; Bob Charles Holcomb, "Senator Joe Bailey" (Ph.D. diss.), pp. 302–350; Adrian Norris Anderson, "Albert Sidney Burleson" (Ph.D. diss.), p. 78; Robert Wiebe, *Businessmen and Reform*, pp. 51–56; Gabriel Kolko, *Railroads and Regulation*, pp. 102–127.

[20] For a detailed study of the period following see James A. Tinsley, "The Progressive Movement in Texas" (Ph.D. diss.).

voters, especially Negroes and Mexicans. Texas progressives successfully backed measures on both the state and national levels aimed at regulation of business, insurance, and banking. They also supported legislation to improve labor conditions, public schools, health services, and tax distribution. The laws typified the extent and limitations of the state's progressivism, based on the Anglo evangelical values of growing urban middle-class business and professional groups and labor organizations, as well as farmers, in North, Central, and East Texas, who collectively constituted a majority of the electorate. Texas progressives, like their counterparts throughout the nation, sought to establish control over the seemingly unrestrained and dehumanizing forces of industrialization and accompanying urbanization for varied reasons. Some hoped for a greater share in the material fruits of a more diverse and dynamic economy. Others tried to preserve the social and religious values of a less complex rural past. Still others wanted to apply new professional standards and organizational methods to both economic and social problems.

The progressive movement in early twentieth-century Texas basically revived the brief coalition of diverse urban and rural interests that had supported Hogg so successfully in 1890, though there had been some shifts in strength in fifteen years and even greater organization of interest groups. By the end of 1906 Texas progressives had begun to ameliorate to varying degrees some problems faced by the state's society. But, equally important, they had changed the makeup of the state electorate and the practice of Texas politics to the extent that one political era had ended and another had begun.

16. CONCLUSIONS

Texas politics from 1876 to 1906 involved primarily issues which arose from changes in the national and state economies. The diversity of the state economy in turn provided a fertile field for clashes of economic interests. Campaigns might involve coalitions of North, East, and Central Texas farmers with urban labor or business groups, but more often they developed into conflicts within or between groups of farmers, West and South Texas cattle and sheep raisers and land dealers, in- and out-of-state railroad men, East Texas and out-of-state oil interests, and East Texas lumbermen. Ethnic and religious groups—the dominant Anglo Baptists and Methodists of North, East, and Central Texas, the Mexican Catholics of South Texas, the German Lutherans and Catholics of South Central Texas, and the Negro Baptists and Methodists of East Texas—also became important factors in most elections, as political parties appealed to voters on the basis of their own cultural interests and prejudices against other groups. Disputes between the principal political figures of the period at times heightened and at other times obscured differences of interests.

In 1876 Texas politics still reflected many of the passions and issues raised by the Civil War and Reconstruction, although the huge, diverse Democratic party controlled the state and most local government. Democrats would employ reminders of the E. J. Davis administration with its real and imagined failings against all opponents, especially those in areas of considerable Negro population, for years to come. The Republican party, among the weakest in the South with only one-fourth of the state's voters, devoted itself to efforts at fusion with third parties, struggles over federal patronage, and debates about whether or not the black majority in the party should provide its leadership. Negro Norris Wright Cuney controlled party affairs from Davis's death in 1883 to 1896. His defeat in a leadership battle through the influence of McKinley supporters in the national Republican convention cleared the way for increasing white dominance on the state level.

The national panic of 1873 and the depression that ran on for years thereafter worsened the condition of most Texans. The pressure upon the Anglo evangelical farming majority, many of whom had just shifted from subsistence to commercial crops, moved the farmers to group action with the intent of improving their situation by changes in government policy. The state Grange, one of the two strongest in the South, and like-minded agrarians operated within the Democratic party primarily to secure tax relief through measures aimed at extreme economy in government. Certainly their views, in conjunction with those of most business-oriented Texas politicians, dominated the administrations from Richard Coke to O. M. Roberts in the late 1870's and early 1880's.

Hostility to tight credit and a limited supply of money in circulation stimulated additional demands by Anglo and Negro evangelical tenant farmers, organized laborers, and some men in expanding businesses, which gave rise to the Greenback party in the campaigns of 1878 and 1880 and to an Independent movement in 1882 and 1884. These strong groups began to divide the white vote and helped force Democrats to face new issues. In their effort to defeat the new groups, the Democrats had continued Grange support, as they attempted to lower tariffs and to increase silver coinage. Adding to their strength were old fears by many whites of Republican rule, and by German Lutherans and Catholics of prohibitionist and inflationist views. The Democratic dominance of Mexican-American Catholics through local leadership and economic controls further bolstered the party.

For a period in the mid-1880's farmers fought with only limited success ranchers, sheepmen, and land dealers over the sale or use of public lands, and over fencing and fence-cutting. The failure of statewide prohibition in 1887 loosened Democratic party ties for many Anglo Baptists and Methodists who met defeat at the hands of a temporary coalition which included some Anglo Protestants and most Negro Baptists and Methodists, Mexican Catholics, and German Lutherans and Catholics. Renewed problems of falling farm prices, increasing tenancy, drought, tight credit, discriminatory freight rates, and low wages in the 1880's stimulated the development of the Farmers' Alliance, the Knights of Labor, and local business groups seeking to enhance their sometimes divergent interests. Democratic Congressman John H. Reagan responded to such views by helping write and press through to passage the Interstate Commerce Act in 1887. Congressman Roger Q. Mills became chairman of the House Ways and Means Committee, which drew up a bill to reduce tariffs in an unsuccessful effort to build a national Democratic majority based on the desire of northeastern commercial interests and southern and western agrarians to increase the volume of foreign trade while reducing the cost of imports. In the early 1890's James Hogg led an ambitious group of younger Democrats, not so wedded as their predecessors to antebellum legalism and fears of government action, to mobilize the unrest and push through a long-sought state railroad commission, to strengthen the state's antitrust laws, and to try to restrict large landholdings by non-Texans. Hogg's major challenger for political prominence in the South during the 1890's, "Pitchfork" Ben Tillman of South Carolina, had risen to power on the basis of similar issues and support, but proved to be less progressive and more racist in attitude. Some railroad, ranching, land, and lumber interests, fearing the effects of commission controls, made concerted efforts to defeat Hogg in the campaign of 1892. They failed, even with Republican support, as each side resorted to passionate appeals based on race and class antagonism. Thereafter the lines developed a generally positive working relationship with the commission, which sought to compromise conflicting interests between railroads and shippers. The frontier need for railroads caused Texas to lag behind southern states east of the Mississippi in the creation of a railroad commission, but its greater powers established a pattern followed by many southern and midwestern states in the 1890's and 1900's.

Demands by Farmers' Alliance leaders for more direct influence in state affairs and for government-backed farm credit soon went beyond anything the Hogg administration could or would do and brought about the organization of the People's party in Texas during 1891. Through three campaigns the predominantly Anglo evangelical small farmers and urban laborers of the Populist party consistently polled the (numerically) largest third-party vote in the South to challenge the Democrats more strongly on the state level than would be done by any other opposition until the mid–twentieth century. Labor support for Populism in Texas and the South ran counter to the trend in the northeast where labor became more strongly Republican. Populists finally drifted back to the Democratic fold because of their failure to develop more than limited support among large farmers, businessmen, ranchers, sheepmen, or minority groups other than Negroes in Texas, and the adoption of many of their platform planks by the better organized Democrats.

Absence of the Populists from the Democratic party weakened its agrarian wing but forced it toward more progressive stands to avoid further defections. To retain their state dominance and to build a more ideologically agreeable national party Texas and southern Democrats shifted from tariff reduction to silver coinage as their key issue in a successful drive to develop a South-West alliance and oust eastern party leadership. The Democrats failed, however, to win the older midwestern agricultural states, where silver had less appeal because they had moved away from a one-crop economy, and lost the national election of 1896.

Out of the heated campaigns of the 1890's came one of the most adept political organizations in Texas history. E. M. House, a masterly organizer and shrewd campaign manager, gained tremendous influence by gathering around him men of similar ability who played key roles in several campaigns for state and congressional offices. The House group coalesced loosely with supporters of popular, volatile Joe Bailey to dominate Texas politics at the turn of the century. After the Hogg-Clark campaigns House and Bailey consistently supported the more conservative wing of the Democratic party, and their moderate business views and friends gradually permeated the administrations of Culberson, Sayers, and Lanham. Those views reflected in part the increasing importance of business and industrial elements in the Texas economy and politics, especially after the rise of oil production in the 1890's and early 1900's. The success of House and Bailey paralleled similar events in other southern states, such as Virginia, where the Thomas Martin machine accepted limited reforms to retain power. Bailey, however, more nearly matched the flamboyant appearance and style of another Mississippian, James K. Vardeman. Bailey's financial connections with H. C. Pierce of the Waters-Pierce Oil Company thrust him into controversy when the state successfully prosecuted the company under antitrust laws in 1906 for its ties to Standard Oil. Though the Legislature absolved him of any illegal action, the case clearly indicated a conflict of interest and dimmed his political future at the same time House withdrew from state politics.

In the early twentieth century a variety of old and new civic and professional organizations, working separately toward some goals and in loose coalition for others, began to re-create the broad support for reform which had existed briefly under Hogg. Anglo evangelical prohibitionist groups—the Texas Local Option Association and the Women's Christian Temperance Union—often held together the somctimes diverse interests represented by the recently organized and urban-oriented State Federation of Labor and Texas Federation of Women's Clubs and the rural Farmers' Union. These groups promoted new state taxes and both state and national regulatory laws aimed at corporations in 1905 and brought about the election as governor in 1906 of Thomas M. Campbell, a former Hogg supporter, to carry out additional administrative, educational, labor, health, and tax reforms on the state level. Their efforts closely approximated in scope and date of passage most progressive measures adopted in Wisconsin under the leadership of Robert M. La Follette, though Texas did not pass civil service, conservation, or state income tax bills. Texas businessmen participated in the progressive movement by developing the commission form of city government and supporting civic improvement and good-road associations. The state medical, banking, and legal associations broadened the progressive spectrum with efforts to legalize state banks, to establish better methods of licensing doctors and attorneys, and to improve health conditions. Some progressive groups operated as part of national organizations; others had counterparts throughout the nation; all represented the continuing shift from geographical to occupational political identifications.

As a result of the bitterly and often illegally waged campaigns of the 1890's came movements affecting the suffrage and elections. An attempt to remove Negroes from politics began on the local level in the form of white men's associations in areas of black majorities and quickly spread through the state in the form of white primaries for the Democratic party. This intent to eliminate Negroes plus a desire to hold down the number of poor Populist farmers who would rejoin the Democratic party led to adoption of the poll tax as a prerequisite for voting. Yet the poll tax and lengthy and complex election laws which required uniform primaries also aimed at ending voting irregularities and political manipulation. These changes did result in more candidates in Democratic primaries for state offices. But mandatory primaries for parties polling 100,000 votes placed a burden on small opposition parties and helped perpetuate the one-party system which developed at the turn of the century. One-party politics produced a state of apathy in which less than 50 per cent of Texas voters participated in both primary and general elections during the first half of the twentieth century. Although Texas trailed seven southern states in adopting a uniform primary system, it acted at the same moment as Wisconsin in 1903. The progressive movement in Texas, in its efforts to attack certain political and social problems, thus changed the state's political processes so completely that it brought an end to an era in Texas politics.

Throughout the period 1876–1906 the Democratic party generally maintained strong support from the state's Anglo evangelical majority by identifying itself with southern states' rights and white supremacy traditions. Yet it ensured its continued control of state government and most Texas congressional seats by creating a coalition of diverse economic, regional, and ethnic and religious groups with flexible appeals to varied local interests. Texas Democrats proved themselves individual and party pragmatists as they frequently led efforts in Congress to produce for their constituents favorable federal action. They reinforced that image by helping to mold the national Democratic party in support of demands by varied groups of Texas voters for harbor improvements, lower tariffs, transportation regulations, and silver coinage. In these efforts they worked with other southern Democrats and, depending on the issue, sought eastern or western Democratic alliances to further their interests. Texas Democrats, like their counterparts throughout the South, made extensive use of intimidation and importation of voters and manipulation of election returns in the 1890's to overcome successfully their first major opposition since Reconstruction. To avoid the recurrence of that threat the party then reduced the electorate by eliminating large numbers of black and poor white voters, although it did not resort to the literacy tests, property requirements, and grandfather clause enacted by southern states with higher percentages of Negro population. Thus the Texas Democratic party succeeded through a pattern of practices similar in most ways to those of its counterparts in the late-nineteenth-century South. It differed primarily because of greater ethnic diversity. In a broader sense, ignoring which party controlled state politics, Texas followed the general course of most southern and midwestern predominantly farming states, which in this era began to reshape their political views to meet the challenge of growing commercialization in agriculture, industrialization, and urbanization, as well as individual specialization and interdependence in the state and national economy and society.

Texas and its leaders, trained and tested in the increasingly complex state politics of the late nineteenth and early twentieth centuries, played an important if generally predictable role in national politics during the period to follow. Senator Bailey remained a lightning rod of Texas politics until his resignation from the Senate in 1913. Senator Culberson lingered on to meet defeat in 1922. Both had fallen steadily behind the sweep of progressivism during their later years in public office. Morris Sheppard, a congressman from Northeast Texas since 1902, took Bailey's place in the Senate in time to reflect the state's progressivism by supporting all major reform legislation of the period and by introducing the national prohibition amendment. On the national scene also appeared E. M. House, in the role of political adviser to Woodrow Wilson, and House confidants Albert S. Burleson as postmaster general and dispenser of increasingly segregated patronage, T. W. Gregory as attorney general, and David F. Houston as secretary of agriculture. Again, as in the 1890's, they rode the political tide toward power and generally acted as conservative influences on the Wilson administration. John Nance Garner, another product of the House-Wells-Bailey machine, advanced his own fortunes and one phase of the Texas progressive spirit as a leading advocate of the graduated income tax who eventually became speaker of the house and vice-president. The continued rise of business and industry to dominance in post–World War II Texas politics produced the shift of pragmatist Lyndon Johnson from a New Deal congressman in line with his Populist-progressive heritage to a moderate senator who consistently defended the oil and gas industries.

State politics after the elimination of most black voters continued to involve ethnic-religious voting blocs formed by persons of German Lutheran and Catholic ancestry and of Mexican Catholic background, which were larger than similar groups in most southern states. Yet disfranchisement of Negroes generally allowed the Anglo evangelical majority to further emphasize its internal differences based on economics, morality, and personality. Changes in the election law also allowed individuals to rise more readily without the support of an elaborate political machine or organization. Those factors clearly influenced the campaigns which placed business-oriented, "wet" Oscar B. Colquitt in the governor's chair in 1911, followed by flamboyant, "wet" "Farmer Jim" Ferguson, who would dominate the period from World War I to the Depression. Although business and industry did not become the most important influences in Texas politics until after World War II, the economic and political trends of the late nineteenth and early twentieth centuries had suggested both the direction and distance Texas might move away from the Civil War and Reconstruction politics of section, race, and even agriculture.

BIBLIOGRAPHY

Manuscripts

(Unless otherwise noted, all manuscript collections are in The University of Texas Archives, Austin, Texas)

Bailey, Joseph W. Papers. 1880–1930. Dallas Historical Society, Hall of State, Dallas. Bailey, Democratic congressman, 1893–1901, and senator, 1901–1913, left only a limited amount of correspondence concerning state and national politics.

Baird, James W. Papers. 1882–1900. Baird, a North Texas Populist leader, left only a few letters concerning politics.

Ballinger, William Pitt. Papers. 1816–1899. Ballinger, a Democratic attorney of Galveston, kept candid diaries that are enlightening on state and congressional campaigns and politicians.

Barry, James B. Papers. 1847–1917. Barry, a Democratic legislator, 1883, and later a Populist, left only a few papers concerning politics.

Bayard, Thomas F. Papers. 1796–1899. Library of Congress. Bayard, Democratic senator and secretary of state from Delaware, corresponded with Congressmen Schleicher and Hancock of Texas.

Brackenridge, John T. Papers. 1840–1906. Brackenridge, a Democratic gubernatorial candidate in 1886, preserved a few letters from supporters.

Bryan, Guy M. Papers. 1837–1901. Bryan, a Democratic legislator, 1879–1881 and 1887–1889, kept correspondence with several political figures.

Bryan, William Jennings. Papers. 1877–1931. Library of Congress. Bryan, Democratic presidential candidate in 1896, 1900, and 1908, corresponded with several young Texas Democrats.

Buchanan, A. W. Papers. 1874–1892. Buchanan, a Grange leader, left a few papers of limited value on politics.

Burges, Richard F. Papers. 1897–1940. Burges, a Democratic reform leader at El Paso, kept a few interesting letters concerning the poll tax.

Burleson, Albert Sidney. Papers. 1863–1937. Library of Congress. Microfilm copies in The University of Texas Library. Burleson, Democratic congressman, 1899–1913, and postmaster general, 1913–1921, left correspondence that is useful in understanding the operations of E. M. House and his friends.

Butler, Marion. Papers. 1854–1937. Southern Historical Collection, University of North Carolina Library. Butler, Populist senator from North Carolina and chairman of the Populist national executive committee in 1896, corresponded with leaders of the party in Texas.

Campbell, Thomas M. Papers. 1898–1921. Campbell, a Hogg supporter and progressive Democratic governor, 1907–1911, left a limited amount of material pertaining to his political career.

———. Papers. 1906–1913. In possession of William Campbell, Sewanee, Tennessee. This collection contains material on T. M. Campbell's 1906 campaign and his gubernatorial administration.

Carothers, Durell. "Roger Q. Mills." Paper, Rice Institute, 1930.

Chandler, William E. Papers. 1862–1917. Library of Congress. Chandler, Republican leader from New Hampshire, corresponded with many southern Republicans including some Texans.

Chilton, Horace. Diaries. 1888–1919. Chilton, Democratic senator, 1891–1892 and 1895–1901, kept diaries which include comment on several political events of the period.

Clarkson, James S. Papers. 1851–1917. Library of Congress. Clarkson, who dispensed patronage for the Harrison and Roosevelt administrations, corresponded about Republican campaigns in Texas.

Cleveland, Grover. Papers. 1859–1945. Library of Congress. Microfilm copies in The University of Texas Library. Cleveland, Democratic President, 1885–1889 and 1893–1897, preserved correspondence with Texas senators, congressmen, and gold Democrats.

Coke, Richard. Biographical File. Texas Collection, The University of Texas Library. Included are newspaper clippings about Coke's political career.

Coke, Richard. Scrapbook. Coke, Democratic governor, 1874–1877, and senator, 1877–1895, can be traced to some extent through these newspaper clippings.

Colquitt, Oscar Branch. Papers. 1875–1940. Colquitt, Democratic state senator, 1895–1899, railroad commissioner, 1903–1911, and governor, 1911–1915, left extensive correspondence on state and local campaigns.

Davenport, Harbert. "Life of James B. Wells." Paper. Archives, The University of Texas.

Davis, Nathaniel Hart. Papers. 1840–1900. Davis, a Republican and Greenbacker, left a few interesting papers on local politics.

Dienst, Alexander. Collection. 1765–1927. Included are letters to George C. Pendleton, Democratic lieutenant governor, 1891–1893, congressman, 1893–1897, and antiprohibitionist after 1900, and others, concerning gold Democrats and Republicans in the 1890's.

Elliott, Claude. Papers. 1822–1937. Archives, Texas State Library. This collection includes letters to George C. Pendleton in 1894.

Executive Correspondence. 1876–1906. Archives, Texas State Library. Included are a few scattered letters on local politics and the political correspondence, 1891–1895, of Charles A. Culberson, Democratic attorney general, 1891–1895, governor, 1895–1899, and senator, 1899–1923.

Faulk, J. J. Papers. 1849–1935. Dallas Historical Society, Hall of State, Dallas. Faulk, a Democratic legislator, 1881–1883 and 1903–1907, left correspondence with several political figures of the period.

Ford, John S. Letters. In possession of Sam Lanham, Galveston, Texas. Ford, a Democratic legislator, 1876–1879, comments on affairs in the 1890's in these letters.

Fulton, G. W., and James. Papers. 1836–1911. The Fultons, coastal ranchers, left papers reflecting their interest in land politics and harbor improvement.

Garfield, James A. Papers. 1852–1881. Library of Congress. Republican President Garfield, 1881, received letters from Texas concerning patronage.

Gillespie County [Texas] Farmers' Alliance. Minutes. 1886–1896. Included are comments on local and state politics and figures.

Gilmer, Alexander. Papers. 1872–1929. Gilmer, a Texas lumberman, left some letters concerning his support of Clark in 1892 and the Republican party in 1896.

Gresham, Walter. Papers. 1834–1897. Rosenberg Library, Galveston. Gresham, Democratic state senator, 1889–1893, and congressman, 1893–1895, left detailed correspondence with supporters while in congress.

Hamman, William H. Papers. Fondren Library, Rice University. Hamman, Greenback gubernatorial nominee in 1878 and 1880, left correspondence and scrapbooks of his political career.

Harrison, Benjamin. Papers. 1787–1938. Library of Congress. Microfilm copies in The University of Texas Library. Republican President Harrison, 1889–1893, corresponded with Texas Republicans and Democrats concerning federal patronage.

Hart, V. T. Scrapbook. Included are a few letters and broadsides on politics.

Hawkins, Walace. "Col. Jacob Carl DeGress." Paper. Archives, University of Texas.

Henderson, Thomas Stalworth. Papers. 1852–1936. Henderson, a Democratic legislator, 1893–1895, left extensive correspondence concerning state and local campaigns.

Hill, Louis Hamilton. Papers. 1883–1945. Southwest Collection, Texas Tech University. These papers include letters from Hill's partner in a land company, Sam Webb, who supported Clark in 1892, opposed Populism, and backed Culberson and McKinley in 1896.

Hogg, James Stephen. Papers. 1836–1946. Hogg, Democratic attorney general, 1887–1891, and governor, 1891–1895, kept voluminous correspondence with a variety of local, state, and national political leaders.

Hopkins, George E. "The Origin of Jim Crow Laws in Texas." Paper. Presented, Phi Alpha Theta session, Annual Meeting, Texas State Historical Association, April 30, 1966.

House, E. M. Papers. 1891–1938. Yale University Library. Microfilm copies in The University of Texas Library. House, Democratic campaign manager for four governors, 1892–1904, left extensive correspondence with state and national political leaders.

Hudson, R. W. Papers. 1900–1912. Hudson, a Democratic supporter of Hogg, left a few letters of interest on state politics.

Hutcheson, J. C. Scrapbooks. In possession of Edward C. Hutcheson and Mrs. Rosalie Hutcheson Bosworth, Houston. Hutcheson, Democratic legislator, 1881–1883, and congressman, 1893–1897, may be traced to some extent through these newspaper clippings and one letter.

Ireland, John. Copybook. 1884–1891. Ireland, Democratic governor, 1883–1887, and candidate for Congress and the Senate, apparently left only these copies of correspondence including little political comment.

Kirby, John Henry. Papers. 1885–1930. Texas Gulf Coast Historical Association, University of Houston. Kirby, a Texas lumber and oil man, left extensive correspondence with Congressman S. B. Cooper, 1893–1905, and lesser amounts with Senator Bailey and on politics of the 1890's and 1900's.

Kleberg, Rudolph. Papers. 1843–1930. Kleberg, Democratic legislator, 1883–1887, and congressman, 1896–1903, left some correspondence and scrapbooks from his political career.

Labor Movement in Texas. Collection, 1883–1944. Included are copies of newspaper articles and some correspondence concerning politics.

Lanham, S. W. T. Letter. 1882. In possession of Samuel Lanham, Galveston, Texas. Lanham, Democratic congressman, 1883–1893, 1897–1903, and governor, 1903–1907, wrote this letter after his first election to Congress.

Lathrop, Barnes F. "The Life and Character of John Ireland." Paper. Archives, The University of Texas.

Long, John B. Papers. 1858–1924. Long, a Grange leader and Democratic congressman, 1891–1893, left a few political papers.

McKinley, William. Papers. 1847–1902. Library of Congress. Microfilm copies in The University of Texas Library. McKinley, Republican president, 1897–1901, received letters from Texas Republicans concerning patronage.

Macune, C. W. Memoir. "The Farmers' Alliance." Macune, president of the state and national alliances, describes the organization before it evolved into the People's party.

Matador Land and Cattle Company. Papers. 1882–1953. Southwest Collection, Texas Tech University. These papers include some correspondence between leaders of the American Cattlemen's Association and political figures in the early twentieth century.

Maxey, Sam Bell. Papers. 1849–1888. Photocopies. Archives, Texas State Library. Maxey, Democratic senator, 1875–1887, left a large collection of family letters in which he often discussed politics, as well as a limited amount of political correspondence and scrapbooks.

Mills, Roger Q. Papers. 1813–1938. Mills, Democratic congressman, 1872–1892, and senator, 1892–1899, left a manuscript on the tariff question and some speeches, but little correspondence on politics.

———. Papers. 1850–1911. Dallas Historical Society, Hall of State, Dallas. This collection contains a short autobiography and a few letters and clippings on politics.

Mills, W. W. Papers. 1856–1922. Mills, a Republican leader in El Paso, preserved a few letters received from other party members.

Milner, R. T. Papers. 1852–1913. Milner, a Democratic legislator, 1887–1893, left some newspaper clippings and a few letters on politics.

Muse, P. B. Papers. 1823–1916. Muse, a Democratic legislator, 1885–1887, preserved a few letters on politics of the period.

Newcomb, James P. Papers. 1839–1941. Newcomb, Republican secretary of state, 1870–1874, and postmaster of San Antonio, 1883–1885, left extensive correspondence with state and national party leaders, from Edmund J. Davis to the Lily-whites.

Paddock, Buckley B. Papers. 1865–1925. Paddock, a railroad promoter, newspaperman, and mayor of Fort Worth, 1892–1900, left considerable correspondence on his efforts to oppose business regulation by the state government and on Clark's campaign for governor in 1892.

Pease, Elisha Marshall. Papers. 1639–1905. Austin Public Library. Pease, Republican governor, 1867–1869, and customs collector at Galveston, 1879–1881, left correspondence on his party's factional struggles.

Polk, Leonidas L. Papers. 1862–1892. Southern Historical Collection, University of North Carolina Library. Polk, president of the Southern Farmers' Alliance, corresponded with several members in Texas about politics.

Raguet, Henry. Papers. 1786–1923. Included are several letters from Amory R. Starr, a Democratic leader of Marshall and Northeast Texas.

Reagan, John H. Papers. 1847–1905. Archives, Texas State Library. Reagan, Democratic congressman, 1875–1887, senator, 1887–1891, and railroad commissioner, 1891–1903, left correspondence concerning both state and national politics.

Roberts, Oran M. Papers. 1815–1953. Roberts, Democratic chief justice of the Supreme Court of Texas, 1874–1879, and governor, 1879–1883, left extensive correspondence with a variety of state political figures.

Robertson, James Harvey. Papers. 1895–1906. Robertson, a Democratic judge and legislator, and law partner of Hogg, left a few letters containing state politics.

Roosevelt, Theodore. Papers. 1870–1940. Library of Congress. Republican President Roosevelt, 1901–1909, corresponded with Texas Republicans about federal offices and factional fights.

Rose, A. J. Papers. 1830–1903. Rose, master of the state Grange and a Hogg supporter, corresponded also with Coke and other Texas politicians.

Ross, Lawrence Sullivan. Papers. 1820–1900. Texas Collection, Baylor University. Ross, Democratic state senator, 1881–1883, and governor, 1887–1891, left only a few letters pertaining to state politics.

Rushing, John B. Papers. Included is limited material on Populism in Texas.

Sayers, Joseph D. Papers. 1834–1911. Sayers. Democratic lieutenant governor, 1879–1881, congressman, 1885–1899, and governor, 1899–1903, left only a few letters and scrapbooks containing information on politics.

Sheppard, Morris. Papers. 1894–1942. Sheppard, Democratic congressman, 1902–1913, and senator, 1913–1941, left little material from his early political career.

Sherman, John. Papers. 1846–1894. Library of Congress. Sherman, Republican leader from Ohio, corresponded with Texans who supported his efforts to get the presidential nomination in the 1880's.

Smith, Ashbel. Papers. 1823–1926. Smith, a Democratic legislator, preserved extensive correspondence on several state political issues and campaigns.

Teagarden, William B. Papers. 1888–1942. Teagarden, a Democratic attorney, left correspondence on gold Democratic and antiprohibitionist efforts.

Terrell, Alexander Watkins. Papers. 1877–1912. Terrell, a Democratic legislator, 1876–1883, 1891–1893, and 1903–1907, and a candidate for the Senate in 1887, left correspondence and printed material from his lengthy career in state politics.

———. Papers. 1865–1905. Archives, Texas State Library. Included are a few letters and broadsides on politics.

Terrell, Ben. Scrapbooks. In possession of Mrs. Richard T. Betts, San Antonio. Terrell, an Alliance and Populist leader, may be traced through these clippings.

Texas Historical Survey. "Index to Biographical Studies of Texans." Ms. 7 vols. Texas Collection, University of Texas Library.

Throckmorton, James W. Papers. 1838–1888. Throckmorton, Democratic congressman, 1875–1879 and 1883–1889, and candidate for governor and senator, left a few scattered letters concerning state and national politics.

Truit, James W. Papers. 1806–1918. Truit, a Democratic legislator, 1881–1883, 1891–1895, preserved correspondence with several local and state political leaders.

Tyler, George W. Papers. 1840–1926. Tyler, a Democratic legislator, 1889–1893, preserved several letters concerning state and local politics.

U.S., Department of Justice. Appointment Papers. National Archives. These papers provide insight into the distribution of patronage in Texas.

U.S., Tenth Census, 1880, Population, for Texas. Microfilm, University of Texas Library.

U.S., Treasury Department. Appointment Papers. National Archives. These papers also contain information on Texas patronage.

Vandale, Earl. Collection. 1819–1947. Included are several letters from Richard Coke about his campaigns for governor and senator in 1876 and a few letters from other political figures.

Washington, Booker T. Papers. 1884–1922. Library of Congress. Washington, a prominent Negro educator, corresponded with Texas and national Republican leaders.

Wells, James B. Papers. 1865–1926. Wells, chairman of the state Democratic executive committee, 1900–1904, and political leader of the Rio Grande Valley, left voluminous correspondence concerning state and local politics.

Whitney, William C. Papers. 1757–1904. Library of Congress. Whitney, Democratic secretary of the navy, corresponded with Congressman Sayers.

Wilson, W. B. Papers. 1896–1939. Wilson, a Populist, left diaries and scrapbooks on local politics.

Wright, Samuel J. Papers. Wright, a leader of the Republican Lily-whites who became a Populist, left a few letters and extensive scrapbooks relating to both parties.

Theses and Dissertations

Anderson, Adrian Norris. "Albert Sidney Burleson: A Southern Politician in the Progressive Era." Ph.D. dissertation, Texas Technological College, 1967.

Bailey, Lelia. "The Life and Public Career of O. M. Roberts, 1815–1883." Ph.D. dissertation, University of Texas, 1932.

Billington, Monroe Lee. "Thomas P. Gore: Oklahoma's Blind Senator." Ph.D. dissertation, University of Kentucky, 1955.

Bowles, Willie D. "The History of the Woman Suffrage Movement in Texas." M.A. thesis, University of Texas, 1939.

Brooks, Glynn Austin. "A Political Survey of the Prohibition Movement in Texas." M.A. thesis, University of Texas, 1920.

Budd, Harrell. "The Negro in Politics in Texas, 1867–1898." M.A. thesis, University of Texas, 1925.

Cannon, Charles A. "The Ideology of Texas Populism, 1886–1894." M.A. thesis, Rice University, 1968.

Chamberlain, Charles Kincheloe. "Alexander Watkins Terrell, Citizen, Statesman." Ph.D. dissertation, University of Texas, 1956.

Cocke, Ione. "Texas and the Federal Tariff." M.A. thesis, University of Texas, 1921.

Demme, Genevieve Pyle. "Owen Pinkney Pyle, Champion of the Farmer." M.A. thesis, Rice Institute, 1958.

Dixon, Frederick Kemp. "A History of Gonzales County in the Nineteenth Century." M.A. thesis, University of Texas, 1964.

Dugas, Vera Lea. "A Social and Economic History of Texas in the Civil War and Reconstruction Periods." Ph.D. dissertation, University of Texas, 1963.

Duke, Escal Franklin. "The Political Career of Morris Sheppard, 1875–1941." Ph.D. dissertation, University of Texas, 1958.

Edwards, Martin Leon. "The Farmers' Movement in Delta County." M.A. thesis, East Texas State College, 1964.

Ellis, Louis Tuffly. "The Texas Cotton Compress Industry: A History." Ph.D. dissertation, University of Texas, 1964.

Evans, Samuel Lee. "Texas Agriculture, 1880–1930." Ph.D. dissertation, University of Texas, 1960.

Garner, William Fletcher. "The Primaries in Texas." M.A. thesis, University of Texas, 1920.

Gray, Sondra Wyatt. "The Political Career of James Luther Slayden." M.A. thesis, University of Texas, 1962.

Greene, Howard Mell. "Legal Regulation of Political Parties in Texas." M.A. thesis, University of Texas, 1923.

Gulley, Steve D. "M. M. Rodgers the Politician, 1877–1909." M.A. thesis, Prairie View (Texas) A. & M. College, 1955.

Hazel, Sybal. "Statewide Prohibition Campaigns in Texas." M.A. thesis, Texas Technological College, 1942.

Hinze, Virginia Neal. "Norris Wright Cuney." M.A. thesis, Rice University, 1965.

Holcomb, Bob Charles. "Senator Joe Bailey: Two Decades of Controversy." Ph.D. dissertation, Texas Technological College, 1968.

Howard, Richard Winston. "The Work of Albert Sidney Burleson as Postmaster General." M.A. thesis, University of Texas, 1938.

Huckaby, George P. "Oscar Branch Colquitt: A Political Biography." Ph.D. dissertation, University of Texas, 1946.

Jarmon, Inez. "A Calendar of E. S. C. Robertson Papers, 1842–1879." M.A. thesis, University of Texas, 1937.

Kerr, Homer Lee. "Migration Into Texas, 1865–1880." Ph.D. dissertation, University of Texas, 1953.

Kochan, Millie L. "The Jaybird-Woodpecker Feud: A Study in Social Conflict." M.A. thesis, University of Texas, 1929.

Laughlin, Henry M. "The Election Laws of Texas, 1876 to 1928." M.A. thesis, University of Texas, 1928.

Margraves, Nina Benware. "The Jaybird Democratic Association of Fort Bend County: A White Man's Union." M.A. thesis, University of Houston, 1955.

Martin, Ruby Lee. "The Administration of Governor S. W. T. Lanham, 1903–1907." M.A. thesis, University of Texas, 1937.

Miller, Benjamin H. "Elisha Marshall Pease: A Biography." M.A. thesis, University of Texas, 1927.

Moore, Sue E. "The Life of John Benjamin Long." M.A. thesis, University of Texas, 1924.

Murphy, Leonard Brewster. "A History of Negro Segregation Practices in Texas, 1865–1958." M.A. thesis, Southern Methodist University, 1958.

Nash, Gerald. "A Chapter from an Active Life: John H. Reagan and Railroad Regulation." M.A. thesis, Columbia University, 1952.

Nielsen, George Raymond. "Richard Bennett Hubbard: 'The Demosthenes of Texas.' " M.A. thesis, University of Houston, 1957.

Norton, Frank Edgar. "The Major Administrative Policies of Oran Milo Roberts: With an Introduction to His Life." M.A. thesis, University of Texas, 1925.

Payne, John Wesley. "David F. Houston: A Biography." Ph.D. dissertation, University of Texas, 1953.

Perry, Douglass Geraldyne. "Black Populism: The Negro in the People's Party." M.A. thesis, Prairie View University, 1945.

Peterson, Robert Lewis. "State Regulation of Railroads in Texas, 1836–1920." Ph.D. dissertation, University of Texas, 1960.

Pool, Oran Jo. "A History of Hamilton County." M.A. thesis, University of Texas, 1954.

Purifoy, Russell A., Jr. "Statesman from Texas: Roger Q. Mills." M.A. thesis, North Texas State University, 1954.

Purinton, Frances B. "The Texas Gubernatorial Campaign of 1896." M.A. thesis, University of Texas, 1955.

Rice, Lawrence D. "The Negro in Texas, 1874–1900." Ph.D. dissertation, Texas Technological College, 1967.

Roberts, Myrtle. "Roger Quarles Mills." M.A. thesis, University of Texas, 1929.

St. Clair, Grady Stafford. "The Hogg-Clark Campaign." M.A. thesis, University of Texas, 1927.

Sanford, William R. "History of the Republican Party in the State of Texas." M.A. thesis, University of Texas, 1954.

Seale, Everett Young. "John Ireland and His Times." M.A. thesis, University of Houston, 1955.

Shelton, Edgar Greer, Jr. "Political Conditions among Texas Mexicans along the Rio Grande." M.A. thesis, University of Texas, 1946.

Smith, Ada Margaret. "The Life and Times of William Harrison Hamman." M.A. thesis, University of Texas, 1952.

Smith, Maggie Ruhamah. "The Administration of Governor John Ireland, 1883–1887." M.A. thesis, University of Texas, 1925.

Smith, Ralph A. "A. J. Rose, Agrarian Crusader in Texas." Ph.D. dissertation, University of Texas, 1938.

Snow, Laura. "The Poll Tax in Texas: Its Historical, Legal, and Fiscal Aspects." M.A. thesis, University of Texas, 1936.

Sochia, Maurice Henry. "The Progressive Movement in Texas, 1900–1914." M.A. thesis, Southwest Texas State College, 1959.

Tenney, James Leighton. "The Public Services of Joseph Draper Sayers." M.A. thesis, University of Texas, 1933.

Thompson, James H. "A Nineteenth Century History of Cameron County, Texas." M.A. thesis, University of Texas, 1965.

Tinsley, James A. "The Progressive Movement in Texas." Ph.D. dissertation, University of Wisconsin, 1953.

Wagner, Robert Lancaster. "The Gubernatorial Career of Charles Allen Culberson." M.A. thesis, University of Texas, 1954.

Webb, Juanita Oliver. "The Administration of Governor L. S. Ross, 1887–1891." M.A. thesis, University of Texas, 1935.

Whiteside, Myrtle. "The Life of Lawrence Sullivan Ross." M.A. thesis, University of Texas, 1938.

Williams, Marshall L. "The Political Career of Cyclone Davis." M.A. thesis, East Texas State College, 1937.

Yelderman, Pauline. "The Jaybird Democratic Association of Fort Bend County." M.A. thesis, University of Texas, 1938.

Younker, Donna Lee. "Thomas B. Love's Service in the Texas Legislature and in State Government During the Lanham and Campbell Administrations." M.A. thesis, Southern Methodist University, 1958.

BOOKS

Acheson, Sam Hanna. *Joe Bailey: The Last Democrat.* New York: The Macmillan Co., 1932.

———. *35,000 Days in Texas: A History of the Dallas News and Its Forebears.* New York: The MacMillan Co., 1938.

Adams, Frank Carter, ed. *Texas Democracy: A Centennial History of Politics and Personalities of the Democratic Party, 1836–1936.* 4 vols. Austin: Democratic Historical Association, 1937.

Adams, Frederick Upham. *The Waters-Pierce Case in Texas: Battling with a Great Corporation.* St. Louis: Skinner & Kennedy, 1908.

Alden, Edwin & Bro. *American Newspaper Catalogue.* Cincinnati: Edwin Alden & Bro., 1884.

Allen, Emory Adams. *The Life and Public Services of James Baird Weaver.* N.p.: People's Party Publishing Co., 1892.

Allen, Ruth A. *Chapters in the History of Organized Labor in Texas.* University of Texas Publication no. 4143. Austin, 1941.

———. *The Great Southwest Strike.* University of Texas Publication No. 4214. Austin, 1942.

Anti-Saloon League. *The Brewers and Texas Politics.* 2 vols. San Antonio: Passing Show Printing Co., 1916.

Atwell, William Hawley. *Autobiography.* Dallas: Warlick Law Printing Co., 1935.

Ayer, N. W. *American Newspaper Annual.* Philadelphia: N. W. Ayer & Son, 1882–1887.

Bain, Richard C. *Convention Decisions and Voting Records.* Washington, D. C.: Brookings Institution, 1960.

Ball, Thomas H. *The Port of Houston: How It Came to Pass.* Houston:

N. pub., n.d.; reprinted from articles appearing in the *Houston Chronicle* and *Houston Post*, August 2–November 1, 1936.

Barker, Eugene C., and Ernest W. Winkler, eds. *A History of Texas and Texans, by Frank W. Johnson*. 5 vols. Chicago and New York: American Historical Society, 1914.

Barnes, James A. *John G. Carlisle, Financial Statesman*. New York: Dodd, Mead & Co., 1931.

Barrett, Charles Simon. *The Mission, History and Times of the Farmers' Union*. Nashville: Marshall & Bruce, 1909.

Benson, Lee. *Merchants, Farmers, and Railroads: Railroad Regulation and New York Politics, 1850–1887*. Cambridge: Harvard University Press, 1955.

Bentley, H. L., and Thomas Pilgrim. *The Texas Legal Directory for 1876–77*. Austin: Democratic Statesman Office, 1877.

Biographical Encyclopedia of Texas. New York: Southern Publishing Co., 1880.

Blair, E. L. *Early History of Grimes County*. N.p.: Privately printed, 1930.

Bogue, Allan G. *Money at Interest: The Farm Mortgage on the Middle Border*. Ithaca: Cornell University Press, 1955.

Breneman, C. K. *In the Republican National Convention, St. Louis, Missouri: Contest from the Twelfth Congressional District of Texas*. San Antonio: Daily Light, 1896.

Brewer, J. Mason. *Negro Legislators of Texas*. Dallas: Mathis Publishing Co., 1935.

Brown, George R. *The Speaker of the House: The Romantic Story of John N. Garner*. New York: Brewer, Warren & Putnam, 1932.

Bryan, William J. *The First Battle: A Story of the Campaign of 1896*. Chicago: W. B. Conkey Co., 1896.

Bryan, William J., and Mary Baird Bryan. *The Memoirs of William Jennings Bryan*. Chicago: John C. Winston Co., 1925.

Buck, Solon J. *The Agrarian Crusade: A Chronicle of the Farmer in Politics*. New Haven: Yale University Press, 1920.

Bundy, William Oliver. *Life of William Madison McDonald*. Fort Worth: Bunker Printing & Book Co., 1925.

Burnham, W. Dean. *Presidential Ballots, 1836–1892*. Baltimore: The Johns Hopkins Press, 1955.

Bushick, Frank H. *Glamorous Days*. San Antonio: Naylor Co., 1934.

Cardwell, John. *Fifteenth Legislature. Sketches of Legislators and State*

Officers, 1876–1878. Austin: Democratic Statesman Steam Print, 1876.

Carlson, Avery L. *A Monetary and Banking History of Texas from the Mexican Regime to the Present Day, 1821–1929.* Fort Worth: Fort Worth National Bank, 1930.

Casdorph, Paul D. *The Republican Party in Texas, 1865–1965.* Austin: Pemberton Press, 1965.

Christian, Stella L. *The History of the Texas Federation of Women's Clubs.* Houston: Texas Federation of Women's Clubs, 1919.

Clancy, Herbert J. *The Presidential Election of 1880.* Chicago: Loyola University Press, 1958.

Clark, George. *A Glance Backward.* Houston: Rein & Sons Co., 1914.

Clark, Ira G. *Then Came the Railroads: The Century from Steam to Diesel in the Southwest.* Norman: University of Oklahoma Press, 1958.

Cocke, William A. *The Bailey Controversy in Texas.* San Antonio: Cocke Co., 1908.

Coletta, Paolo E. *William Jennings Bryan: Political Evangelist, 1860–1908.* Lincoln: University of Nebraska Press, 1964.

Connally, Tom, and Alfred Steinberg. *My Name is Tom Connally.* New York: Thomas Y. Crowell Co., 1954.

Cotner, Robert C. *James Stephen Hogg: A Biography.* Austin: University of Texas Press, 1959.

———, ed. *Addresses and State Papers of James Stephen Hogg.* Austin: University of Texas Press, 1951.

Cranfill, J. B. *Dr. J. B. Cranfill's Chronicle.* Chicago: Fleming H. Revell Co., 1916.

———. *From Memory.* Nashville: Broadman Press, 1937.

Craven, Avery O. *The Growth of Southern Nationalism, 1848–1861.* Baton Rouge: Louisiana State University Press, 1953.

Crenshaw, Ollinger. *The Slave States in the Presidential Election of 1860.* The Johns Hopkins University Studies in Historical and Political Science, series 63, no. 3. Baltimore, 1945.

Daniell, L. E., comp. *Personnel of the Texas State Government.* Austin: City Printing Co., 1887.

———. *Personnel of the Texas State Government.* San Antonio: Maverick Printing House, 1892.

Davis, James Harvey "Cyclone." *Memoir.* Sherman: Courier Press, 1935.

———. *A Political Revelation.* Dallas: Advance Publishing Company, 1894.

Democratic Executive Committee, Bexar County, Texas. *The Democratic Situation in Bexar County Explained.* San Antonio: Guessaz and Ferlet, 1892.

Democratic Executive Committee, Fayette County, Texas. *A Statement of the "Split" in the Fayette County Democracy.* LaGrange, 1892.

Democratic Executive Committee, Lamar County, Texas. *A Response to Greenbackism: The Record of the Democracy.* Paris: Banner Office, 1880.

Democratic Executive Committee, Texas. *Call for State Democratic Convention, August 14, 1906.* Houston: State Printing Co., 1906.

Democratic Party, National Convention. *Proceedings,* 1876–1904.

Democratic Party, Texas, Galveston. *To the People of the Fifth Congressional District, State of Texas.* [Galveston (?), 1878(?)]

De Santis, Vincent P. *Republicans Face the Southern Question: The New Departure Years, 1877–1897.* Baltimore: The Johns Hopkins Press, 1959.

Dohoney, E. L. *An Average American.* Paris (Texas): E. L. Dohoney, 1907.

Dunn, Arthur Wallace. *From Harrison to Harding.* 2 vols. New York: G. P. Putnam's Sons, 1922.

Dunning, N. A., ed. *The Farmers' Alliance History and Agricultural Digest.* Washington, D.C.: Alliance Publishing Co., 1891.

Durden, Robert F. *The Climax of Populism: The Election of 1896.* Lexington: University of Kentucky Press, 1965.

Eby, Frederick. *The Development of Education in Texas.* New York: The Macmillan Co., 1925.

Elliott, Claude. *Leathercoat: The Life History of a Texas Patriot* [James W. Throckmorton]. San Antonio: Standard Printing Co., 1938.

Farrow, Marion H. *The Texas Democrats.* San Antonio: Naylor Co., 1944.

Faulkner, Harold U. *Politics, Reform, and Expansion, 1890–1900.* New York: Harper & Brothers, 1959.

Finty, Tom, Jr. *Anti-Trust Legislation in Texas.* Dallas and Galveston: A. H. Belo and Co., 1916.

Fitzgerald, Hugh Nugent. *Governors I Have Known.* Austin: Austin American-Statesman, 1927.

Forbes, Gerald. *Flush Production: The Epic of Oil in the Gulf-Southwest.* Norman: University of Oklahoma Press, 1942.

Fornell, Earl Wesley. *The Galveston Era: The Texas Crescent on the Eve of Secession.* Austin: University of Texas Press, 1961.

Friedman, Milton, and Anna Jacobson Schwartz. *A Monetary History of the United States, 1867–1960.* Princeton: Princeton University Press, 1963.

Gammel, H. P. N., comp. *The Laws of Texas, 1822–1897.* 10 vols. Austin: Gammel Publishing Co., 1898.

Gantt, Fred, Jr. *The Chief Executive in Texas: A Study in Gubernatorial Leadership.* Austin: University of Texas Press, 1964.

Gard, Wayne. *Rawhide Texas.* Norman: University of Oklahoma Press, 1965.

Garraty, John A. *The New Commonwealth, 1877–1890.* New York: Harper & Row, 1968.

Garvin, W. L., and S. O. Daws. *History of the National Farmers' Alliance and Co-operative Union of America.* Jacksboro, Texas: J. N. Rogers & Co., 1887.

George, Alexander L., and Juliette L. *Woodrow Wilson and Colonel House: A Personality Study.* New York: The John Day Co., 1956.

Ginger, Ray. *Age of Excess: The United States From 1877 to 1914.* New York: The Macmillan Co., 1965.

Glad, Paul W. *McKinley, Bryan, and the People.* New York: J. B. Lippincott Co., 1964.

———. *The Trumpet Soundeth: William Jennings Bryan and His Democracy, 1896–1912.* Lincoln: University of Nebraska Press, 1960.

Gooch, John Young. *Speech of Jno. Young Gooch.* Palestine, Texas: W. G. Atkins, 1880.

Gracy, David B. II, ed. *Maxey's Texas.* Austin: Pemberton Press, 1965.

Grantham, Dewey W., Jr. *The Democratic South.* Athens: University of Georgia Press, 1963.

Gressley, Gene M. *Bankers and Cattlemen.* New York: Alfred A. Knopf, 1966.

Grodinsky, Julius. *Jay Gould: His Business Career: 1867–1892.* Philadelphia: University of Pennsylvania Press, 1957.

Haley, J. Evetts. *Charles Goodnight: Cowman & Plainsman.* Boston: Houghton Mifflin Co., 1936.

Hamilton, Holman. *Prologue to Conflict: The Crisis and Compromise of 1850.* Lexington: University of Kentucky Press, 1964.

Hancock, John. *Reply to the Attacks Made on Him by Col. Giddings on 4th November, and Col. Flournoy on 6th November, 1876, at Galveston, Texas.* Galveston: Galveston News Steam Book Print, 1876.

Hardy, Dermot H., and Ingham S. Roberts. *Historical Review of South-East Texas.* 2 vols. Chicago: Lewis Publishing Co., 1910.

Hare, Maud Cuney. *Norris Wright Cuney: A Tribune of the Black People.* New York: Crisis Publishing Co., 1913.

Haynes, Fred E. *Third Party Movements since the Civil War: With Special Reference to Iowa.* Iowa City: State Historical Society of Iowa, 1916.

Hays, Samuel P. *The Response to Industrialism, 1885–1914.* Chicago: University of Chicago Press, 1957.

Henderson, Nat Q., comp. *Directory of the Members and Officers of the Fourteenth Legislature of the State of Texas.* Austin: Cardwell & Walker, 1874.

Hicks, John D. *The Populist Revolt: A History of the Farmers' Alliance and the People's Party.* Minneapolis: University of Minnesota Press, 1931.

Hirshson, Stanley P. *Farewell to the Bloody Shirt: Northern Republicans and the Southern Negro, 1877–1893.* Bloomington: Indiana University Press, 1962.

Hofstadter, Richard. *The Age of Reform: From Bryan to F. D. R.* New York: Alfred A. Knopf, 1955.

Hollingsworth, J. Rogers. *The Whirligig of Politics: The Democracy of Cleveland and Bryan.* Chicago: University of Chicago Press, 1963.

Hoogenboom, Ira. *Outlawing the Spoils: A History of the Civil Service Reform Movement, 1865–1883.* Urbana: University of Illinois Press, 1961.

Hunt, Robert Lee. *A History of Farmer Movements in the Southwest, 1873–1925.* College Station: Texas A. & M. Press, 1935(?).

Ivy, H. A. *Rum on the Run in Texas: A Brief History of Prohibition in the Lone Star State.* Dallas: Temperance Publishing Co., 1910.

Johnson, Allen, and Dumas Malone, eds. *Dictionary of American Biography.* 22 vols. New York: Charles Scribner's Sons, 1928–1958.

Jones, Stanley L. *The Presidential Election of 1896.* Madison: University of Wisconsin Press, 1964.

Jordan, Terry G. *German Seed in Texas Soil: Immigrant Farmers in Nineteenth-Century Texas.* Austin: University of Texas Press, 1966.

Key, V. O., Jr. *Southern Politics in State and Nation.* New York: Alfred A. Knopf, 1949.

King, C. Richard. *Wagons East: The Great Drouth of 1886.* Austin: School of Journalism, The University of Texas, 1965.

King, John O. *The Early History of the Houston Oil Company of Texas, 1901–1908.* Houston: Texas Gulf Coast Historical Association, 1959.

Kinzer, David L. *An Episode in Anti-Catholicism: The American Protective Association.* Seattle: University of Washington Press, 1964.

Kittrell, Norman G. *Governors Who Have Been, and Other Public Men of Texas.* Houston: Dealy-Adey-Elgin Co., 1921.

Knight, Oliver. *Fort Worth: Outpost on the Trinity.* Norman: University of Oklahoma Press, 1953.

Knoles, George H. *The Presidential Campaign and Election of 1892.* Stanford: Stanford University Press, 1942.

Kolko, Gabriel. *The Triumph of Conservatism: A Reinterpretation of American History, 1900–1916.* London: Collier-Macmillan, Free Press of Glencoe, 1963.

———. *Railroads and Regulation, 1877–1916.* Princeton: Princeton University Press, 1965.

LaFeber, Walter. *The New Empire: An Interpretation of American Expansion, 1860–1898.* Ithaca: Cornell University Press, for the American Historical Association, 1963.

Lambert, Will, comp. *Pocket Directory of the Eighteenth Legislature of Texas.* Austin: Deffenbaugh & Co., 1883.

———. *Pocket Directory of the Seventeenth Legislature of Texas.* Austin: Swindells Book & Job Office, 1881.

Lang, A. S. *Financial History of the Public Lands in Texas.* Baylor University Bulletin 35, no. 3. Waco, 1932.

Lathrop, Barnes F. *Migration into East Texas, 1835–1860.* Austin: Texas State Historical Association, 1949.

Leathers, Frances Jane. *Through the Years: A Historical Sketch of Leon County and the Town of Oakwood.* Oakwood, Texas: N.p., 1946.

Lee, Charles Robert, Jr. *The Confederate Constitutions.* Chapel Hill: The University of North Carolina Press, 1963.

A Legislative Manual for the State of Texas. 2 vols. Austin: E. W. Swindells, 1879–1883.

Lewis, Arthur H. *The Day They Shook the Plum Tree.* New York: Harcourt, Brace & World, 1964.

Lewis, Lloyd, and Henry Justin Smith. *Oscar Wilde Discovers America.* New York: Harcourt, Brace and Co., 1936.

Link, Arthur S. *Wilson: The New Freedom.* Princeton: Princeton University Press, 1956.

Logan, Rayford W. *The Negro in American Life and Thought: The Nadir, 1877–1901.* New York: Dial Press, 1954.

———, ed. *The Attitude of the Southern White Press toward Negro Suffrage, 1932–1940.* Washington, D.C.: Foundation Publishers, 1940.

Lotto, F. *Fayette County, Her History and Her People.* Schulenburg, Texas: Sticker Steam Press, 1902.

Loughery, E. H. *Personnel of the Texas State Government for 1885.* Austin: L. E. Daniell, 1885.

Love, Annie Carpenter. *History of Navarro County.* Dallas: Southwest Press, 1933.

McCall, Abner V. "History of Texas Election Laws." In *Vernon's Annotated Revised Civil Statutes of the State of Texas,* IX,, xvii–xxxvi. Kansas City, Mo.: Vernon Law Book Company, 1952.

McCallum, Henry D., and Frances T. *The Wire That Fenced the West.* Norman: University of Oklahoma Press, 1965.

McCraw, William. *Professional Politicians.* Washington, D.C.: Imperial Press, 1940.

McKay, Seth Shepard. *Seven Decades of the Texas Constitution of 1876.* Lubbock: Texas Technological College Press, 1942.

McKitrick, Reuben. *The Public Land System of Texas, 1823–1910.* University of Wisconsin Bulletin no. 905. Madison, 1918.

McPherson, Edward. *A Handbook of Politics,* 1876–1894. Washington, D.C.: Solomons and Chapman, 1876–1878; J. J. Chapman, 1880–1892; R. Beall, 1894.

Madden, James William. *Charles Allen Culberson.* Austin: Gammel's Book Store, 1929.

Martin, Roscoe C. *The People's Party in Texas: A Study in Third Party Politics.* University of Texas Bulletin no. 3308. Austin, 1933.

Maxey, S. B. *Speech Delivered at Fort Worth, Texas, September 13, 1886.* Paris, Texas: Daily News Steam Printing House, 1886.

May, Ernest R. *Imperial Democracy: The Emergence of America as a Great Power.* New York: Harcourt, Brace & World, 1961.

Meier, August. *Negro Thought in America, 1880–1915.* Ann Arbor: University of Michigan Press, 1963.

Meinig, D. W. *Imperial Texas: An Interpretive Essay in Cultural Geography.* Austin: University of Texas Press, 1969.

Memorial and Biographical History of Dallas County, Texas. Chicago: Lewis Publishing Co., 1892.

Memorial and Biographical History of Johnson and Hill Counties, Texas. Chicago: Lewis Publishing Co., 1892.

Memorial and Biographical History of McLennan, Falls, Bell, and Coryell Counties, Texas. Chicago: Lewis Publishing Co., 1893.

Merchants' Association of New York. *The Natural Resources and Economic Conditions of the State of Texas.* New York, 1901.

Merrill, Horace Samuel. *Bourbon Leader: Grover Cleveland and the Democratic Party.* Boston: Little, Brown and Co., 1957.

Miller, Edmund Thornton. *A Financial History of Texas.* University of Texas Bulletin no. 37. Austin, 1916.

Morgan, H. Wayne, ed. *The Gilded Age: A Reappraisal.* Syracuse: Syracuse University Press, 1963.

Morgan, W. Scott. *History of the Wheel and Alliance, and the Impending Revolution.* Fort Scott, Arkansas: J. H. Rice & Sons, 1889.

Morrison and Fourmy's General Directory of the City of Austin, 1893–94. Galveston, 1893.

Morrison and Fourmy's General Directory of the City of Dallas, 1891–92. Galveston, 1891.

Morrison and Fourmy's General Directory of the City of Fort Worth, 1899–1900. Galveston, 1899.

Morrison and Fourmy's General Directory of the City of Houston, 1889–90. Galveston, 1889.

Morrison and Fourmy's General Directory of the City of San Antonio, 1892–93. Galveston, 1892.

Neilson, James W. *Shelby M. Cullom: Prairie State Republican.* Urbana: The University of Illinois Press, 1962.

Nevins, Allan. *Grover Cleveland: A Study in Courage.* New York: Dodd, Mead & Co., 1933.

Nixon, Pat Ireland. *A History of the Texas Medical Association, 1853–1953.* Austin: University of Texas Press, 1953.

Noblin, Stuart. *Leonidas LaFayette Polk, Agrarian Crusader.* Chapel Hill: The University of North Carolina Press, 1949.

Nugent, Catharine, ed. *Life Work of Thomas L. Nugent.* Stephenville, Texas: C. Nugent, 1896.

Nugent, Walter T. K. *The Tolerant Populists: Kansas Populism and Nativism.* Chicago: University of Chicago Press, 1963.

Nunn, W. C. *Texas under the Carpetbaggers.* Austin: University of Texas Press, 1962.

Ogden, Frederic D. *The Poll Tax in the South.* University: University of Alabama Press, 1958.

Otken, Charles H. *The Ills of the South.* New York: G. P. Putnam's Sons, 1894.

Overdyke, W. Darrell. *The Know-Nothing Party in the South.* Baton Rouge: Louisiana State University Press, 1950.

Overton, Richard C. *Gulf to Rockies: The Heritage of the Fort Worth and Denver–Colorado and Southern Railways, 1861–1898.* Austin: University of Texas Press, 1953.

Paddock, B. B., ed. *History of Texas: Fort Worth and Texas Northwest.* 4 vols. Chicago and New York: Lewis Publishing Co., 1922.

Parker, Richard Denny. *Historical Recollections of Robertson County, Texas.* Edited by Nona Clement Parker. Salado, Texas: Anson Jones Press, 1955.

Pease, E. M. *Speech Delivered at Turner Hall, Galveston, Texas, July 12th, 1880.* Galveston: Republican County Committee, 1880.

Polk, R. L. *Texas State Gazetteer and Business Directory.* 2 vols. Detroit, 1891–1892.

Pollack, Norman. *The Populist Response to Industrial America: Midwestern Populist Thought.* Cambridge: Harvard University Press, 1962.

———, ed. *The Populist Mind.* Indianapolis: The Bobbs-Merrill Co., 1967.

Pool, William C. *Bosque Territory: A History of an Agrarian Community.* Kyle, Texas: Chaparral Press, 1964.

Pool, William C., Emmie Craddock, and David E. Conrad. *Lyndon Baines Johnson: The Formative Years.* San Marcos, Texas: Southwest Texas State College Press, 1965.

Potts, Charles S. *Railroad Transportation in Texas.* University of Texas Bulletin no. 119. Austin, 1909.

Pressly, Thomas J., and William H. Scofield. *Farm Real Estate Values in the United States by Counties, 1850–1959.* Seattle: University of Washington Press, 1965.

Procter, Ben H. *Not Without Honor: The Life of John H. Reagan.* Austin: University of Texas Press, 1962.

Ramey, Wm. Neal, ed. *Texian (Annual)*, 2, no. 17. Austin, 1886.

Ramsdell, Charles W. "The Frontier and Secession." In *Studies in Southern History and Politics*, pp. 63–79. New York: Columbia University Press, 1914.

———. *Reconstruction in Texas*. New York: Columbia University Press, 1910.

Rankin, G. C. *The Story of My Life*. Dallas: Smith and Lamar, 1912.

Ray, Jeff D. *B. H. Carroll*. Nashville: Southern Baptist Convention, 1927.

Reagan, John H. *Memoirs*. Edited by W. F. McCaleb. New York: Neale Publishing Co., 1906.

Reed, S. G. *A History of the Texas Railroads*. Houston: St. Clair Publishing Co., 1941.

Reese, John Walter, and Lillian Estelle Reese. *Flaming Feuds of Colorado County*. Salado, Texas: Anson Jones Press, 1962.

"Reform" Republican Party, Texas. *Basis of Representation Adopted by the Republican State Executive Committee for the Texas Republican State Convention to Convene in Dallas, August 6th, 1894*. Houston: J. J. Pastoriza, 1894.

Renfro, T. J. *Thirteen Years of Radical Misrule: A History of the Montgomery County Troubles from 1865 to 1879*. N.p.: Courier Print, 1879.

Republican Party, National Convention. *Proceedings*, 1876–1904.

Republican Party, Texas. *Proceedings of the Republican Convention of the State of Texas, Held at the City of Houston, January 12, 13 and 14, 1876*. Austin: Evening News Book and Job Office, 1876.

———. *Proceedings of the Republican State Convention, Held in the Hall of the House of Representatives in the City of Austin, March 24, 1880*. Austin: J. M. Snyder, 1880.

Richardson, Rupert Norval. *Colonel Edward M. House: The Texas Years, 1858–1912*. Hardin-Simmons University Publications in History, I. Abilene, Texas: 1964.

Ridge, Martin. *Ignatius Donnelly: The Portrait of a Politician*. Chicago: University of Chicago Press, 1962.

Ripley, William Z. *Railroads: Finance and Organization*. New York: Longmans, Green and Co., 1915.

———. *Railroads: Rates and Regulation*. New York: Longmans, Green and Co., 1923.

Roberts, Oran M. "The Political, Legislative, and Judicial History of Texas for its Fifty Years of Statehood, 1845–1895." In *Comprehensive History of Texas, 1685–1897*. Edited by Dudley G. Wooten, 2: 7–329. 2 vols. Dallas: W. G. Scarff, 1898.

Robinson, Edgar Eugene. *The Presidential Vote, 1896–1932*. Stanford: Stanford University Press, 1934.

Rosser, Charles McDaniel. *The Crusading Commoner: A Close-up of William Jennings Bryan and His Times*. Dallas: Mathis, Van Nort & Co., 1937.

Rowell, George P. *American Newspaper Directory*. New York: George P. Rowell & Co., 1876–1882.

Saloutos, Theodore. *Farmer Movements in the South, 1865–1933*. Berkeley: University of California Press, 1960.

Shannon, Fred A. *The Farmer's Last Frontier: Agriculture, 1860–1897*. New York: Farrar & Rinehart, 1945.

Siegel, Stanley. *A Political History of the Texas Republic, 1836–1845*. Austin: University of Texas Press, 1956.

Simkins, Francis Butler. *Pitchfork Ben Tillman, South Carolinian*. Baton Rouge: Louisiana State University Press, 1944.

Simpson, Harold B., ed. *Touched with Valor: Civil War Papers and Casualty Reports of Hood's Texas Brigade, Written and Collected by General Jerome B. Robertson*. Hillsboro: Hill Junior College Press, 1964.

Sleeper, John, and J. C. Hutchins. *Waco and McLennan County, Texas, Containing a City Directory of Waco*. Waco, 1876. Reprint. Waco: Texian Press, 1966.

Sonnichsen, C. L. *I'll Die Before I'll Run: The Story of the Great Feuds of Texas*. New York, 1951. Reprint. New York: Devin-Adair Co., 1962.

———. *Pass of the North: Four Centuries on the Rio Grande*. El Paso: Texas Western Press, 1968.

Soukup, James R., Clifton McCleskey, and Harry Holloway. *Party and Factional Division in Texas*. Austin: University of Texas Press, 1964.

Spain, Rufus B. *At Ease in Zion: Social History of Southern Baptists, 1865–1900*. Nashville: Vanderbilt University Press, 1967.

Speer, William S., ed. *The Encyclopedia of the New West*. Marshall, Texas: United States Biographical Publishing Company, 1881.

Spratt, John S. *The Road to Spindletop: Economic Change in Texas, 1875–1901*. Dallas: Southern Methodist University Press, 1955.

Steen, Ralph W. *Twentieth-Century Texas: An Economic and Social History.* Austin: The Steck Company, 1942.
Stieghorst, Juann J. *Bay City and Matagorda County: A History.* Austin: Pemberton Press, 1965.
Stone, Harold A., et al. *City Manager Government in Nine Cities.* Chicago: Public Administration Service, 1940.
Summers, Festus P. *William L. Wilson and Tariff Reform.* New Brunswick: Rutgers University Press, 1953.
Tansill, Charles C. *The Congressional Career of Thomas Francis Bayard, 1869–1885.* Washington, D.C.: Georgetown University Press, 1946.
Taylor, Carl C. *The Farmers' Movement, 1620–1920.* New York: American Book Co., 1953.
Taylor, I. T. *The Cavalcade of Jackson County.* San Antonio: Naylor Co., 1938.
Terrell, C. V. *The Terrells: Eighty-five Years, Texas from Indians to Atomic Bomb.* Austin: C. V. Terrell, 1948.
Terry, J. W. *Terry on Crowley: Massachusetts' Gift to Texas.* Galveston: Allied Printing Trades Council, 1894.
Texas, Legislature. *General Laws of the State of Texas,* 26th Legislature–30th Legislature, 1899–1907.
Texas, Legislature. *Members of the Legislature of the State of Texas from 1846 to 1939.* [Austin, 1939].
Texas, Legislature, House of Representatives. *House Journals,* 15th Legislature–30th Legislature, 1876–1907.
———. *Rules of Order of the House of Representatives of the Twenty-first Legislature.* Austin: Smith, Hicks & Jones, 1889.
———. *Rules of Order of the House of Representatives of the Twenty-second Legislature.* Austin: Henry Hutchings, 1891.
———. *Rules of Order of the House of Representatives of the Twenty-third Legislature.* Austin: Ben C. Jones & Co., 1893.
Texas, Legislature, Senate. *Rules of Order of the Senate of the Twenty-second Legislature.* Austin: Henry Hutchings, 1891.
———. *Rules of Order and Standing Committees of the Senate: Fourteenth Legislature.* Austin: Cardwell & Walker, 1874.
———. *Senate Journals,* 15th Legislature–30th Legislature, 1876–1907.
Texas, Railroad Commission. *Annual Reports,* 1892, 1895.
Texas, Secretary of State. *Reports.* 1876–1906.
Texas Almanac. Dallas: A. B. Belo and Co., 1904, 1942, 1966–1967.

Texas Legislative Manual for 1893. Austin: Hutchings Printing Co., 1893.

Texas Legislative Manual for 1897. Austin: Ben C. Jones & Co., 1897.

Texas Legislative Manual for 1899. Austin: Von Boeckmann, Moore, Schutze, 1899.

Texas Legislative Manual for 1901. Austin: Von Boeckmann, Schutze & Co., 1901.

Texas Legislative Manual for 1903. Austin: Von Boeckmann-Jones Co., 1903.

Texas Legislative Manual for 1905. Austin: Gammel-Statesman Publishing Co., 1905.

Texas Legislative Manual for 1907. Austin: Von Boeckmann-Jones Co., 1907.

Thomas, Harrison Cook. *The Return of the Democratic Party to Power in 1884*. New York: Columbia University Press, 1919.

Timmons, Bascom N. *Garner of Texas: A Personal History*. New York: Harper & Brothers, 1948.

Tinsley, James A., ed. *Letters from the Colonel: Edward M. House to Frank Andrews, 1899–1902*. Houston: Texas Gulf Coast Historical Association, 1960.

Tyler, George W. *The History of Bell County*. Edited by Charles W. Ramsdell. San Antonio: Naylor Co., 1936.

Unger, Irwin. *The Greenback Era: A Social and Political History of American Finance, 1865–1879*. Princeton: Princeton University Press, 1964.

U.S., Census Bureau. *Abstract of the Twelfth Census of the United States, 1900*. Washington, D.C.: Government Printing Office, 1904.

U.S., Census Bureau. *Report on Statistics of Churches in the United States at the Eleventh Census: 1890*. Washington, D.C.: Government Printing Office, 1894.

U.S., Census Bureau. *Tenth Census of the United States: 1880*. Washington, D.C.: Government Printing Office, 1883.

U.S., Congress. *Biographical Directory of the American Congress, 1774–1961*. Washington, D.C.: Government Printing Office, 1961.

U.S., Congress. *Congressional Record*, 44th Congress–59th Congress, 1875–1906.

Wallace, Ernest. *Charles DeMorse: Pioneer Editor and Statesman*. Lubbock: Texas Technological College Press, 1943.

Watson, Thomas E. *The People's Party Campaign Book, 1892: Not a Revolt; It is a Revolution.* Washington, D.C.: National Watchman Publishing Co., 1892.

Webb, Walter Prescott, and H. Bailey Carroll, eds. *The Handbook of Texas.* 2 vols. Austin: Texas State Historical Association, 1952.

Webb, Walter Prescott, and Terrell Webb, eds. *Washington Wife: Journal of Ellen Maury Slayden from 1897–1919.* New York: Harper & Row, 1962.

Wharton, Clarence R. *History of Fort Bend County.* San Antonio: Naylor Co., 1939.

Wheeler, Kenneth W. *To Wear a City's Crown: The Beginnings of Urban Growth in Texas, 1836–1865.* Cambridge: Harvard University Press, 1968.

Wiebe, Robert. *Businessmen and Reform: A Study of the Progressive Movement.* Cambridge: Harvard University Press, 1962.

———. *The Search for Order, 1877–1920.* New York: Hill and Wang, 1967.

Williams, Annie Lee. *A History of Wharton County, 1846–1961.* Austin: Von Boeckmann-Jones Co., 1964.

Winkler, Ernest William, ed. *Platforms of Political Parties in Texas.* University of Texas Bulletin no. 53, Austin, 1916.

Woodward, C. Vann. *Origins of the New South, 1877–1913.* Baton Rouge: Louisiana State University Press, 1951.

———. *Reunion and Reaction: The Compromise of 1877 and the End of Reconstruction.* New York: Little, Brown and Co., 1951.

———. *Tom Watson, Agrarian Rebel.* New York: The Macmillan Co., 1938.

Wooster, Ralph A. *The Secession Conventions of the South.* Princeton: Princeton University Press, 1962.

Wooten, Dudley G., ed. *Comprehensive History of Texas, 1685–1897.* 2 vols. Dallas: W. G. Scarff, 1898.

Work Projects Administration. *Houston: A History and Guide.* Houston: Anson Jones Press, 1942.

Yearns, Wilfred Buck. *The Confederate Congress.* Athens: University of Georgia Press, 1963.

Young, Allyn A. *An Analysis of Bank Statistics for the United States.* Cambridge: Harvard University Press, 1928.

Articles

Abramowitz, Jack. "The Negro in the Populist Movement." *Journal of Negro History* 38 (July 1953): 257–289.

———. "John B. Rayner—A Grass-Roots Leader." *Journal of Negro History* 36 (April 1951): 160–193.

Alvord, Wayne. "T. L. Nugent, Texas Populist." *Southwestern Historical Quarterly* 57 (July 1953): 65–81.

Barr, Alwyn. "B. J. Chambers and the Greenback Party Split." *Mid-America* 49 (October 1967): 276–284.

———. "Ben Terrell: Agrarian Spokesman." *West Texas Historical Association Year Book* 45 (1969): 58–71.

Baughman, James P., ed. "Letters From the Texas Coast, 1875." *Southwestern Historical Quarterly* 69 (April 1966): 499–515.

Billington, Monroe. "T. P. Gore and Agricultural Legislation." *Agricultural History* 31 (January 1957): 29–40.

Brandon, Ida. "The Tax Payers' Union in Brazoria County." *Texas History Teachers' Bulletin* 14 (1926): 86–92.

Bryant, Keith Lynn, Jr. " 'Alfalfa Bill' Murray: The Formative Years." *East Texas Historical Journal* 3 (October 1965): 103–118.

Campbell, Randolph. "The Whig Party of Texas in the Elections of 1848 and 1852." *Southwestern Historical Quarterly* 73 (July 1969): 17–34.

Cockrell, Fred. "Pioneering in Politics on the Plains." *West Texas Historical Association Year Book* 6 (1930): 94–108.

Connor, Seymour V. "Early Land Speculation in West Texas." *Southwestern Social Science Quarterly* 42 (March 1962): 354–362.

Cotner, Robert C., and Watt P. Marchman, eds. "Correspondence of Guy M. Bryan and Rutherford B. Hayes: Additional Letters." *Ohio State Archaeological and Historical Quarterly* 63 (October 1954): 349–377.

Crane, M. M. "Recollections of the Establishment of the Texas Railroad Commission." *Southwestern Historical Quarterly* 50 (April 1947): 478–486.

Diggs, Annie L. "The Farmers' Alliance and Some of Its Leaders." *Arena* 5 (1891–1892): 590–604.

———. "The Women in the Farmers' Alliance." *Arena* 6 (1892): 161–179.

Duncan, Merle Mears. "An 1890 Richard Coke Letter." *Southwestern Historical Quarterly* 66 (July 1962) : 68–72.

Dunn, Roy Sylvan. "Drouth in West Texas, 1890–1894." *West Texas Historical Association Year Book* 37 (1961) : 121–136.

Ericson, J. E. "The Delegates to the Convention of 1875: A Reappraisal." *Southwestern Historical Quarterly* 67 (July 1963) : 22–27.

Gard, Wayne. "The Fence-Cutters." *Southwestern Historical Quarterly* 51 (July 1947) : 1–15.

Going, Allen J. "The South and the Blair Education Bill." *Mississippi Valley Historical Review* 44 (September 1957) : 267–290.

Greenwood, Helen. "Anderson, the Rome of Texas." *Texas History Teachers' Bulletin* 13 (1925) : 97–103.

Gressley, Gene M. "Broker to the British: Francis Smith and Company." *Southwestern Historical Quarterly* 71 (July 1967) : 7–25.

Hall, Claude H. "The Fabulous Tom Ochiltree: Promoter, Politician, and Raconteur." *Southwestern Historical Quarterly* 71 (January 1968) : 347–376.

Handlin, Oscar. "Reconsidering the Populists." *Agricultural History* 39 (April 1965) : 68–74.

Hollingsworth, J. Rogers. "Commentary: Populism: The Problem of Rhetoric and Reality." *Agricultural History* 39 (April 1965) : 81–85.

Holt, R. D. "Texas Had Hot County Elections." *West Texas Historical Association Year Book* 24 (1948) : 3–26.

Langston, Rosalind. "The Life of Colonel R. T. Milner." *Southwestern Historical Quarterly* 44 (April 1941) : 407–451; 45 (July 1941) : 24–73.

Lentz, Sallie M. "Highlights of Early Harrison County." *Southwestern Historical Quarterly* 61 (October 1957) : 240–256.

Lightfoot, Billy Bob. "The Human Party: Populism in Comanche County, 1886." *West Texas Historical Association Year Book* 31 (1955) : 28–40.

———. "The Negro Exodus from Comanche County, Texas." *Southwestern Historical Quarterly* 56 (January 1953) : 407–416.

Link, Arthur S. "Progressive Movement in the South, 1870–1914." *North Carolina Historical Review* 23 (April 1946) : 172–195.

McKay, Seth Shepard. "John Nance Garner." *West Texas Historical Association Year Book* 37 (1961) : 3–44.

———. "The Texas State Democratic Convention of 1878." *West Texas Historical Association Year Book* 12 (1936) : 3–10.

Martin, Roscoe C. "The Grange as a Political Factor in Texas," *Southwestern Social Science Quarterly* 6 (March 1926): 363–383.

———. "The Greenback Party in Texas." *Southwestern Historical Quarterly* 30 (January 1927): 161–177.

Maxwell, Robert S. "The Pines of Texas: A Study in Lumbering and Public Policy, 1880–1930." *East Texas Historical Journal* 2 (October 1964): 77–86.

Miller, E. T. "The Historical Development of the Texas State Tax System." *Southwestern Historical Quarterly* 55 (July 1951): 1–29.

Miller, Thomas L. "Texas Land Grants to Confederate Veterans and Widows." *Southwestern Historical Quarterly* 69 (July 1965): 59–65.

Moseley, J. A. R. "The Citizens White Primary of Marion County." *Southwestern Historical Quarterly* 49 (April 1946): 524–531.

Myres, S. D., Jr. "Mysticism, Realism, and the Texas Constitution of 1876." *Southwestern Social Science Quarterly* 9 (September 1928): 166–184.

Nash, Gerald. "Origins of the Interstate Commerce Act of 1887." *Pennsylvania History* 24 (July 1957): 181–190.

———. "The Reformer Reformed: John H. Reagan and Railroad Regulation." *Business History Review* 29 (June 1955): 189–196.

———, ed. "Selections from the Reagan Papers: The Butler-Reagan Ticket of 1884." *Journal of Southern History* 21 (August 1955): 379–386.

Nelson, Henry. "Political Situation in the South." *International Review* 12 (April 1882): 411–418.

Nichols, Jeannette Paddock. "The Politics and Personalities of Silver Repeal in the United States Senate." *American Historical Review* 41 (October 1935): 26–53.

Ogletree, D. W. "Establishing the Texas Court of Appeals, 1875–1876." *Southwestern Historical Quarterly* 47 (July 1943): 5–18.

Peterson, Robert L. "Jay Gould and the Railroad Commission of Texas." *Southwestern Historical Quarterly* 58 (January 1955): 422–432.

Pollack, Norman. "Fear of Man: Populism, Authoritarianism, and the Historian." *Agricultural History* 39 (April 1965): 59–67.

Ramsdell, Charles W., Jr. "Memories of a Texas Land Commissioner, W. C. Walsh." *Southwestern Historical Quarterly* 44 (April 1941): 481–497.

Reese, James V. "The Early History of Labor Organizations in Texas,

1838–1876." *Southwestern Historical Quarterly* 72 (July 1968): 1–20.

Rippy, J. Fred. "British Investments in Texas Lands and Livestock." *Southwestern Historical Quarterly* 58 (January 1955): 331–341.

Saloutos, Theodore. "The Professors and the Populists." *Agricultural History* 40 (October 1966): 235–254.

Saunders, Robert. "Southern Populists and the Negro, 1893–1895." *Journal of Negro History* 54 (July 1969): 240–261.

Schott, Christine. "Gustavus Schleicher: A Representative of the Early German Emigrants in Texas." *West Texas Historical Association Year Book* 28 (1952): 50–70.

Scott, Anne Firor. "A Progressive Wind from the South, 1906–1913." *Journal of Southern History* 29 (February 1963): 53–70.

Smith, Ralph A. "The Farmers' Alliance in Texas, 1875–1900." *Southwestern Historical Quarterly* 48 (January 1945): 346–369.

———. "The Grange Movement in Texas, 1873–1900." *Southwestern Historical Quarterly* 42 (April 1939): 297–315.

Spindler, Frank MacD. "Concerning Hempstead and Waller County." *Southwestern Historical Quarterly* 59 (April 1956): 455–472.

Splawn, W. M. W. "Valuation and Rate Regulation by the Railroad Commission of Texas." *Journal of Political Economy* 31 (October 1923): 675–707.

Strong, Donald S. "The Poll Tax: The Case of Texas." *American Political Science Review* 38 (August 1944): 693–709.

Taylor, A. Elizabeth. "The Woman Suffrage Movement in Texas." *Journal of Southern History* 17 (May 1951): 194–215.

Trelease, Allen W. "Who Were the Scalawags?" *Journal of Southern History* 29 (November 1963): 445–468.

Tucker, William P. "Populism Up-to-Date: The Story of the Farmers' Union." *Agricultural History* 21 (October 1947): 198–208.

Unger, Irwin. "Critique of Norman Pollack's 'Fear of Man.'" *Agricultural History* 39 (April 1965): 75–80.

Weeks, O. Douglas. "The Direct Primary System." *Southwestern Social Science Quarterly* 13 (September 1932): 95–120.

———. "The Texas-Mexican and the Politics of South Texas." *American Political Science Review* 24 (August 1930): 606–627.

Weinstein, James. "Organized Business and the City Commission and Manager Movements." *Journal of Southern History* 28 (May 1962): 166–182.

Wilcox, Seb S. "The Laredo City Election and Riot of April, 1886." *Southwestern Historical Quarterly* 45 (July 1941): 1–23.

Winkler, Ernest William, ed. "The Bryan-Hayes Correspondence." *Southwestern Historical Quarterly* 27–30 (July 1923–July 1926).

Wooster, Ralph A. "An Analysis of the Texas Know-Nothings." *Southwestern Historical Quarterly* 70 (January 1967): 414–423.

NEWSPAPERS AND PERIODICALS

Abilene Reporter, 1892.

Austin Evening Call, 1886.

Austin Statesman, 1876, 1878, 1879, 1894, 1903, 1966.

Austin *State Topics*, 1904–1906.

Austin *Texas Capital*, 1877–1880.

Austin *Texas Farm and Ranch*, 1884.

Bastrop Advertiser, 1879–1884.

Brownsville *Herald*, 1896.

Dallas *Advance*, 1893–1894.

Dallas Herald, 1867, 1876, 1884.

Dallas News, 1886, 1891, 1894, 1896, 1903, 1905, 1906.

Dallas *Norton's Intelligencer*, 1876–1895.

Dallas *Southern Mercury*, 1891–1902.

Dallas *Texas State Labor Journal*, 1896.

Fort Worth Gazette, 1887.

Galveston News, 1876–1906.

Houston Post, 1882, 1892, 1894, 1896, 1963.

Houston *Southern Industrial and Lumber Review*, 1902–1905.

Houston Telegraph, 1876.

Houston *Western Star*, 1900.

Longview *Texas New Era*, 1879–1886.

Marshall *Herald*, 1878–1879.

Palestine (Texas) *Bagpipe*, 1906.

Paris (Texas) *Herald*, 1892.

St. Louis Globe Democrat, 1886.

San Antonio *Campaign News*, 1888.

San Antonio Express, 1890, 1894, 1896, 1903.

San Antonio Light, 1897, 1898.

San Antonio *White Republican*, 1890.

Waco Examiner, 1876, 1878.

Washington, D. C., *National Economist*, 1889–1892.

Weatherford Times, 1882.

INDEX